RECKLESS

Philip Augar worked in investment banking for over twenty years. He led NatWest's global equity and bond business before becoming a Group Managing Director at Schroders. Since 2000 he has combined consulting and writing. This is his fifth book. He can b~

www.philip~

PHILIP AUGAR

Reckless

The Rise and Fall of the City, 1997–2008

VINTAGE BOOKS
London

Published by Vintage 2010

2 4 6 8 10 9 7 5 3 1

Copyright © Philip Augar 2009

Philip Augar has asserted his right under the Copyright, Designs
and Patents Act 1988 to be identified as the author of this work

First published in Great Britain in 2009 by
The Bodley Head

Vintage
Random House, 20 Vauxhall Bridge Road,
London SW1V 2SA

www.vintage-books.co.uk

Addresses for companies within The Random House Group Limited
can be found at: www.randomhouse.co.uk/offices.htm

The Random House Group Limited Reg. No. 954009

A CIP catalogue record for this book
is available from the British Library

ISBN 9780099524045

The Random House Group Limited supports The Forest Stewardship
Council (FSC), the leading international forest certification organisation. All our titles that are printed on Greenpeace approved FSC
certified paper carry the FSC logo. Our paper procurement policy can
be found at www.rbooks.co.uk/environment

Printed and bound in Great Britain by
CPI Cox & Wyman, Reading RG1 8EX

For Denise, William and Rachel

In memory of John Augar 1928–2003 and in appreciation of Helen Augar

And to my fellow Leeds fans, amongst the first victims of all this

CONTENTS

PREFACE: CHASING ALPHA

'Alpha' is shorthand in the City for supercharged profit and 'chasing alpha' is what Britain's bankers, investors and corporate chief executives did in the last two decades of the 20th century and the opening years of this millennium, culminating between 2003 and 2007 in an orgy of leverage and reckless growth plans.

But to most participants and observers the years 1997–2007 seemed to show that chasing alpha worked. Britain reinvented itself as a service-led economy, and a new paradigm of steady growth, low interest rates and predictable employment was proclaimed. The City attained unprecedented wealth and power. Its influence spread first to Westminster and Whitehall and then out into the country at large. Its earnings drove the whole economy, its values infiltrated Britain's culture, and its sophisticated methods of financial engineering enabled the banks to offer apparently limitless credit to consumers eager to buy homes, cars and retail goods with borrowed money. The City became widely admired as an international leader in the increasingly complex and interconnected world of finance and was held up as a shining example of Britain's new knowledge economy.

It seemed too good to be true and it was. Falling house prices and defaulting borrowers in America unstitched the new global financial system in the closing months of 2007. In the ensuing mayhem, the British government found itself owning two mortgage banks as well as stakes in two big high street banks. The banking crisis of 2008 rapidly spread to the rest of the economy, starving consumers of credit and businesses of working capital, causing house prices to plunge and sending the country into recession. Bankers were reviled and the City lost its recently acquired cachet. Alpha went out of the window and in its place came beta, the City's term for reliable, predictable profits no more or no less than the economy could comfortably sustain.

This book is the story of the rise and the fall. Both happened on New Labour's watch but the foundations were laid in the last quarter of the 20th century when free market forces and shareholder value – the elevation of shareholders' interests above those of other stake-holders – were unleashed as the guiding lights of the British and American economies. New Labour might have got a bit carried away in its devotion to the City between 1997 and 2007 and there was a crucial moment back in 1996 when the party nearly went in another direction, but there is no party-political angle in this book. The Conservatives did nothing to distance themselves from undiluted free market economics and went out of their way to court the City. Not even the Liberal Democrats, whose economics spokesman Vincent Cable predicted the credit crunch, get full marks for they failed to develop Cable's scepticism into a coherent alternative model.

The government went to some lengths to emphasise that the financial crisis was a global event not of its own making. The public partly got the message but noted that the UK was affected more than most countries. Its fifth, eighth and twelfth largest banks, HBOS, Northern Rock and Bradford & Bingley, in effect failed, and an even larger bank, the Royal Bank of Scotland, needed the state to come in as a majority shareholder to survive. Britain was the only major country where a run on a bank led to mass panic and queues in the high street, a situation that led people to ask how such a situation had arisen.

It was understood that the UK had a greater reliance on capital markets and banking business than other countries. British finan-cial institutions were so plugged into the global financial system that it was inevitable that some of them at least would be at the cutting edge of the modern techniques that caused the problems, and it was not unexpected that some of them would trip up. The collapse of Iceland's entire banking system in October 2008 helped to bring perspective. If the financial system of a remote country on the fringes of the global economy was caught up in the mess, it was not surprising that the UK, the world's self-proclaimed international financial services capital, took some blows. But the violence of the downturn and the inability of the authorities to control it begged some questions and in particular whether the much-trumpeted success of the City between 1997 and 2007 was really only a binge.

At the time of writing it is too early to be certain of the consequences of the banking crisis. It is not clear whether we are in 1929, the year of the Wall Street Crash, or 1933, the year governments began to get a grip on the financial crisis and the ensuing Great Depression.[1] The financial services industry will be much changed by the crisis and will no doubt undergo a period of contrition and caution before eventual recovery. Again, at the time of writing the timing and nature of this recovery is not clear and neither is the extent to which the City will be able to regain its influence in government and over the economy. This book does not try to provide definitive answers to these questions but the author hopes that the story told here will help readers to understand what happened and to form their own opinions.

The City hosts a panoply of financial businesses including insurance, shipping and bullion trading, but this book focuses on investment banking, asset management, hedge funds and private equity. These are the capital markets activities that were at the heart of the global financial system, were most central to the firing up of the recent British economy and were most involved in the subsequent banking crisis.

'The City' is a geographical term that denoted the financial services industry when it was located in the square mile around London EC2. Now the industry has spread to Canary Wharf, Mayfair, Edinburgh and regional financial centres such as West Yorkshire. In this book the term is used as a catch-all term for Britain's financial services industry wherever it is located.

I wish to acknowledge the many men and women who have given their time to meet me and discuss this subject and in some cases read draft text. Some of them are referred to by name in the book, others wished to remain anonymous. I am deeply grateful to them all for their candour and patience. Helen Wells painstakingly transcribed many hours of taped interviews and Dan Hind has been an inspiring editor. As usual, my wife Denise has been patient and tolerant of my eccentricities, which are always most pronounced at book writing time.

Philip Augar,
Cambridge, England
December 2008

PART ONE

INTRODUCTION

Our answer, consciously or unconsciously, reflects our own position in time, and forms part of our answer to the broader question, what view we take of the society in which we live.

What is History?, E.H. Carr, Penguin, 1964, p. 8

PART ONE

INTRODUCTION

1

THE BIG END OF TOWN: SUMMER 2007

Despite the unseasonably cool damp weather, the City of London was the place to be in the summer of 2007. It was the space where many of Britain's brightest and most ambitious people gathered in a pulsating mass of wealth creation, and it had become so powerful that it was known in government circles as 'the big end of town'. Not only was it the driving force in the British economy, the motor behind the country's rampant housing boom and consumer credit spree, it was acknowledged to be Europe's, some said the world's, financial services capital.

The people who worked there lived in a bubble that insulated them from the rest of the world. That summer, while the country shivered and sheltered from the elements and in a few places watched helplessly as floods swept away their belongings and seeped into their living rooms, the kings and queens of Britain's financial services industry looked down from their commanding heights. In their homes in Chelsea, Notting Hill, Hampstead and the smartest London suburbs they enjoyed a gilded existence. City people used cabs not the bus, and flew business class not economy. Their wealth shielded them from shoddy goods and indifferent service. They rarely had to queue. They worked hard but their money made life easy for them. They could afford small armies of hirelings to help juggle their demanding careers and home lives. Their world was one of good schools, private medicine, domestic help and the best holidays that money could buy. Younger City types sometimes went over the top but this was no wild thrash. In general the brokers, bankers and fund managers that made up the City's hard core were self-assured and had grown accustomed to having money. They believed that they deserved their success and were confident it would last.

One reason for this was that influential people told them so, including Gordon Brown, the man who in the summer of 2007 had every reason to share their self-congratulatory glow. After impatiently waiting his turn during Tony Blair's ten years at the top, Gordon Brown finally achieved his ambition of becoming prime minister that June. Brown's elevation was welcomed in the City. He had already declared his admiration for Britain's financial services industry when he was Chancellor of the Exchequer, once telling an audience of bankers, 'What you have achieved for the financial services sector we, as a country, now aspire to achieve for the whole of the British economy,' and other politicians got the message. When Brown moved next door, the new occupant of 11 Downing Street, Alistair Darling, was quick to follow his predecessor's lead, immediately paying tribute to the City's role 'not just in London's health but the UK's health' and describing it as 'absolutely critical' to the economy.

It was evidently New Labour orthodoxy to revere the City as the jewel in the crown, a remarkable turnaround from the days when top-hatted City toffs had been regarded as the enemies of the party. In 2006 in one of his first speeches as economic secretary to the Treasury, the former *Financial Times* journalist Ed Balls, who had risen through New Labour from a position as Brown's special adviser, delivered a eulogistic history of the City going back some thirty years. The tone was set by his opening remarks: 'I have absolutely no hesitation when I say to you that London is – now, today – the world's greatest global financial centre.'[1]

New Labour's admiration for the City – an admiration matched by the Conservatives, who had traditionally regarded the square mile as their natural constituency – apparently knew no bounds. Senior members of the government, for example Tony Blair at Goldman Sachs and Gordon Brown at Lehman Brothers, had appeared at events organised by leading financial institutions. The Ed Balls speech quoted above was made at the London offices of the financial services information company Bloomberg. City grandees were consulted at breakfast meetings held at 11 Downing Street and were invited to join the advisory councils that Gordon Brown set up early in his premiership to discuss issues of national importance. For example, Damon Buffini, the managing partner of the private equity firm Permira, featured on two such bodies, sitting on both the Business Council for Britain and the National Council for Educational Excellence.

A two-way street opened up between Westminister and the City. After fourteen years at the investment bank UBS Warburg, Shriti Vadera spent eight years advising Gordon Brown when he was Chancellor and was a member of his Council of Economic Advisers from 1999 to 2007. She was made a life peer shortly after Brown became prime minister. In 2002, James Sassoon, another former Warburg investment banker, became managing director of finance and regulation at the Treasury, becoming its most senior outside recruit in decades. In December 2005 he was appointed the Chancellor and Treasury's representative for promotion of the City, a part-time role in which he championed internationally the interests of the UK's financial and business services firms and markets. Sassoon was eventually knighted for his services to the finance industry and for public service.

The career of Jeremy Heywood spoke volumes for the City's newly found influence and gravitas. Heywood was a career civil servant who held a variety of positions at the Treasury, including time as principal private secretary to two Chancellors of the Exchequer and as head of the team that oversaw the regulation of financial markets. From 1999-2003 he was principal private secretary to the Prime Minister, Tony Blair. In 2003 he took unpaid leave from the civil service to become a managing director at the US investment bank Morgan Stanley, and then in June 2007 he switched back to the public sector as head of domestic policy and strategy in the Cabinet Office.

At the time of Gordon Brown's election as prime minister, apart from during a brief panic about the growing influence of private equity, New Labour and Conservative politicians and mainstream commentators scarcely had a bad word for the City. Once regarded as the epitome of greed and excess, it had even developed a philanthropic face. According to the *Sunday Times* annual Rich List survey for 2008, fifteen of the UK's fifty largest philanthropists had made their fortunes in the City.[2] The sums were staggering. The recent donations of Christopher Hohn, a young hedge fund manager who had set up the Children's Investment Fund Foundation, were listed as £235.8 million, more than double his own wealth. Private equity tycoons such as Jon Moulton (£8.6 million) and Sir Ronnie Cohen (£5.3 million) also emerged as significant donors.

City benefactors began to organise themselves into charitable institutions to achieve maximum impact, and some supported government initiatives. In 2002 several senior figures from London's hedge fund industry set up the charity Absolute Return for Kids (ARK) with the initial objective of addressing global issues such as HIV/Aids and children in care. The charity developed a UK dimension in 2004 when ARK Schools was created to become a major supporter of the government's flagship academies programme in Britain's inner city areas. The first ARK academy started admitting students in September 2006, and ARK aimed to have 10,000 young people enrolled in twelve academies by the end of 2012, thus making a sizeable contribution to the government's academies programme.

Not only did the City surprise everyone by revealing its softer side, it also became unbelievably trendy. During New Labour's first decade in power the City's centre of gravity had moved away from the dusty streets and narrow alleyways of the old square mile around the Bank of England. Further east, out in Docklands, the Canary Wharf development took off as a financial centre. By 2007 some 87,000 people worked there, over a quarter of the total number of City jobs in the capital, compared to just 25,000, less than 10 per cent, in 1997. New York-style skyscrapers, underground shopping malls and an array of cool cafes, wine bars, restaurants and gyms served the needs of these high-flyers. Many of the period's top names of finance, including Morgan Stanley, Lehman Brothers, HSBC and Barclays Capital, set up shop in Canary Wharf. With its spectacular waterfront setting, the area developed a cosmopolitan buzz thanks in part to the thousands of European and American financial experts employed by the global banks and fund managers. Canary Wharf defined the City in its pomp: soaring buildings, glitzy eating and watering holes and thousands of confident young people in a hurry.

But if Canary Wharf was cool, the emerging financial districts of Mayfair and St James's were hot. These were the favoured locations of the hedge funds, the dynamic force that, as we shall see, were integral to the City's story in these years. Along Davies Street and Curzon

Street and around Berkeley Square and St James's Square, discreet brass nameplates appeared, often containing the words 'capital' and 'asset management' but otherwise giving little away about the firms behind them. As the secretive hedge funds multiplied and office rents rose, the West End became an important destination for brokers and investment bankers wishing to visit their clients. The hedge fund people kept a low profile and blended into the crowd but they and their acolytes gathered at venues such as The Wolseley cafe-restaurant on Piccadilly, giving off unmistakable vibes of understated power and serious money. Upmarket retailers appealing to the affluent thirty-year-olds appeared alongside more traditional shops, and the area took on that indefinable aura of money, chic and success that characterises all financial districts that are on form.

The traditional financial district of the old City needed to respond to the challenge from Canary Wharf and the West End. It became a roaring hubbub of construction as the office blocks hastily put up after the Second World War were torn down. From the precincts of St Paul's Cathedral, where the 1960s development derided by one lord mayor of London as a 'ghastly monolithic construction' was replaced by an elegant design of linked squares, to the regeneration of the area around Spitalfields Market, the square mile and its environs redefined itself. It clung on to some big names in finance including Merrill Lynch, Schroders and UBS Warburg, all of which kept their London head-quarters in the City. It retained critical mass, and this was most evident on Thursday evenings, when the traders and their clients jammed into the pubs and bars in a raucous celebration of the end of another successful week and the approach of a precious weekend to recharge the batteries.

Each of the three financial districts had its own distinct atmosphere. In St James's and Mayfair you had to look hard to find the hedge fund set, but they were unmistakable when sighted. Understated but self-assured, these were the men and a few women sitting at the best corner table before sliding into their kerbside chauffeur-driven car with one eye on the street scene and the other on their BlackBerry.

The City was all hustle and bustle, and a walk through the square mile took you past old churches, historic streets with names like Old Jewry and Pudding Lane and the spectacle of office architecture through the ages. It contained a variety of financial types. Over by

Leadenhall Market the insurance brokers hurried through the streets, making their way from the Lloyd's building to their offices clutching bulging files containing details of the day's deals. At Broadgate Circle above Liverpool Street station smart investment bankers and brokers rubbed shoulders with their fund management clients, and in the streets off Cheapside between St Paul's Cathedral and the Bank of England the City's workforce sampled its traditional public houses and trendy minimalist bars.

Canary Wharf was a world apart, best accessed by the Jubilee Line, the newest Underground route in London and the one with the most modern trains and stations. Changing onto the Jubilee Line during the rush hour is like stepping into a different world. The people, particularly the women, are likely to be smarter than those on the train you have just left and nearly all are over twenty-five and below forty-five years old. The station where they all get off, Canary Wharf, has the feel of an award-winning airport. The most dramatic way to leave the station is to follow the signs to Upper Bank Street, go up the escalator and look up through the transparent domed roof to the circle of skyscrapers that appears to be tumbling in on you.

It is a strange place. Patrick Wellington, a well-respected investment analyst who started working in Canary Wharf in 2000 after fifteen years in the square mile, likens it to a 'safari park, an artificial creation in an alien environment. Here are we, a load of fabulously paid investment banking types and over there, half a mile away, is Poplar High Street and the real East End.' He describes the car parks as being 'jammed with Lotuses and other top-notch cars', and the shops 'so busy at lunchtimes that you have to push and shove your way through the crowds'. But at weekends it is a different story: 'the bankers have gone and the shops are full of normal people'.

Most of the action at Canary Wharf takes place below ground in the underground shopping malls or up in the sky in the office blocks; there are relatively few people walking around at street level. The exception is on summer evenings, when the terraces outside the cafes and bars are thronged with diners and drinkers, and the square behind Jubilee Place bounded by establishments such as Carluccio's, the Slug and Lettuce and Smollensky's is so crowded on Thursday and Friday evenings that it is a job to reach the entrance to the Tube.

London was internationally admired and considered a desirable posting for financial services people eager to get on. Over a third of the employees of the top London investment banks were non-British nationals.[3] London was winning business from New York and European rivals such as Frankfurt and Paris, much to the consternation of the authorities there. In 2007 New York senator Charles Schumer and the city's mayor Michael Bloomberg commissioned a study from the consulting firm McKinsey to address the issue of New York's global competitiveness, a study that was littered with references to London's success. The French finance minister Christine Lagarde spoke frequently about the example set by London and encouraged Parisian institutions and authorities to rise to the challenge.

London's regulatory system was particularly praised. It was held up as an example of light-touch, principles-based regulation and contrasted with what financial services practitioners alleged was the heavy-handed, rules-obsessed approach of US regulators. The McKinsey study reported evidence from interviews with a wide range of senior financial executives and their customers: 'For many executives, London has a better regulatory model: it is easier to conduct business there, there is a more open dialogue with practitioners and the market benefits from high-level, principles-based standards set by a single regulator for all financial markets.'[4]

City institutions and City people began to win plaudits and recognition. Even the clearing banks, previously regarded as stumbling giants when it came to the sharp end of the financial services industry, found themselves winning unaccustomed praise for their achievements: 'Investment banking used to be a dirty word for Britain's high street banks. No longer. After repeatedly failing to establish themselves in the City of London and on Wall Street in the 1980s and 1990s, the UK's biggest banks are now increasingly dependent on their investment banking arms for profits – and for growth.'[5]

The new financial firms springing up in the hedge fund and private equity sectors adopted aggressive strategies that made people sit up and take notice. When a British hedge fund, the Children's Investment Fund, set up only two years before, forced the venerable Deutsche Börse to drop its bid for the even more venerable London Stock Exchange, and the private equity firm Permira emerged as the new owner of the iconic British institution the Automobile Association, it was clear that vital new forces were at work.

A fresh generation of City managers emerged to replace the gentlemanly capitalists of the Big Bang era. A headline in the *Financial Times*, WEALTH OF TALENT IN THE UK'S BANKS, would have been unthinkable a decade before.[6] The US investment banks were still dominated by Americans but there was a trickle of British people edging forward to join them. Roger Nagioff, a former trader at the London broking firm Smith New Court, became global head of Lehman's powerful fixed income division, and another British trader, Michael Sherwood, emerged at Goldman Sachs to lead that firm's European operations. The British press might have cheered a little too loudly and jingoistically at these and other promotions, but at best British management in financial services was on the up and at worst it was no longer a joke.

With every new set of statistics the media celebrated the City's increased share of global financial transactions as a rare example of British success. Organisations such as the City of London Corporation and International Financial Services London were tasked with promoting the UK financial services industry and did so with gusto: 'The UK is both the leading global financial services centre and the single most internationally focused marketplace in the world . . . [with] . . . an unrivalled contribution of capital and capabilities.'[7] More objective commentators such as Andrew Hilton, director of the Centre for the Study of Financial Innovation, also confessed to being 'stunned by how far London is perceived to be ahead of its Continental European rivals'.[8]

And the figures were there to back up the claims. In the economy the financial services industry started the period as a major force and just grew in scale and significance relative to other sectors. In the years 1996 to 2006 the financial services industry's self-proclaimed share of GDP grew from 6.6 to 9.4 per cent, its trade surplus rose from £8.7 billion to about £25 billion and City jobs grew from 265,000 to 338,000.[9] On nearly all measures London gained market share in this period. McKinsey's study for New York's civic leaders included interviews with senior executives in the financial services industry in New York and London: most agreed that London's momentum in 2006, the date of the report, was far stronger than New York's.[10]

This is borne out by a range of statistics showing how London gained market share in most of the industry's major business segments.

One of the most important areas of modern finance was the inter-professional trade in complex financial instruments known as over-the-counter (OTC) derivatives. London dominated this business, its global market share shooting up from 27 per cent in 1995 to 43 per cent in 2004, by which time the average daily turnover in OTC derivatives in the UK was $643 billion. Hedge funds, aggressively managed pools of investment capital, was another go-go area in which London excelled. London's share of the global hedge fund industry rose from 10 per cent in 2002 to 20 per cent in 2006,[11] and hedge fund assets under management in London grew at the rate of 63 per cent a year, reaching $300 billion in 2006.[12] The London Stock Exchange and its more lightly regulated Alternative Investment Market (AIM) attracted a rising share of the world's initial public offerings (IPOs) and this boosted Europe's share of global IPOs from 33 per cent in 2001 to 63 per cent in 2006.[13]

These growth rates were reflected in the revenues of the financial services industry. For example, in 2004–5 revenue in investment banking and sales and trading rose by 25 per cent in Europe, 19 per cent in Asia and just 6 per cent in the US. The growth of Europe transformed the geographical profile of the industry. Total investment banking, sales and trading revenues in Europe, at one time a mere drop in the investment banks' ocean, were only 10 per cent lower than in the US by 2005.[14]

The City's new status as a 21st-century prodigy was partly attributable to what it liked to call a new paradigm in risk management. Derivatives, it was claimed, had taken the risk out of banking. Lower-risk banking, supporters said, cut the cost of debt for private and corporate borrowers and enabled governments to plan for a smooth economic cycle without the kind of banking crises that had spattered the 20th-century economic landscape. The chief proponent of this new system was Alan Greenspan, chairman of the US Federal Reserve between 1987 and 2006. His influence in the UK was such that he was knighted in 2002 and he used that visit to extol the virtues of the new banking model. 'The broad success of that paradigm,' he told an audience at Lancaster House, 'seemed to be most evident in the US over the past two and a half years. Despite the draining impact of a loss of $8 trillion of stock market wealth, a sharp contraction in capital investment and, of course, the tragic events of September 11 2001, our economy held firm. Importantly, despite significant losses, no major US financial institution was driven to default.'*

At the heart of this supposedly risk-light world was a method of banking known as originate and distribute. Old-style banking involved banks taking deposits from some customers and lending to others, paying careful attention to ensure that they did not lend out more than they had received from their savers. The banks kept the loans on their books and charged interest until they were repaid. For very big deals banks would get together in a syndicate to spread the risk, but each member of the syndicate would keep its portion of the loan on its balance sheet until the loan matured.

In the second half of the 1990s bankers and derivatives experts invented the new originate and distribute model. The breakthrough idea was credit default swaps (CDSs), which enabled banks to exchange risk in one entity for another, effectively a form of insurance against a company defaulting. This idea was used to expand the established technique of securitisation from a specialism used mainly by American banks into a global banking phenomenon. Instead of keeping the loans on their own balance sheets, a risky business that tied up lots of capital under banking regulations, banks pooled their loan books into special investment vehicles (SIVs) and sold shares in them on to investors. SIVs contained a blend of low-yielding investment-grade debt and riskier and therefore higher-yielding lower-grade debt. Ratings agencies, organisations that classified securities according to the risk they carried, were persuaded that the whole entity was low risk and gave the SIVs the coveted AAA rating. The overall package produced a higher yield than was available on conventional bonds; investors could hedge out the risk of credit default in the CDS market and the extra income appeared to be risk free.

Demand for securitised bonds was enormous, growing from $800 billion in 1997 to over $3 trillion ten years later.[15] This growth was triggered by an unusual set of circumstances. At the same time as the derivatives experts worked out how to take the risk out of high-yield securities, global interest rates fell below 5 per cent, stimulating an unprecedented and sustained demand from consumers for credit.

*Remarks by Chairman Alan Greenspan at Lancaster House, London, 25 September 2002, federalreserve.gov

Simultaneously the emerging countries of Asia joined the oil-producing states of the Middle East in generating financial surpluses. There was a wall of money from these countries looking for places to invest and few if any conventional assets offering much in the way of income. Structured financial products connected the borrowers and the investors. They offered investors a premium income with apparently little risk and attracted billions of petrodollars and Asian surpluses either directly or through investments in hedge funds and other players in the credit markets.

Securitisation enabled banks to increase their lending to personal and corporate borrowers, eventually prompting a boom in house prices and record levels of household indebtedness. Britain was in the vanguard. Until the year 2000 the UK total household debt was always less than the country's total gross domestic product. The cross-over came in the second quarter of 2000; and by 2007 household debt exceeded GDP by more than 50 per cent, having grown by an incredible £67 billion since the turn of the century. In less than a decade the country changed from being a nation of producers into a nation of borrowers.

Investors' appetite for securitised assets enabled banks to lend so much, and they did so by shifting vast amounts of debt off their balance sheets (where it had to be matched by prescribed amounts of regulatory capital) into off-balance sheet SIVs, where regulatory capital rules did not apply. Existing and new loans were parcelled out in this way creating a shadow banking system outside the control of regulators. In effect the banks borrowed in the securitisation markets at one price and lent the proceeds on to customers such as mortgage holders, credit card users and corporate borrowers at a higher price. The margin between the two made for a nice profit for the banks but there were three risks involved.

First, if the underlying creditors – the homeowners, credit card holders or corporate borrowers – defaulted, the banks had obligations to the SIVs as their underwriters. Second, the duration of the securitisation was shorter than the duration of the loans – what is called a maturity mismatch. The banks had to renew their funding in the securitisation markets several times during the course of each loan; if the markets closed, they were in trouble. Third, there was so much money around and it was so easy for the banks to borrow cheaply and mark up the interest rate that they were tempted to lend out more and more. As a result, the old discipline of balancing loans and deposits was lost and banks became highly leveraged institutions themselves and vulnerable to either of the first two risks.

These risks were not appreciated in 2007. Derivates-based originate and distribute banking persuaded practitioners, regulators and investors that the risk characteristics of providing capital to the world had been fundamentally changed by structured finance, and nowhere was this new paradigm more enthusiastically proclaimed than in Britain. Investment bankers had the most to gain as the providers of these products and they were aggressive in promoting their use. One leading investment bank modestly presented its derivatives strategy with a slide showing itself on one side of the picture and its clients on the other side. The two were linked by a box labelled 'risk transformation', and the bank claimed that through its clever 'solutions' risk could be repackaged in such a way that it disappeared out of the system.[16]

When accidents did happen, such as the collapses of the US energy giant Enron in 2001 and the Italian food company Parmalat in 2003, financiers were quick to cry foul, blaming deliberate manipulation and deception and praising the new system for containing the damage. Government in Britain and America gave the banks the benefit of the doubt and continued to talk up the modern financial services industry. One of Ed Balls's predecessors as Britain's economic secretary to the Treasury, Ruth Kelly, drew comfort from the collapse of Parmalat, an event, she said, that 'passed with relatively few repercussions at least in part due to the increasingly widespread use of credit default swaps'. She concluded, 'If used carefully [derivatives] have the power to spread risk. More has been lost from bad real estate investments than from derivatives.'[17]

Not everyone agreed. In his 2003 letter to shareholders in his investment group Berkshire Hathaway, Warren Buffett, regarded as one of the world's most shrewd investors, warned that derivatives were 'financial weapons of mass destruction' that could harm the whole economic system, but in the years leading up to 2007 few people were prepared to listen to him or other critics. In Britain and America the financial services industry was on a roll, and it was neither fashionable nor, in the heat of the moment, considered credible to question its business model.

The City knew that it was in the ascendant and began to get cocky. In the spring of 2006 the *Financial Times* produced a special report on what it dubbed the New City, leading off with the accurate observation: 'There is a certain swagger about the City of London these days – a self-confidence born of success as it has strengthened its position as Europe's leading financial centre and as a magnet for capital and talent from around the world.'[18] Barely six months later the twentieth anniversary of Big Bang was marked by a degree of backslapping that has scarcely been surpassed even in an industry that could hardly be described as self-effacing: 'The self-congratulation has been epic. In newspaper articles, in lectures and in private meetings with cabinet ministers, extremely rich men have reminded us how the Big Bang ushered in 20 glorious years of success.'[19]

However, closer scrutiny of the twenty years after Big Bang reveals that the picture was not quite as glorious as City publicists made out. The City's record between 1987 and 1997 was so uneven that its elevated status in the years and months leading up to June 2007 was remarkable given what had gone on before and what was to come. When we deal with the credit crunch and the collapse of Northern Rock in the second half of 2007 in the closing chapters of this book we shall see the striking contrast with the euphoria of the previous few years. But first it is important to consider another contrast: that between the triumphant New City of early 2007 and the shambolic face it presented in 1997 when New Labour first came to power.

2

GROUND ZERO: 1987–97

In 1995 The *City Research Project*, a report for the City of London Corporation, produced a glowing account of its client's place in the global financial services industry. In nearly every major segment of the world's capital markets the City's market share of cross-border trading was impressive: 64 per cent in international equities, 27 per cent in global currency trading, 35 per cent in swaps, 65–75 per cent in Eurobond issues, 75 per cent in secondary Eurobond trading and 81 per cent in international fund management.[1] A subsequent report for the Corporation of London said the City was one of the world's top three financial capitals and 'whereas the other two centres, New York and Tokyo, are primarily financial centres for their domestic markets, London's major activities are predominantly international. London is in fact the world's largest centre for international financial transactions.'[2]

The same year as the City Research Project was completed a rather different opinion on the City emerged with the publication of Will Hutton's best-seller *The State We're In*. The first page accused the City of London of being 'sullied by malpractice and a reputation for commercial misjudgment' and five pages later Hutton proclaimed, 'The City of London has become a byword for speculation, inefficiency and cheating.'[3]

Both views were right. The City was indeed riding high as a global financial services capital, but this was in spite of rather than because of its principal institutions, many of which displayed all the characteristics that Hutton observed. A flurry of losses and scandals suggested that banks, brokers and fund managers were unable to manage their own businesses. The City's regulators including the Bank of England appeared out of their depth and unable to control the industries they were meant to supervise. The stock exchange's attempts to modernise lurched from crisis to crisis, spoiled by infighting and poor project management. The Lloyd's insurance market was on its knees as losses threatened its very survival. Senior businessmen and their advisers were under investigation as a series of corporate scandals suggested that the City's culture was deteriorating fast. Malpractice? Misjudgment? Speculation? Inefficiency? Cheating? It was difficult to argue with any of Hutton's charges.

For most of the 1980s the City had appeared to be synonymous with Britain's economic recovery in the first flush of Thatcherism, flexing its muscles for the first time after two decades in which governments of a socialist or timid Conservative hue had held it in check. Measures such as the abolition of exchange controls in 1979 and the Big Bang deregulation of financial markets in 1986 had enhanced the City's international competitiveness. A global bull market in equities, the government's privatisation of state assets such as BT and a permissive attitude to merger and acquisitions boosted capital markets business. The arrival of hard-charging American investment banks transformed the City's culture, work ethic and pay.

Conspicuous consumption in bars and restaurants and the flaunting of badges of wealth such as Rolex watches and Porsches alerted the press and public to the big bonuses on offer to the City's high rollers. It was the high-spending, high-earning yuppie era in which greed was good and lunch was for wimps. Public perception of the City stereotype changed from the gent in his bowler hat and pinstripes to the gesticulating options trader in his brightly coloured jacket.

But these high-octane days came to a shuddering halt in October 1987 when the equity market crashed in spectacular fashion, falling by more than 20 per cent in just two days. For the next ten years the City succeeded as an economic entity in spite of pitiful performances by many of its leading institutions. It was a curious paradox. On the one hand the City extended its position as a modern global financial services centre, sucking in increasing amounts of valuable overseas earnings. On the other hand it was difficult to find a single major British financial institution that was an unqualified success, while many failed dismally.

Investment banking was the most high profile of the disaster zones in the decade after Big Bang. Investment banks advised corporate and institutional clients, offering guidance to chief executives on strategic issues such as mergers and acquisitions and pension funds on which shares to buy and sell. Big Bang on 27 October 1986 was intended to modernise Britain's investment banking and broking industry and equip it to compete in a fast globalising industry. The City before Big Bang had many merits, including a culture that put its clients interests' first and a structure that avoided conflict of interest, but it also had a reputation for being inward-looking, not especially hard-working and for protecting its own interests. This was exemplified by the stock exchange, a closed shop with fixed rates of commission and restrictions on membership.

The new rules swept these away, deregulating commissions, opening up the stock exchange to outside members and adopting the US practice of allowing brokers to trade in markets for themselves as well as for customers. Britain's clearing and merchant banks were allowed to buy brokers, and it was expected that this would enable them to compete with the American investment banks such as Goldman Sachs, Merrill Lynch and Morgan Stanley. Between 1983 and 1986 the big banks of the day, including Barclays, NatWest, HSBC and Midland, and merchant banks like Warburgs, Schroders and Kleinwort Benson bought, built or converted to investment banks.

After a successful first year, the crash of 1987 revealed that the bankers, brokers and dealers had been flattered by a rising equity market and had neglected to put in place appropriate business controls. The year's profits were wiped out, and some of the new owners lost confidence in the businesses they had bought and swiftly reversed their strategy. From that moment on, investment banking in the City by UK-owned firms was on the run, unloved by shareholders and under pressure from big American banks.

They moved in for the kill between 1995 and 1997, when six of the City's top investment banks were sold to overseas competitors in little more than eighteen months. Barings was the first to go in February 1995. It was not the most important institution to fall but its demise was the most shocking because of the management weaknesses that were exposed. The man directly responsible for Barings' demise was Nick Leeson, a part-qualified trader sent out to Singapore to run the bank's derivatives operations there. He fraudulently ran up and concealed losses of £850 million, busting the bank so that it was sold in distress for the nominal sum of £1. Leeson's trial in Singapore and regulators' reports revealed that Barings' management had made several fundamental errors. Senior executives seemed to have only a hazy understanding of the products being traded and appeared lackadaisical at following up on warning signs. Barings' directors, including members of the Baring family and some of the City's most respected investment bankers, were humiliated.

Three months later, in May 1995, the City's leading investment bank bit the dust when S. G. Warburg was sold to SBC of Switzerland. Warburg had assembled a strong business in the run-up to Big Bang and had ridden the volatile markets of the late 1980s and early 1990s with aplomb. It was believed that the Treasury and the Bank of England had decided that if any British firm was going to be able to take on the giants of Wall Street it would be Warburg, and the firm received a steady flow of government business. But following profit warnings after an unwise expansion into the bond markets in 1994 and botched merger discussions with the US investment bank Morgan Stanley at the end of that year, Warburg was forced to merge with SBC as the junior partner in the deal. The fall of Warburg led other credible independent British investment banks to throw in the towel, and there was a spate of mergers, including Smith New Court with Merrill Lynch and Kleinwort Benson with Dresdner Bank later in 1995.

The year Labour came to power, 1997, saw the end of the Big Bang experiments in investment banking. The big British clearing banks had rushed into the sector but Midland withdrew after the crash of 1987 and soon merged with HSBC. HSBC had made an ambitious investment banking play, buying up the UK's leading broker James Capel, but by the early 1990s was restricting its ambitions and appeared to be running the business down. NatWest and Barclays, the last two clearing banks with expansion plans in investment banking, sold their equities businesses to American competitors in ignominious circumstances in 1997. NatWest lost all credibility with shareholders when it revealed a long-standing hole in its options books just days after reporting its full-year results, and Barclays suddenly withdrew from full-scale investment banking in the midst of a hiring spree.

There was an element of inevitability about the investment banks' demise. Globalisation and clients' demands for capital meant that UK institutions lacked the scale to compete. The Americans' ability to cross-subsidise their European businesses from their more profitable domestic activities and their long-established investment banking culture gave them a decisive advantage. But these factors were compounded by mismanagement, and the City looked inept as, one after the other, its leading investment banks fell.

While all this was going on in the investment banks, another of the City's flagship activities, investment management, was also showing signs of strain. Investment managers were responsible for investing the assets of pension funds and retail savers in the markets. By the late 1990s the industry's reputation was suffering from poor investment performance and business control issues.

Pension fund management was the investment management industry's core product and in the 1990s the sector was dominated by five firms: Schroders, Mercury, Gartmore, Phillips & Drew and Morgan Grenfell. Pension fund trustees usually allocated their whole fund to one or two of these firms or others like them and left asset allocation between different classes of investment – bonds or equities, British or European, American or emerging markets – to the appointed managers. The broadly based portfolios in which the fund managers decided the asset allocation were known as balanced funds.

Giving the fund managers such wide discretion might have produced bold and imaginative investment strategies but in fact the reverse occurred. The industry was highly competitive with investment performance relative to other fund managers the principal factor in determining whether business was won or lost. Fund managers became scared of underperforming, and as Paul Myners, chairman of Gartmore, explained in a Treasury review of the investment manager industry published in 2001, by the mid-1990s this had led to risk-averse fund management: 'the managers hired tended to gravitate to holding the same asset classes as one another, in roughly the same proportions, thus reducing the business risk of losing the account by reason of returns noticeably lower than those of their peers'.[4]

This defensive strategy served clients badly. In the five years to the end of 1998, more than 80 per cent of actively managed UK funds failed to beat the targets they had been set, according to CAPS, a consultancy specialising in fund management performance. The further one digs into the figures the worse the performance looks. Pooled funds – small pension funds pooled under the control of a single asset manager – managed by the leading pension fund managers performed dreadfully in 1997. The FT All Share Index was a reasonable and common benchmark, and this rose 23.6 per cent in 1997. None of the biggest firms produced returns above 14 per cent in 1997 for their pooled funds; the median for UK fund managers was 16.6 per cent and only the top few performers produced 23.6 per cent, according to CAPS.[5]

The Myners report gave a bleak but accurate description of the situation: 'By the middle of the 1990s, the balanced mandate was seen to have produced disappointing results. Among the perceived problems was the persistent underexposure of most managers to the particularly highly performing American equity market. Replacing one balanced manager by another, or by multiple balanced managers, did not appear to alleviate the problem.'[6] There is safety in numbers but not when the numbers turn soft. As the years of underperformance rolled by, pension funds and the consultants that advised them grew unhappy. Throughout the 1990s the abject performance of the UK's pension fund managers was an open secret in the financial services industry and became public knowledge in 1998.

This was the year that Unilever began proceedings against Mercury, the firm that managed its pension fund. In 1996 Mercury and Unilever had agreed investment guidelines for the portfolio. Unilever specified that the fund managed by Mercury should be structured so as to beat a named benchmark by 1 per cent and never to underperform it by more than 3 per cent. For a sophisticated fund manager such as Mercury this was an achievable target, and Unilever probably expected Mercury to construct a broadly based portfolio to deliver these conservative aims. But Mercury was more individualistic than most other leading fund management firms and ran a concentrated portfolio of forty stocks for the Unilever fund. Unfortunately it underperformed the benchmark by over 10 per cent before Unilever terminated the contract in 1998.[7]

Unilever alleged that Mercury had not stuck to the agreed mandate, and public interest was stimulated by the fact that the principal protagonists, Wendy Mayall, Unilever's chief investment officer, and Carol Galley, one of Mercury's top executives, were two of the most powerful women in the City. Mayall quoted a conversation with a Mercury fund manager who 'suggested that the source of the problems lay with Carol Galley's reluctance to intervene and exercise control over the managers'. Mayall recalled a meeting in November 1997 where 'Carol Galley was unable to offer an explanation for why Mercury had put in place in November/December 1996 a portfolio structure which was inconsistent with our specified objectives and risk tolerance. She was only able to offer comments such as "no excuse" and "no explanation".'[8]

Mercury denied the allegations and cited exceptional stock market conditions. The case was settled out of court but the publicity given to Unilever's allegations harmed the reputation of the pension fund management industry. This reputation had already been damaged by some high-profile scandals surrounding Morgan Grenfell Asset Management, another of the big five firms.

The Peter Young affair broke in 1996, when Morgan Grenfell discovered that Young, the manager of its European Growth unit trust, had been investing excessively in hard-to-sell and hard-to-value high-risk, high-technology firms. Prosecutors alleged a smokescreen of shell companies in Luxembourg and collusion with a Scandinavian stockbroker. The affair cost Keith Percy, Morgan Grenfell's chief investment officer, and four other employees their jobs. Morgan Grenfell paid a total of £400 million to compensate investors and shore up the funds. Fraud charges were brought against Young, a colleague and two stockbrokers. Young appeared at a pretrial hearing dressed as a woman and using the name Elizabeth. He later claimed to have heard voices urging him to change sex and carried out self-mutilation. The stockbrokers and Young's colleague were acquitted and a jury found Young unfit to stand trial. The case against him was dismissed under the 1964 Insanity Act.[9]

In 1997 Morgan Grenfell suffered more adverse publicity when it suspended Nicola Horlick, one of its star fund managers. Horlick was alleged to have been negotiating with another firm to move her team, a charge she denies. Horlick was told to go home, let everything cool down and return to work a few days later: 'Nobody outside will ever know,' she was told.[10] But Horlick was barely inside her front door when a friend rang to commiserate, having read about her suspension on Reuters.

A crowd scene quickly developed outside Horlick's house: 'There were about fifty journalists, satellite television vans and television crews everywhere. From then on the whole thing just exploded. Morgan Grenfell underestimated how newsworthy it was for a thirty-five-year-old woman who earns a lot and who was quite good at her job with five children one of whom has leukaemia to be suspended from work.' Horlick suspected that senior management at Morgan Grenfell were briefing against her and was determined to meet them and have her say. The top people in London would not see her, so she flew to Frankfurt to the head office of Morgan Grenfell's parent company Deutsche Bank, followed by a pack of reporters. Horlick says she was treated professionally and courteously in Frankfurt, but by then it was too late and she left the firm.

Poor investment performance, the Peter Young and Nicola Horlick affairs at Morgan Grenfell, the Unilever–Mercury case and other events convinced many observers that investment managers in the City could not look after themselves. In the words of one contemporary fund manager it was 'ironic that there we were, analysing companies, criticising companies, yet our own industry was appallingly badly run. You had people trampling over each other to get to the top and then staying there five minutes before they were deposed. When it came to management, it was a terrible industry.'[11] Taken together with the failure of so many investment banks over the same period, mismanagement in the City appeared rife.

Managerial incompetence in these two core businesses was accompanied by a whiff of sleaze in the space where the City met the corporate sector. The Guinness affair, in which several senior City figures, including the company's high-profile chief executive Ernest Saunders, were sent to jail for their part in an illegal share support operation during the takeover battle for Distillers Company, came to trial in 1990. The furore around another share support operation, in which the investment banks County NatWest and Phillips & Drew were accused of misleading the market by secretly buying Blue Arrow shares during its 1986 rights issue, culminated in a year-long trial (and no convictions) ending in 1992. News of corruption at the failed bank BCCI and the looting of pension funds in the Maxwell group of companies broke in 1991. In 1993 Asil Nadir, the Turkish-Cypriot entrepreneur whose

Polly Peck group had seen its share price rise from five pence to thirty-five pounds before collapsing in 1991, fled to Northern Cyprus, a country with which Britain had no extradition treaty, with sixty-six charges of theft involving £34 million hanging over him. The unsavoury smell lingered over the City throughout the mid-1990s, and even during the 1997 election campaign there was a controversial attempt backed by Hambros Bank to break up the Co-operative Group. Hambros was caught with leaked confidential documents in its Tower Hill offices; three of its executives resigned over the debacle and Hambro's chairman Sir Chips Keswick had to make a public apology. The bank and the three executives were fined and reprimanded by regulators.

Those in charge of keeping the system running smoothly did not come out of the 1990s well either. There were problems at many of the City's central institutions, including the Bank of England, where Sir Chips was a member of the governing body. The bank was embarrassed when a deputy governor resigned having smuggled his girlfriend into the building under an alias for sex in the governor's dressing room, but more serious issues were raised by the Barings affair, which revealed weaknesses amongst Britain's banking and securities industry regulators. The Board of Banking Supervision, a body that consisted largely of City insiders, carried out the official inquiry into what happened. The report was gentle to say the least but exposed a regulatory system that lacked clarity of responsibility and sufficient determination and expertise to chase down potential problems.

The Bank of England, which was 'at all relevant times the consolidated supervisor of the Barings Group', 'had confidence in Barings' senior management, many of whom were longstanding Barings' employees' and as a result of this misplaced confidence 'with regard to Barings' overseas subsidiaries the Bank undertook no reviews'. Too much trust, too much complacency and an organisational form unsuited to regulating complex financial groups meant that Barings' lead regulator was unable to spot either Leeson's deception or management's ineptitude. According to the Board of Banking Supervision's generally powder-puff report, 'There does not appear to have been any guideline or system in place within the Bank for determining whether the situation with regard to a member of a banking group for which the Bank was responsible for consolidated supervision was material such that it could affect the wellbeing of the bank.'[12] It was another blow to the Bank of England's reputation, which was already under pressure from BCCI creditors, who had launched a $1 billion claim against it alleging inadequate supervision.

Responsibility for supervising Barings was shared with the Securities and Futures Authority (SFA), a body which evidently took a narrow view of its responsibilities for regulating the UK securities industry. It showed little interest in what Barings was doing overseas, a remarkable misjudgement given the interconnected, global financial services industry of the late 20th century, as the Board of Banking Supervision recognised: 'We consider that the SFA's responsibility for monitoring a member firm's obligation to maintain adequate financial resources to meet its investment business commitments and to withstand the risks to which its business is subject requires it to have regard to the activities and financial soundness of a member firm's subsidiaries insofar as they are capable of materially affecting the financial integrity of the member firm.'[13] Neither the Bank of England nor the SFA had the regulators' vital instinct for sensing where danger might lay. Overlapping responsibilities led to insufficient focus on high-risk areas and to a lack of clarity as to exactly who was responsible for what.

The SFA's counterpart in investment management was the Investment Management Regulatory Organisation (IMRO). Like the SFA it had a reputation amongst practitioners of being weak, bureaucratic and not very well staffed. In 1995 an embarrassing row broke out between Phillip Thorpe, IMRO's chief executive, and Andrew Large, chairman of the Securities and Investment Board (SIB), an umbrella organisation in charge of the financial services industry's various regulators. IMRO sent a paper to the influential Treasury Select Committee of MPs criticising the SIB's effectiveness but Thorpe clammed up on the matter when he appeared before the committee. Critics said he had been gagged.

The stock exchange was another of London's central institutions that ran into trouble in the early and middle 1990s. It had lost its supervisory functions in Big Bang and later shed its information services business. Although its position as a market for equities, particularly international equities, strengthened during these years, the stock exchange was riddled with factions and its performance blighted by technology problems. In 1993 the exchange was forced to abandon

TAURUS, a long-running project to introduce an electronic system for the settlement of securities trades. The idea had been first mooted back in 1981, but a combination of poor IT management and infighting amongst the investment banks and brokers led to delays and cost over-runs. By the time the project was shelved the exchange had spent £75 million, its members £320 million, and there was nothing to show for it. Some 350 staff were made redundant and its chief executive, Peter Rawlins, resigned. Perhaps the most telling indictment of the stock exchange's ineptitude came from the Bank of England, which took over the project and produced a new system inside three years at a cost of less than £30 million.[14]

The TAURUS episode forced the exchange to re-evaluate its role in the financial services industry, and it began to turn round, but not before another embarrassing spat in 1996. Rawlins's successor as chief executive, Michael Lawrence, attempted to introduce a modern method of dealing in stocks known as electronic order-driven trading, but the vested interests amongst the traditional market makers and broker-dealers were not to be coerced. They rebelled against the proposed system and in January 1996 Lawrence suddenly resigned. To outside observers of these events, City firms resembled an unruly rabble with the stock exchange cast in the role of a schoolteacher that had lost control of the class.[15]

A few hundred yards to the east of the stock exchange stood the headquarters of London's insurance market: the shiny new Lloyd's building, designed by the architect Richard Rogers and opened in 1986. The substance of Lloyd's business, however, did not match the style of its surroundings. In the 1980s unexpectedly large awards in the US courts for punitive damages on asbestos, pollution and health hazard (APH) policies strained the resources of the Lloyd's underwriting syndicates. After paying out on a run of disasters including the Piper Alpha oil rig explosion of 1988 and Hurricane Hugo in 1989, annual losses were approaching £2 billion.

Several US states and private investors – names – alleged that Lloyd's kept secret their knowledge of APH claims until they could recruit more investors to take on these claims. Enforcement officials in eleven US states also charged Lloyd's and some of its associates with various wrongs such as fraud and selling unregistered securities. Eventually a new management team restructured the Lloyd's market with a

£3.2 billion recovery plan in 1996 and managed to buy off the names, but the reputational damage of the earlier episodes was severe.[16]

The novelist Julian Barnes's description of the mismanagement at Lloyds – 'negligence, fraud, complacency, and sardonic uncaringness'[17] – was evident in different places and at different times in other parts of the City during the less than glorious decade before 1997. Many of the City's institutions were struggling, and except in odd pockets such as at LIFFE, London's dynamic derivatives exchange, there was no sign of the vibrancy that came to characterise the coming decade. Although the City talked a good game, playing up its gains in trading market share and its importance to the UK economy, the failures of so many of its leading institutions gave the place a losing feel in 1997 as the UK stood on the brink of its first Labour government for nearly twenty years.

PART TWO

RENAISSANCE:
1997–JUNE 2007

The force that through the green fuse drives the flower
Drives my green age; that blasts the roots of trees
Is my destroyer.

> 'The force that through the green fuse drives the
> flower', Dylan Thomas
> Dylan Thomas, Miscellany One, J M Dent, 1963,
> Page 7

3

THE PERFECT CALM

Britain and the City moved along parallel and sometimes inter-connected lines during the Blair years, each undergoing undoubted changes in style and more debatable changes in substance. These parallel journeys were no coincidence for, as we have already seen, City people had an open door to the government, and the financial services industry was a prime mover in the British economy.

The fresh faces of Tony Blair and his ministerial team represented a generational change in British politics. New Labour's leaders looked younger, acted younger and in many cases were younger than the outgoing Conservatives. Blair was able to pull off hobnobbing with 'Cool Britannia' icons such as Oasis and playing football with Kevin Keegan in a way that would have eluded John Major. Patriotism gave way to globalism. Despite staying out of monetary union, Britain became more European once the Conservatives' Euro-sceptics had moved from the government to the opposition benches in the House of Commons.

Suddenly it seemed less embarrassing to be British. The Premier-ship became a magnet for world soccer stars, England's rugby team won the World Cup and its cricket team beat the Australians to regain the Ashes. These sporting achievements were nothing to do with New Labour or the City (although brokers, bankers and certain politicians could be found in the best seats at the key moments) but they seemed to sum up the nation's new confidence.

This was all underpinned by a strong economy. Chancellor Gordon Brown presided over a decade of stable growth, low inflation and low interest rates. His stern Scottish manner as he intoned the golden rules of fiscal responsibility gave reassurance to a nation that valued sobriety – at least from its public leaders. Apparently secure in their jobs and with no threat of high taxes or rising prices, consumers went on a credit binge. Household debt nearly trebled during Brown's time as Chancellor as consumers borrowed to buy houses, cars and digital technology. The high street was transformed into a ribbon of coffee shops, mobile phone retailers and bars as traditional shops decamped to out-of-town retail parks. It was the age of the Internet, and online shopping became a national hobby. This was particularly true of the travel industry, where budget airlines such as easyJet and Ryanair smashed the conventional operating model and brought overseas travel into nearly everyone's budget. There was a thrusting self-confidence about Britain in the Blair years epitomised by Stansted Airport on a typical Saturday morning, where hordes of people, mobiles in hand, jammed the retail outlets and picked up coffees from Starbucks before jostling to catch flights to the sun or the ski slopes.

The City was intimately connected with all this. City bonus payments rose from £1.7 billion in 1997 to £8.5 billion in 2007 and this wealth rippled out into the rest of the economy.[1] The City's lifestyle, attitudes and behaviour helped to determine the new national culture. Mobile technology, the 'work hard, play hard' ethic, Europeanisation and conspicuous consumption were City attributes that the rest of society soon followed. It was summed up in *How To Spend It*, a magazine launched by the *Financial Times* in 1994. The paper said it was 'essential reading for the educated, the affluent and the influential. Unashamedly glamorous, it holds real appeal to discerning consumers who like to stay ahead of the game.'[2] City people could afford and the rest of the country aspired to the products of regular *How To Spend It* advertisers such as Rolex, Cartier, Burberry and Louis Vuitton.

Events were to prove that the permanence of Britain's prosperity was illusory, and the same was to be true of the City, but superficially, and it was to turn out temporarily, the financial services industry experienced a stunning organisational revival between 1997 and 2007. Cutting-edge investment banks replaced stumbling merchant banks. Razor-sharp hedge funds challenged conventional investment management. Private equity threatened established corporate governance structures. Regulators became facilitators. The Bank of England, the stock exchange and Lloyd's moved forward with renewed vigour. And City people made money, bags and bags of it, beyond their wildest dreams.

Rising markets and benign economic conditions gave everyone and everything the appearance of success, and for the entire ten years between 1997 and 2007 the City believed in its own genius. This was only partly justified. The new focus and clarity in fund management, the global perspective and range of the best hedge funds and the efficiencies generated by certain private equity teams were for real. But the City also contained many lacklustre hedge funds borrowing cheap money to buy high-yield bonds, some highly leveraged buyout funds masquerading as turnround experts, deal-hungry investment bankers colluding with chief executives looking for a short cut to a higher share price and complacent regulators. Thus the very real improvements in the quality of the work being done in some parts of the City contrasted with the 'bubble' elements that flattered to deceive.

The City was the temporary beneficiary of four separate but related factors. Firstly, market forces were exceptionally favourable during these years. Secondly, good luck determined that the City was in the right place at the right time while its competitors chose a bad moment to fluff their lines. Thirdly, history endowed the City with a talent pool and an infrastructure that enabled it to seize the moment. Fourthly, the New Labour government, through a mixture of good luck and good judgement, enabled the City to make the most of these opportunities. These factors produced a perfect calm in which Britain's financial services industry prospered as never before.

The decade after 1997 turned out to be one of the most buoyant ever for the world's financial services industry. Finance had been capturing ever higher percentages of output from the early 1980s onwards – Britain's financial services industry contributed only 15 per cent of corporation tax in the 1980s; by 2005 this had risen to over 30 per cent – and this was reflected in a long boom in asset prices.[3] And as those closest to capital captured more of the value of economic activity, others turned to debt to achieve rising living standards. This is evident in the rise in total household debt, which was only two thirds of the nation's total household disposable income at the beginning of the period but matched it by the end.

Finance was all-pervasive in these years. The value of the world's stock markets and annual share trading quadrupled in less than ten years. UK equity market turnover was broadly equal to the country's GDP in 1997; by 2007 it was treble GDP.[4] New products burst onto the scene, offering solutions to problems clients scarcely knew they had and creating vast profits for financial institutions and fortunes for the rocket scientists who invented them. One number sums it up: the global market in derivatives, around which many of the new products were based, grew from $41 trillion to an astonishing $677 trillion in these years.[5]

Globalisation was the driving force behind this activity, and the fastest growth came in international deals that played right into London's strengths. The world converged on free-market capitalism as communism crumbled and the stakeholder economies of France, Germany and Japan struggled. The Eurozone countries and the emerging economies of eastern Europe and Asia turned to the capital markets to fund their expansion and eventually to invest their savings. Nearly every single financial product in every single financial centre grew apace, but cross-border deals, which quadrupled in value in a decade, grew faster than any other category. This completely changed the US-centricity of the financial world. US total financial stock, the sum of equities, debt and bank deposits, grew at 6.5 per cent per annum in the first few years of the 21st century, an unprecedented rate for such a mature economy over such a sustained period. But the Eurozone beat it at 6.8 per cent; the UK achieved 8.4 per cent; and non-Japan Asia grew at an annual rate of 15.5 per cent in these years.[6]

As the emerging markets boomed, London's great advantage was that it was in the right time zone to do business with Asia. American markets were closed during Asia's trading hours and London's trading day straddled Asia's close and America's opening bell. Bankers and traders based in London were able to become the point of connection between East and West. They held the balance of power, could claim to be working round the clock and for a while were at the centre of the financial universe.[7]

The City received another slice of good fortune from the poor performance of its competitors, especially New York. The dot.com crash of 2001–2 exposed mismanaged conflict of interest and insider dealing on Wall Street. In a backlash, Congress passed the Sarbanes Oxley Act, contributing to the 800 different regulations covering banks and financial institutions introduced between 1989 and 2005. The cost of complying with these regulations was prohibitive, rising from $13 billion in 2002 to $25 billion in 2005 for the securities industry alone, according to the Securities Industry Association.[8]

The US appeared to be litigious and bureaucratic, and so businesses looked elsewhere for a place to operate. Federal and state prosecutors hounded the executives held responsible for the dot.com scandals and long prison sentences and heavy fines were handed down. Aggrieved investors seeking restitution for their losses mounted class actions. Section 404 of Sarbanes Oxley required management to prepare an internal control report and to maintain 'adequate internal control procedures for financial reporting', and auditors to 'attest to and report on the assessment made by management'. The act exposed chief executives, chief financial officers, audit partners and others to the risk of criminal prosecution in the US, regardless of where their company was headquartered or where they resided.[9] According to one former senior investment banker, 'The Sarbanes Oxley Act and the litigious environment are creating a more risk averse culture in the United States.' The consequence was plain: 'We are simply pushing people to do more business overseas.'[10]

Luckily for London, none of its competitors was in a position to take advantage of New York's problems. Frankfurt had won much praise during the dot.com bubble for its Neuer Markt, a stock exchange for high-tech companies, but the Neuer Markt imploded during the dot.com crash and soon closed down. This left a nasty taste in the mouths of some German bankers and politicians, who made disparaging comments about the activities of hedge and buy-out funds, thus causing these high-octane players to doubt that Frankurt would provide the level playing field they needed.

Paris had tried to challenge London as a financial centre through Paris Europlace, a government-backed organisation involving the Banque de France, the bourse, the Paris city council and the leading banks and financial institutions. But its attempts to win global capital markets business were undermined by the French government's determination to cling to social market policies and national protectionism. It had areas of expertise, particularly in derivatives, but many of its bright young people went off to work in London, and surveys that ranked cities' talent pools placed Paris behind New York, London and

Frankfurt.[11] And when Christine Lagarde, France's finance minister, launched a series of measures to enhance the standing of Paris as a financial centre in October 2007, the aim was no longer to knock London off the top spot but to win a bit of its financial culture.[12]

Japan failed to develop the status it had in the 1980s as a strong domestic financial centre into an equivalent international position. The reasons were protectionism for domestic players in the corporate and financial sectors and an ailing domestic economy. While an outward-looking and globally competitive Japanese financial sector might have won a large share of the capital markets business coming out of Russia and the former Soviet republics, that business instead went west to London's liquid and transparent markets.

History was kind in that London already had a well-developed infrastructure (including an unrivalled offshore network of tax havens such as the Cayman Islands) and a deep pool of skills. London also spoke English, the international language of finance. It had a great ability to attract new talent in comparison with New York-based firms hampered by restrictive US immigration policies and cumbersome, unpredictable visa application procedures. London was able to take full advantage of EU freedom of movement laws and used European talent to achieve market leadership in the fastest growing and most lucrative sectors such as derivatives. A report for the Corporation of London in 2003, written by the independent think tank the Centre for the Study of Financial Innovation (CSFI), put skilled labour at the top of its list of London's strengths: 'The flexibility of labour practices and the depth of the talent pool are among its biggest pluses.'[13] The report added that virtually every skill required by international finance and its support services could be found in London. A European banker rammed the point home when interviewed for the same report: 'If you want a Greek quant, you'd look in London not Athens', and a British banker agreed: 'You can build intellectual capital very easily in London'.[14]

The City's established position as a global trading centre meant that it had the right financial infrastructure to support the growth. Questions about the City's office stock were answered by the stunning success of Canary Wharf. Privatisation and digital technology had jet-propelled the UK's telecommunications services into the 21st century, and despite lengthening delays at Heathrow, London is a global transport hub reached easily from Europe, the US and Asia. Legal, accounting and management consultancy services were in ready supply and contributed to the critical mass that goes to make up a financial services centre.

London had a good reputation for the quality of its markets, clearing and settling processes and ethical standards. The CSFI ranked the City above other European centres (but below New York) on market quality and quoted one respondent as saying, 'In the main the culture of my word is my bond lives on.' Another said, 'Someone who has survived in the City is tried and tested, can be trusted, knows the language, can initiate a deal with a handshake'[15] – a case of perception above reality if ever there was one.

On 12 June 1997, six weeks after becoming Chancellor of the Exchequer in the new Labour government, Gordon Brown appeared at one of the City's annual set pieces, the Lord Mayor's Banquet for Bankers and Merchants or the Mansion House Dinner as it is more commonly called. By tradition it was a glittering affair, attended by the City's great and good and addressed on financial affairs of state by both the governor of the Bank of England and the Chancellor. Guests were expected to wear formal dress but Brown had let it be known that he would not be wearing a dinner jacket and black tie that night. Wearing a business suit and accompanied by his special advisers Charlie Whelan (dark green double-breasted suit) and Ed Balls (lounge suit with red tie), he made his way to the top table to the traditional slow handclap from the 350 guests.[16] It looked like a deliberate snub – when asked for an opinion Brown's predecessor as Chancellor Ken Clarke dryly commented, 'I personally always turn up in what I was invited to wear'[17] – and a bad omen for the new government's relations with the City. However, appearances can be deceptive, for the gesture was aimed not at the financial community but at the trade unions and Labour's left wing, which were suspicious about New Labour's comfort with the City and market forces.

Their suspicions were well founded, for the replacement of socialism with market-friendly policies was the watershed between Old and New Labour. Out went renationalisation, high taxes and intervention in business; in came free enterprise, market forces and deregulation. It was a defining moment. The Labour governments after 1997 turned out to be even more pro-business than the outgoing Conservatives.

The acceleration of free-market economics provided a platform for a new wave of London's financial institutions to succeed where their predecessors had failed during the previous decade.

The change in Labour's attitude to the market economy was born out of electoral necessity. While Margaret Thatcher's Conservatives were cutting taxes, privatising state assets and smashing the trade unions, Labour had remained a socialist party. The party's 1992 manifesto included commitments to renationalisation, the European Social Chapter for employees and a 50 per cent tax rate on incomes above £40,000. During the 1980s Tony Blair and Gordon Brown, Labour's market-friendly leaders of the future, sounded like old-school socialists when referring to the City. Blair, at the time Labour's spokesman on the City, savaged the stock exchange's report on the crash of 1987 as 'an exercise in self-congratulation rather than self-criticism'.[18] Brown's 1989 tract against Thatcherism, *Where There Is Greed*, denounced privatisation, the 'extraordinary transfer of resources from poor to rich' and the 'huge concentrations of private unaccountable power' that he saw emerging in Britain.[19] But the 1992 election defeat, influenced by the *Sun*'s headline IF NEIL KINNOCK WINS TODAY, WILL THE LAST PERSON TO LEAVE BRITAIN PLEASE TURN OUT THE LIGHTS, convinced Labour that it would have to change if it was ever to be elected. Serious reform began under the leadership of John Smith and was continued by Tony Blair and Gordon Brown after Smith's death.

In the 1980s the urbane Blair had been more interested in the City while the left-leaning Brown focused on manufacturing, believing that Britain's future lay in a state-inspired industrial revival. By the early 1990s Brown's view had changed: 'I came to economics principally through the concern about social justice my father taught me. As the early Fabian socialists did, I felt it was a failure of economics, so the answer was Keynesian – more demand, at least making jobs possible. In the eighties, I saw that we needed a more flexible economy to create jobs. My understanding of an inclusive globalization is that we must combine stability, free trade, open markets and flexibility with investment in equipping people for jobs of the future, principally through education.'[20] Soon after Smith's death in the autumn of 1994, Brown and Blair visited Alan Greenspan, chairman of the US Federal Reserve. At the meeting 'Brown espoused globalization and free markets and did not seem interested in reversing much of what Thatcher had changed in Britain.'[21]

It was Brown's view that mattered on economic affairs. In return for standing aside for Blair to become leader of the party in 1994, he secured control over economic and social policy in a future Labour government, and he guarded this jealously. Greenspan recalled: 'It appeared to me that Brown was the senior person. Blair stayed in the background while Brown did most of the talking about a "new" Labour.'[22] When Blair did venture into the economic sphere, Brown was quick to re-establish his authority. In 1996 Blair created ripples in New Labour circles when he appeared to endorse Will Hutton's stakeholder views, telling an audience in Singapore, 'It is surely time to assess how we shift the emphasis in corporate ethos from the company being a mere vehicle for the capital market to be traded, bought and sold as a commodity, towards a vision of the company as a community or partnership in which each employee has a stake.'[23] However, according to Alastair Campbell, Brown was having none of it and poured cold water on any notion that New Labour would dabble with such radical ideas: 'it was pretty clear that GB did not believe in the basic stakeholder economy message at all . . . [and] . . . he successfully troubled TB, who began to wonder whether we had the right definition of the stakeholder economy.'[24]

It was a sudden and crucial decision in the history of New Labour and the City. 'One minute the then-editor of the *Observer* [Will Hutton] was sitting in Blair's kitchen watching Tony Blair push down the plunger on the cafetière as he said "Will, stakeholding is going to be our Bible" . . . Just six weeks later Hutton found his idea had been dropped.'[25] A New Labour adviser, Geoff Mulgan, told the entrepreneur and academic Shann Turnbull that 'the stakeholder idea had frightened the big end of town and so it had been dropped. Company directors were concerned that they would be made accountable to people other than shareholders and institutional investors were frightened that it would destroy shareholder value.'[26] This change of mind was a turning point for the City. It set the scene for the close alliance between the City and New Labour, and the decade would have looked very different if stakeholder governance had been adopted.

Once the decision had been taken to go with market forces, the importance of the City as the government's window on the world became obvious. Not only was it the incoming New Labour government's ally in the operation of a market economy but also – as had been shown in 1991–2 by the drop in tax revenues from the City during the recession – its earnings would help to balance the nation's books. Anti-City rhetoric of the kind that had characterised the 1980s was a thing of the past, and New Labour got down to thinking about how to work with market forces.

Research carried out while the party was in opposition had persuaded Labour's leaders that intervention in markets did not work. One of their advisers at the time recalls that lessons were drawn from events in the US in 1963, when an attempt to protect the US balance of payments by taxing Americans buying foreign securities had unforeseen results: 'There was a paper circulating that looked at what had happened in the US during the Kennedy administration when they put in interest rate controls. This forced the Eurodollar market out of America into Europe and proved to be a very costly mistake. It was accepted that excessive interference in City structures might similarly invoke the law of unintended consequences and could kill the goose that laid the golden egg.'[27]

Proof that non-intervention in markets was to be the order of the day came on 6 May 1997, less than a week after Labour's election victory, when Gordon Brown announced that he was handing over responsibility to the Bank of England to set interest rates. This change had symbolic and practical significance. Clement Attlee's Labour government had nationalised the Bank of England in 1946; setting it free of government control in 1997 was a clear signal that Labour had fully embraced free markets. The economic consequences of the decision were even more important. Power to set interest rates would reside with the new Monetary Policy Committee, a brains trust of the bank's three top officials, two bank executive directors and four expert economists appointed by the Chancellor. Economists not politicians would in future determine interest rates, one of the principal means of controlling the economy. The City liked this message, and gilts, sterling and equities all rose in the belief that the change would keep inflation down.[28] When Brown used his Budget speech of 2 July 1997 to set out Labour's economic agenda including the 'golden rule' that over the economic cycle the government would only borrow to invest, and that public debt would be held at a prudent level, markets gave Labour an emphatic thumbs up, and on 3 July 1997 the FTSE index rose to a new record.[29]

A few City diehards believed that New Labour would turn out to be a wolf in sheep's clothing once it was in power. They feared it would soak the rich by raising personal tax rates on high incomes, and some wealthy individuals made contingency arrangements in case their worst fears were realised. In fact the new government's tax policies for high earners were generous, some said to a fault, and were instrumental in drawing in talent and financial services business to the City.

The Labour Party had learned the lessons of 1992, when its tax plans – which the Conservative press had dubbed 'Labour's tax bomb' – were a key factor in the loss of the election. Between 1992 and 1997 the leadership weaned the party away from the notion that raising tax rates for high earners was the best way to redistribute wealth. According to senior advisers, when Gordon Brown was shadow Chancellor 'he had a chart which he showed MPs that pointed out that less than 1 per cent of the population had taxable income of over £100,000 a year, and that taxing the rich would not raise very much revenue and was likely to damage the economy's ability to produce. Shear the sheep, don't kill them, was the approach. It was a matter of trade-offs.'[30]

The Labour government's first Budget in 1997 contained no nasty personal taxation surprises and the 1998 Budget included the single measure that was to transform the City's tax regime. This was the reduction in capital gains tax from 40 to 10 per cent on business assets held for at least ten, later two, years. It provided a stimulus for hedge fund start-ups and ensured that neither they nor private equity firms would be tempted by lower foreign tax rates to move their businesses overseas.

It was a perfect example of the law of unintended consequences, for it seems that Brown's intention in cutting capital gains tax was to encourage dot.com entrepreneurs not hedge funds. When he announced the tax cuts Chancellor Brown said, 'This government today sends a clear signal of support for enterprise to those who invest in the UK. My message to business is – when you are ready to start out, start up, start investing or start hiring – this government is on your side.'[31] Brown did not specify which sector he had in mind but advisers are absolutely clear why the change was made: 'The government had brought it in because it was in favour of new industry innovation and there had been a lot of lobbying from dot.com personnel. So they brought in taper relief and dropped capital gains tax to 10 per cent.'[32]

According to one hedge fund manager this change had a major impact: 'London became the place to be, to set up businesses. Historically, people did not leave big organisations and start up on their own, but with 10 per cent taper relief it became possible for a new generation of entrepreneurs or individuals who were willing to take risk to set up on their own, and basically risk their careers but possibly make a fortune. The pay-off slope changed. The tax situation meant that the threshold hurdle for taking risks came down.'[33]

Labour's decision to continue with tax breaks for non-domiciled residents of the UK was also important for the hedge fund and private equity communities. Non-domiciled residents are people who live in the UK but are able to show some other country as their real home. This involves filling out a short form in which they provide their family background, list their connections with the country of their birth and state their intention not to stay permanently in the UK. This shelters them from paying UK tax on their earnings in the rest of the world unless they remit the money to the UK. The UK rules are very generous compared to those in many countries. In the US, for example, it does not matter where you were born: if you qualify as a resident of the US, you must pay US tax on all your income and capital gains all over the world.

The Conservatives had a look at the non-dom issue during Margaret Thatcher's premiership. There were no hedge funds around at the time but the Treasury briefed her that an important reason for global shipping insurance being done through London was because many Greek shipowners were encouraged to live in the UK by the generous tax rules. A cost-benefit analysis was done and it was decided that it would be disastrous to abolish the non-dom rules. Ten years later, when the first hedge funds were started in London, the big international players looked hard at the UK. According to one fund manager who was around at the time, 'They could hire good people, the tax regime was kind and whether they were German hedge fund players, French, American this was the place to be.'[34]

The increase in the number of non-doms in London during the City's boom years of the early 21st century is remarkable. Prior to the hedge fund and private equity boom, most of the UK's 60,000 non-doms were shipping magnates, Middle Eastern princes, American corporate heirs and a few highly paid sports, movie and rock stars.[35] By 2008, when Labour Chancellor Alistair Darling announced modest proposals to tax non-doms, the number had risen to 115,000, and it seems highly likely that the financial services industry accounted for the majority of this increase. To put this in context, it seems that between 10 and 15 per cent of the City's total workforce in 2008 may have been non-doms, and that this group accounted for half of the increase in City jobs after 1997.

There was only one area in which Labour's tax policies worked against the City, and that was the abolition of dividend tax credits for pension funds in the 1997 Budget. This eventually became a political issue, but when it was first announced protests from the opposition parties and the pension funds had no traction. Under existing legislation pension funds were entitled to claim a tax credit on dividends paid by UK companies, a concession that the Treasury believed gave 'exempt investors an incentive to press companies to pay dividends rather than retain and reinvest profits'.[36] Abolishing the tax credits was expected to raise £5 billion a year in revenue and achieve one of Gordon Brown's long-standing aims of encouraging British industry to invest for the long term.

The public did not immediately see the withdrawal of the tax credits as a problem that affected them. As a result of the rise in share prices during the long bull market, pension funds seemed able to absorb the loss. Only after the fall in equity prices in the dot.com crash of 2000, and the imposition of tougher requirements in the UK Pensions Act of 2004 and from 2005 by Financial Reporting Standard 17 caused the pension funds to swing round to an actuarial deficit of £120 billion did the pension fund tax credit become a political issue. Pension fund sponsors lengthened the time people would have to work until retirement as a result of the deficit; generous defined-benefit pension schemes were closed to new members and the unions were up in arms. But it never really damaged New Labour's pro-market credentials in the City, and as is their way London's investment bankers saw opportunity in adversity, swiftly developing new products to help solve pension fund problems.

Dividend tax credits apart, the City could hardly have asked for more of New Labour in its economic and taxation policies. It had been generous to high earners, non-doms and entrepreneurs. It had declared its intention of allowing markets a free hand by giving the Bank of England operational independence and achieved a stable economy that made the UK an attractive place in which to invest and do business. Privatisation was continued via schemes such as the private finance initiatives and public–private partnerships in the health and education sectors. But New Labour went even further than this in delivering for the City when it developed a light-touch regulatory regime that proved to be an important asset in attracting and retaining financial services business for London.

Financial services regulation in the UK in 1997 was a mess. It had been set up at the time of Big Bang in 1986, and as a result of industry lobbying included a large element of practitioner input. Three self-regulatory organisations each responsible for supervising a different part of the securities and investment industry reported to an over-arching body called the Securities and Investments Board (SIB). Howard Davies, who became the first chief executive of the Financial Services Authority (FSA), had previously spent two years on the board of the SIB and claims never to have been quite sure what its precise role was.

But the problem was not so much the SIB as the self-regulatory organisations that underpinned it, for the financial services industry had changed beyond recognition since 1986. Davies says, 'The Insurance industry had developed strong links with the banking and investment banking industries. The regulation of insurance was in the wrong place in the Department of Trade and Industry. Many building societies were in the process of demutualising and turning themselves into banks and no longer needed a separate regulator. There were two tiers of regulation in the securities industry. Banks had grown increasingly involved in the securities industry and there was overlap between the Bank of England and the SFA.'[37] Steve Robson, the Treasury official who masterminded reform, agrees that the old system no longer worked: 'There was duplication and overlap. Resources were often in the wrong place. As one regulator left through the back door, another came in through the front. Information did not flow between the silos.'[38]

Ineffective regulation contributed to the wave of scandals that engulfed the City in the decade after Big Bang. Reform was under discussion in the last years of the Conservative government, and the Treasury tried unsuccessfully to persuade Ken Clarke, John Major's Chancellor of the Exchequer, to tackle the issue. Clarke would not engage, and so Treasury officials focused their attention on the City, meeting regulators, practitioners and leading financial institutions. The Treasury, supported by Sir Andrew Large, chairman of the SIB, hoped eventually to fold the myriad of regulators into a single body but stopped short of including the Bank of England. Robson says that the Treasury 'looked longingly over at the Bank of England's role in banking supervision. Logic said that it should be consolidated into one body but we thought that would be too big a fight.'[39]

Details of the Treasury's discussions with the City fed back to the opposition and influenced Labour's thinking on the issue. In 1995, the same year that the collapse of Barings highlighted the overlap between the Bank of England and the securities regulator, Ed Balls, at the time one of Gordon Brown's advisers, produced a paper on the bank's role. According to Geoffrey Robinson, who was to become paymaster general in the first New Labour Government, the paper envisaged a three-way split in the Bank of England in which 'The bank's regulatory functions would be hived off and combined with the various other overlapping organizations to form an integrated new supervisory agency.'[40]

There was no mention of any change in the regulatory arrangements when the Bank of England's new powers as an independent monetary authority were announced on 6 May 1997. That news came a fortnight later, on 20 May 1997, but only after some behind-the-scenes drama. On the weekend of 4–5 May, Gordon Brown told Eddie George, governor of the Bank of England, about the bank's independence. Either George was not told that the bank would lose banking supervision, or if he was, so obliquely that he did not get the message. According to insiders, George 'went back to the Bank of England and did a victory lap, saying that they had won monetary independence and kept banking supervision'.[41]

But on 19 May George was summoned back to 11 Downing Street and told that banking supervision would pass from the bank to the new regulator and that the news would be announced in the House of Commons the next day.[42] George was furious at the lack of consultation, apparently considering it a betrayal of a letter from the Treasury stating that the future of supervision was to be reviewed but 'We will of course consult you on how it happens.'[43]

The same day that George was told about the new arrangements, Howard Davies, the deputy governor of the Bank of England, was offered the job of heading up the new regulator. He was in Argentina speaking at a conference of central bankers when the call came from 11 Downing Street. He was surprised and asked for some time to consider the matter. He spoke to George, who was still fuming about what he perceived to be a betrayal, and the two men considered resigning. In the end they decided that, with the bank having argued for monetary policy independence for thirty years, it would look foolish if the governor and deputy governor then resigned in a fit of pique over a subsidiary issue. And both men could see advantages in the new proposals. The new system would be simpler to operate, and with fewer grey areas could lead to better regulation, more consumer protection and a fairer marketplace. Davies telephoned his 'in principle' acceptance of the new role and flew back to London, landing on 20 May, the day the Chancellor went public with the announcement of the financial services reform and news of his own appointment. While Davies was in the air George had to go back to the bank and say, in the words of one insider, 'Oops, it wasn't quite the victory I told you about.'[44]

Howard Davies was a former McKinsey consultant and civil servant whose experience straddled the public and private sectors. As controller of the Audit Commission, Britain's watchdog over local authorities, between 1987 and 1992 he had famously forced the cancellation of a series of derivatives deals instigated by several local authorities led by Hammersmith and Fulham Council on the grounds that they had exceeded their authority.[45] According to Geoffrey Robinson, 'he had not just the intellectual capacity but also the managerial competence that would be required to integrate the different organizations'.[46]

The new super-regulator was named the Financial Services Authority in September 1997 and started up the following month. The Bank of England transferred banking supervision authority to the FSA in June 1998 and in May 2000 the FSA assumed the role of UK listing authority from the London Stock Exchange. Later the FSA took responsibility for several other activities, including the mortgage industry in 2004 and the general insurance industry in 2005.[47]

Davies went for a policy of rapid integration of the organisations the FSA took over and took a gamble in locating its headquarters at Canary Wharf at a time when the development's success was in the balance. The gamble paid off, for the FSA established itself as part of the City's new wave, and according to Paul Reichmann, the Canadian property developer behind the project, the FSA's arrival proved to be a turning point for Canary Wharf.

Regulators all over the world came to regard the FSA as setting the benchmark in effective and proportionate supervision and in offering the industry a single point of contact. It attempted to regulate by means of a set of broad principles rather than producing a rule for every eventuality, and although it ended up by operating two tiers, one containing principles and the other rules, its approach was widely praised. McKinsey's report on New York's competitive position recommended the US 'developing a clearly articulated vision, strategy, and mandate that is similar to the FSA's two-tiered, principles-based system'.[48] The report admired London's regulatory model and believed that 'the market benefits from high-level, principles-based standards set by a single regulator for all financial markets'.[49] The FSA's principles dealt with firms' responsibilities for managing conduct of business, conflict of interest and risk control, and provided an important framework for regulation, and were supported by a detailed rulebook that contained over 5,000 rules by 2006.[50]

It was not so much the principles or the rules that made the FSA's reputation but the way they were applied. This stemmed from the Financial Services and Markets Act of 2001, which prescribed the FSA's remit. It served as a mandate to protect the UK's financial services industry as well as to regulate it. The regulator was not to discourage the launch of new financial products and had to avoid erecting regulatory barriers, terms of reference that gave it a mission to be as friendly to the firms it regulated as it was to the industry's clients. Just in case it was in any doubt as to where its loyalties lay, it had to consider the international mobility of financial businesses and avoid damaging the UK's competitiveness. It was almost as though the FSA was an extended arm of International Financial Services London, the body that existed to promote London as a global financial capital.

The FSA certainly got the message and prioritised persuasion above compulsion: 'Our preference is for working with the industry to find solutions to market failures and to intervene only where the benefits of doing so are likely to outweigh the costs.'[51] The FSA maintained an easy dialogue with the industry and practitioners soon realised that it was in their interests to cooperate. For example, in 2006 the FSA worked with the hedge fund industry to solve problems arising when some funds gave preferential treatment to certain investors in respect of investing in and withdrawing money from their funds. The FSA said, 'We worked with the Alternative Investment Management Association (AIMA) to seek an industry-led solution and in October 2006 AIMA published guidance for the industry on defining and disclosing the existence of material terms [of this kind].'[52]

Round-table discussions were held with industry representatives to address topical issues such as managing conflict of interest. These meetings were followed up by letters addressed to the chief executives of firms reminding them of their responsibilities in these areas.[53] Discussion papers were written on topical issues – for example on private equity in November 2006. New rules and regulations were made from time to time – for example in 2007 covering investment research, personal account dealing and front running research – taking proprietary positions in advance of an analyst's report – but these were a last resort.

Senior FSA executives took a conciliatory approach to the industry. One former regulator told me that 'Although firms were always anxious to push at the frontiers to gain a competitive advantage, the senior management is in for the long haul and are ready to co-operate.'[54] Hector Sants, who joined the FSA in 2004 after working in the City for twenty years and became the regulator's chief executive in 2007 told an industry conference, 'I firmly believe the vast majority of firms are run by decent honest people.'[55]

The FSA eventually toughened its stance – Sants put more resources into enforcement and moved its mantra from 'not enforcement led' to 'credible deterrence' – but for much of the period its relations with the industry were all very cosy. The CEO of one US securities firm said, 'The FSA is open to discussing issues constructively and resolving problems quietly, without penalizing you for coming forward when you see a potential problem. The multiple US regulators and enforcers, by contrast, play a different game entirely.'[56] Paul Ruddock, founding partner and co-head of Landsdowne Partners, one of London's leading hedge funds, describes the FSA as 'a pleasure to work with',[57] and the regulator's light-touch methods were undoubtedly a factor in so many hedge funds setting up in London. The global head of compliance at one of the big investment banks describes 'a very close and personal relationship with the FSA. I would not dream of going to the US regulators to discuss an issue without taking a lawyer with me; in the UK it is a very different environment.'[58]

The years from 1997 to 2007 were benign years for the financial services industry, although as we shall see in later chapters, there was a sting in the tail, but for much of the decade the FSA played a meaningful role in London's recovery. There are four specific areas where it is possible to attribute the City's success in these years to the FSA.

First, the global investment banks that had bought up British firms in the 1990s stayed here and did not switch business back to New York. A large factor in this was the more favourable regulatory regime in the UK compared to the US. Second, London became the centre for the over-the-counter derivatives business – deals conducted in private and not reported to a recognised stock exchange – that has seen such rapid growth in the last ten years. A key reason for this was the FSA's willingness to allow banks to offset counter-balancing trades in assessing the banks' capital positions. US regulators did not offer this facility to financial institutions, and as a result derivatives dealers preferred to do their business in London. Third, London's share of the international IPO market grew during this period as companies sought to avoid the onerous listing requirements and legal system found in the US. Six of the ten largest IPOs on the London Stock Exchange in 2005 were made by foreign issuers, and many smaller European and emerging market companies listed in London, taking advantage of the lighter listing requirements on the Alternative Investment Market (AIM).[59] Finally, the FSA adopted a sensitive approach to the developing hedge fund sector, ensuring that London was the location of choice for Europe's alternative investment management industry.

It was a rare example of a regulator leading an industry upward, but it was too good to be true. The new regulatory system contained two potential weaknesses. The first concerned its relationship with the industry. Practitioners were so complimentary about their regulators that questions arose as to whether the regulators were really asking the tough questions. The industry was quick to play the relocation card, threatening to up sticks and away whenever a policy was discussed that it did not like. Under these circumstances it was understandable for an organisation such as the FSA, charged with protecting the City's global position, lowering barriers and fostering its ability to innovate, to back off.

The second potential issue was that the FSA did not quite have the field to itself, as the Treasury and the Bank of England were still involved in regulation. A memorandum of understanding was drawn up in October 1997 specifying the role each was to play in what came to be known as the tripartite arrangements. The Bank of England was to be responsible for maintaining the stability of the financial system as a whole, including taking a broad overview, advising the Chancellor of any major problem arising and acting in the markets to deal with fluctuations in liquidity. The FSA took responsibility for the authorisation and prudential supervision of financial institutions, dealing with problem cases and setting regulatory policy. The Treasury was to be responsible for the overall institutional structure of financial regulation and for accounting to Parliament on such matters. The memorandum stated: 'The Treasury has no operational responsibility for the activities of the FSA and the Bank and shall not be involved in them.'[60]

The involvement of the Bank and the Treasury was rarely discussed in the first ten years of the tripartite arrangements, and most commentators and practitioners assumed that the FSA was the only regulator. But not surprisingly, given the controversial circumstances of the Bank of England's loss of banking supervision, overlap between the three parties existed and precise responsibilities were left undefined, as would become clear during the Northern Rock crisis of 2007. This will be discussed in later chapters.

The cracks beneath the surface – the lack of clarity in regulation, the mispricing of risk, and the dangers of originate and distribute banking – were hidden from view during the boom years from 1997 to 2007. The City exulted in pro-market governments, sympathetic regulators and soaring markets. Some of these conditions had existed between Big Bang in 1986 and the fall of the Conservatives in 1997 but without the same symmetry or force. However the biggest difference between the two periods was the response of the firms and the people working in the City. Whereas in the Big Bang decade brokers, bankers and fund managers made a lot of money, even though their firms struggled, in the following decade both the employees and the organisations they worked for appeared triumphant. Established firms adapted better to the changing environment and new businesses sprang up led and staffed by a younger and more entrepreneurial generation. An incredibly dynamic new force led the charge: London's hedge funds.

4

HEDGE FUNDS

London's hedge funds appeared out of nowhere in the opening years of the 21st century. They did not get a single indexed mention in the final 886-page volume of David Kynaston's epic history of the City to the year 2000[1] nor in my own book of that year *The Death of Gentlemanly Capitalism*,[2] and were covered in little more than a page of Paul Myners' comprehensive 200-page review of the UK's institutional investment industry published in 2001.[3] These were not simply oversights, for when these publications were completed there were less than fifty such firms in Britain, and alternative investment management, as hedge funds prefer to be known, was not yet a major factor in UK capital markets. But by the end of 2006 there were nearly 300 alternative investment management firms in London managing a massive $360 billion in 900 separate funds. They became the investment banks' best customers, trading actively in the market and buying other financial services from them. The brokers put their best salespeople on hedge fund accounts, gave them the first call with market intelligence and promoted them above many longer-established fund management houses to the top of their service lists.[4]

Most of the growth occurred between 2003 and 2006, when over 200 new firms and a total of 600 new hedge funds were started in London, and alternative assets managed there grew by an astonishing $250 billion.[5] This upstart industry grabbed a fifth of the increase in the money managed by the entire UK fund management industry in these four years, and around 3,000 of the City's best and brightest people gave up secure and well-paid jobs in investment banks and established asset management firms to move into these bold new ventures.[6]

The hedge funds' impact on the City was sensational. The emergence of new financial services firms that could thrive without the prop of American management and ownership gave the City a validity it had been in danger of losing. The growth of 300 new businesses in less than a decade brought pace, drive and self-respect to London's financial services industry. They put the spring back into the City's step and turned the tables on the dot.com sector, which had competed for its talent in the 1990s. They brought new methods into the capital markets, introduced innovative investment techniques and financial products, and turned accepted theories of portfolio management on their heads. Traditional asset management firms were shocked into responding, becoming more aggressive and less concerned with relative as against absolute performance. The effect on the City was transformational, recharging it after the torrid 1990s and giving it a self-confidence that was eventually to prove intoxicating.

The people behind this movement were 'members of a strange breed', according to David Yarrow, who founded the hedge fund Clareville Capital in 1996. Another expert who has been working with the hedge fund industry for just as long told me:

There is a definite hedge fund type. They have an emotional disconnect with other people. In every situation they want the put and the call. They never give up. If you give them an inch, it's not that they will take a yard; they will already have taken the yard before you can blink. They squeeze and they squeeze. If you agree X with them, it's only the starting point to Y, and Y is only a starting point to Z, and then there's nothing left for you to give. That's how they survive in markets: they extract every last cent from every single trade. Everything is an issue with them. It doesn't matter if their assistant has forgotten to give them their hairbrush or if a trade has just gone wrong, everything is a big deal for them.[7]

They are renowned for being relentless in their focus on business. My source told me, 'If I have a mental picture of a hedge fund manager, it would be 6 p.m. in St James's. He steps out of his office still trading the markets on his handheld, shuffles into his chauffeur-driven car and heads off home to do more of the same.'[8] I sent an email to a hedge fund contact of mine requesting an interview to discuss the origins of the alternative asset management industry. I received a cordial rejection: 'Please excuse me for not wanting to reminisce about the early days. Every day is an opportunity and with growing experience the scope of that opportunity grows. I apply myself daily to the tasks ahead and would never feel that I should comment on the past for fear it limits our potential in the future.'

Such intensity was like an electric shock for the City. The hedge funds were high-trading, capital-hungry and high-maintenance, but in a good year they generated $10 billion in revenue for the investment banking industry and a fortune for themselves.[9] Other professional services firms shared in the fun. Top US law firms such as Baker & McKenzie and Skadden, Arps opened London offices that serviced hedge funds, and accounting firms were equally busy constructing watertight tax structures between offshore hedge funds and their British management companies.

The hedge funds' aggression threatened the old order of things, and to begin with the UK establishment was hostile. Politicians and central bankers identified hedge funds with the devaluation of sterling in 1992 and the run on the Asian currencies in 1997 when Malaysian prime minister Mahathir Mohammed described them as 'highwaymen of the global economy'. Boards of directors in the corporate world blamed hedge funds for unexpected falls in their share prices, and traditional fund managers were uneasy about the challenges hedge funds posed to established investment practices.

Ian Morley, the first chairman of the European Managed Futures Association, the forerunner of the Alternative Investment Management Association, remembers this early hostility very clearly. He attended many lunches in the City with traditional fund managers and describes their attitude to him as 'From under which stone did he crawl?'[10] Criticism rose to a crescendo whenever markets were turbulent. Following the dot.com crash, Robert Talbut, the highly respected chief investment officer of Friends Ivory and Sime, called for an urgent regulatory review of the 'destabilising influence' of hedge funds and their disproportionate effect. 'There is an impression that the tail is wagging the dog,' he said.[11] In the end hedge fund critics had to back off in the face of market power. A few diehards preached conservatism in areas such as risk management, conflict of interest and compensation, but were told that they had misunderstood the new paradigm and should 'lighten up' and 'move on'.

THE HEDGE FUND BUSINESS MODEL

The hedge funds' pitch to investors was simple. If you give us freedom to invest, we will generate absolute returns that will leave traditional asset management standing. We will put up some of our own money alongside yours; we will charge you a flat-rate management fee of 2 per cent; and we will also take 20 per cent of the profit once the fund has passed an agreed benchmark.

It was a shrewd proposition. It gave the hedge fund managers far more flexibility and a much more lucrative business model than were available to conventional fund managers. Whereas pension and mutual fund managers had to stick to the restrictive mandates they had agreed with risk-averse trustees and investment boards, hedge fund managers had a much wider brief. Unlike many pension funds, hedge funds were able to sell shares they did not own in the hope of buying them back more cheaply, a technique known as short selling. This difference between alternative and traditional investment management is so fundamental that traditional fund managers outside the hedge fund circle were dubbed 'long-only' managers.

There were other important differences. Hedge funds could borrow money to invest in the market, thus leveraging up on clients' own money, whereas long-only funds could invest only what investors had given them. With 20 per cent of the profits above the agreed benchmark to consider, leverage became accepted practice for hedge funds, and some funds borrowed and invested many times over the amount of capital investors had originally put up. Hedge funds were also heavy users of derivatives, a tool denied to many pension and mutual funds. By using derivatives, managers were able to magnify the effect of their investment decisions and reduce portfolio risk. Standard derivatives, such as futures and options traded on exchanges and controlled by regulators, grew rapidly but they were only the tip of the iceberg. The real action was in over-the-counter [OTC] derivatives traded in private between hedge funds, investment banks and other financial institutions. This trade was unregulated and opaque: only the parties to each deal knew who was involved and how much was at stake.

The hedge fund business model included one further benefit: light-touch regulation. In the early days pension and mutual funds considered hedge funds too risky to invest in, and two thirds of hedge fund money came from high-net-worth individuals.[12] Regulators decided these sophisticated investors should be able to look after themselves and gave hedge funds a long leash. The FSA was particularly helpful. It held a round-table meeting with the industry and its critics in 2002 and published a supportive discussion paper. It maintained a dialogue with the industry, and although it eventually formed a specialist hedge fund centre and stepped up supervision, its approach remained light touch.

But if the flexibility in the hedge funds' business proposition gave them an advantage in generating alpha, it was their lucrative business model that attracted the talent on which they depended. They scored over long-only fund managers at every level. Their flat-rate management fee of 2 per cent was at least four times more than long-only managers could charge, but the icing on the cake was the incentive structure. Performance fees of any kind were rare in the long-only world, and performance fees of 20 per cent, standard practice in alternative investment, were virtually unknown.

The fee structure meant that hedge funds could offer rewards that trumped compensation levels in long-only investment management and also the huge salary and bonus packages on offer in the investment banks. It did not take quick-witted and confident traders long to calculate that in a bull market two-and-twenty would beat a discretionary bonus, and that they had little to lose from jumping ship. The ratio of risks to rewards between investors and managers was loaded in the managers' favour. They enjoyed a fat slice of the upside, and if everything went wrong the only penalty was the missed opportunity of lucrative employment elsewhere and the loss of the money they themselves put into the fund – this could vary from a token gesture to the bulk of their net worth. The effect was galvanising. One of London's leading hedge fund managers, who asked to remain anonymous, told me, 'I was a senior vice president of a big investment bank with a good income and reasonable security. Out of the blue someone came along and said, "Join us in our emerging markets hedge fund and we will give you a little equity." I reasoned that if I worked really hard for three, four or five years I could make a fortune, and if I got it dead wrong I could go back to broking. I was young enough, foolish enough and I thought, I am going to go for this money management thing.'[13]

THE HISTORY OF LONDON'S HEDGE FUNDS

London's hedge fund story is inextricably linked with events in America, where by 2007 two-thirds of global alternatively managed assets were based. A former US diplomat and journalist turned investor named Alfred Winslow Jones invented hedge funds in the 1950s, but the industry only took off during the bull market of 1982–2000, when famous American hedge fund managers such as Michael Steinhardt, Paul Tudor Jones, Louis Moore Bacon and Julian Robertson became legends of the financial world on account of their wealth and audacity.

The growth of American hedge funds in the 1980s coincided with the opening up of the City to global forces as it prepared for Big Bang in 1986. British brokers opened offices on Wall Street and began to do business with hedge funds, buying and selling shares on their behalf. US investment banks expanded their operations in London, and the brokers, dealers and fund managers who worked for these American banks got a taste for the excitement and wealth generated by hedge funds. In parallel with this, the opening of the London International Financial Futures Exchange in 1982 established London as a derivatives centre. A few foreign institutions set up derivatives-based managed futures funds, precursors of hedge funds, in London, and the alternative investment industry's first UK trade association, the European Managed Futures Association was formed in 1989.

By the end of the 1980s London's most savvy brokers and investors knew all about hedge funds, but it was 16 September 1992 before their potential became widely appreciated in the British financial community. On that day, immediately named Black Wednesday, sterling crashed out of the European Exchange Rate Mechanism. The Bank of England spent £15 billion and interest rates were cranked up to 15 per cent in vain attempts to defend the pound, but currency speculators had the markets on the run and sterling was in effect devalued. News that a US-based hedge fund manager named George Soros and Nick Roditi, who ran money for Soros from a small office in Hampstead, had made $1 billion on the day opened the eyes of a generation to the potential of the hedge fund industry.[14]

The combination of the example of the managed futures funds, British brokers doing business with the big American hedge funds such as Steinhardt, Tiger, Moore Capital and Tudor Jones, and Soros's demonstration of the power of hedge funds in its own backyard stimulated the first phase of London's hedge fund movement in the 1990s. Important early London hedge funds included AHL, a computer-driven managed futures fund founded in 1987 that became the flagship of the Man Group, the UK's largest quoted hedge fund manager, Odey Asset Management (1991), Bayard Partners (1992), Sloane Robinson (1993) and Egerton Capital and Millennium Global (1994).

Enthusiasm for hedge funds was temporarily checked in 1998 when Long Term Capital Management, a highly leveraged bond fund run by an all-star roster of Wall Street and academic luminaries for an elite group of investors, lost nearly all its money when the Russian debt crisis triggered market movements its models had failed to predict. With total positions of nearly $100 billion, most of it borrowed, Long Term briefly threatened to bring down the US banking system, until the Federal Reserve Bank of New York organised an orderly rescue. But Long Term was known for its extreme use of leverage and its collapse did not deter London's budding hedge funds. The next wave of start-ups included Clareville Capital (1996), Lansdowne, Marble Bar and Marshall Wace (1998), Gartmore's AlphaGen Capella (1999) and Centaurus Capital (2000).

The founders of these London-based hedge funds were nearly all people with international equities experience and overseas connections. Bayard's Jeremy Rowlands and Christopher Bouckley had worked for an emerging-markets investment bank; Hugh Sloane and George Robinson were fund managers who had worked in Asia-Pacific; Egerton's John Armitage was a European equity specialist and his partner William Bollinger had spent much of his career in New York; Clareville's David Yarrow was an equity broker who had worked in New York; Marble Bar's Hilton Nathanson was an equities broker from Australia; Lansdowne's Paul Ruddock had been a broker specialising in US equities and his partner Steven Heinz had worked as an equities fund manager for the Harvard Foundation. Paul Marshall had been a European equity fund manager at Mercury Asset Management and Ian Wace had wide experience of global markets as head of international trading at Warburg Securities and Deutsche Morgan Grenfell. The founders of Centaurus, Bernard Oppetit and Randel Freeman, had worked in risk arbitrage and derivatives in London for the French bank BNP but both had previously worked in America.

These equity and equity derivatives specialists were the driving force in the first wave of London's hedge fund industry, and many new funds emulated them in the early years of the 21st century. Meanwhile, added impetus came from debt-based funds, also known as fixed-income funds (including convertible and credit funds). Three factors stimulated the growth of these fixed-income hedge funds: low global interest rates, the perception that the US central bank would bail out markets whenever necessary and the invention of a new type of over-the-counter derivative called credit default swaps.

Once again the origins lay in the US, where interest rates had been cranked up in the 1980s as part of the government's fight against inflation. Investors became accustomed to a high yield from debt securities, but in the 1990s the game changed. The 1991 recession prompted the Federal Reserve to cut rates in order to stimulate the economy and the average yield on ten-year US government securities, which had been over 10 per cent in the 1980s, plunged to little more than 6 per cent in the 1990s.

Investors, particularly pension funds in the US and Japan, looked around for alternative sources of income. Corporate bonds, particularly convertibles, were the obvious place to go. Corporate bonds are company-issued securities that make a fixed annual interest payment but do not carry equity rights. Convertibles (also known as equity-linked bonds) are corporate bonds that pay a fixed rate of interest and offer the holder the option to convert the bonds into ordinary equity shares. Corporate bonds traditionally yield more than government securities to compensate for the risk of the corporate behind them going bust and are scored against this risk by specialist firms called ratings agencies.

In the first half of the 1990s, as hedge funds and proprietary trading desks at the investment banks expanded, traders stepped up their purchases of fixed-income and convertible bonds. Interest rates were falling, there was a bull market in equities and smart traders saw arbitrage opportunities – exploiting price anomalies – and an easy way to pick up some income by leveraging their capital. The only risk for them was credit default, and in the benign economic circumstances of the mid-1990s this seemed to be a risk worth taking.

Then in 1995 a product arrived that promised to take all the risk out of conventional fixed-income trading. The derivatives team at J.P. Morgan developed credit default swaps, an insurance policy against the risk of a corporate going broke. The implications were enormous. Provided the insurance premium did not reduce the net yield to a point below the cost of capital, traders could borrow money, invest it in bonds and convertibles, insure the risk through credit default swaps and sit back and watch the money roll in. With interest rates so low, investors were desperate for sources of income, and the market swiftly extended the idea of default swaps from corporate bonds to other securities backed by interest-paying assets such as mortgages.

A further factor that encouraged credit funds became known as the Greenspan Put. As chairman of the Federal Reserve from 1987 to 2006, Alan Greenspan developed a reputation for cutting US interest rates to stimulate markets whenever events threatened to undermine sentiment. Following the terrorist attack on the World Trade Center in 2001 US interest rates were cut to 1 per cent and with Greenspan at the helm investors thought they could rely on them staying low.

These conditions offered hedge funds and investment banks' proprietary trading desks a guaranteed return. They could borrow at low rates, invest in high-yielding corporate bonds and convertibles, hedge the risk with credit derivatives and sit back to enjoy the ride. The popularity of this strategy is evident from the extraordinary expansion in the global credit derivatives market. It grew from almost zero in 1995 to nearly $1 billion by the year 2000 and then soared to $20 trillion by 2006. Massive US hedge funds such as Angelo Gordon, Bridgewater, Fortress, Highbridge, Och-Ziff, Citadel and Renaissance Technologies drove much of this growth, borrowing from banks to add to their investors' capital.

Although the first wave of debt hedge funds started in America, globalisation meant that the City was heavily involved. Many of these US giants, including Citadel, Highbridge and Och-Ziff, had offices in London, and those that stayed at home traded with London-based investment banks from America. London accounted for nearly half of global credit derivatives turnover in 1998 and still over a third of the greatly expanded market in 2006, and much of this activity came from UK fixed-income and convertible hedge funds.[15]

Noam Gottesman, Pierre Lagrange and Jonathan Green, who had worked together as private bankers at Goldman Sachs since the late 1980s, started one of the earliest. In 1995 they founded the hedge fund GLG as a division of Lehman Brothers. Although now a multi-strategy fund, its origins were in the convertibles world. The first fund was launched in 1997, and in 2000 the firm became an independent business with Lehman holding a minority interest, before going on to list on the New York Stock Exchange.

But GLG was an early starter, and the main wave of fixed-income hedge funds hit London between 1999 and 2006. CQS started life in 1999 as a convertibles fund run by Michael Hintze, an Australian trader who had worked for the American investment banks Goldman Sachs and CSFB. A crop of fixed-income and convertibles hedge funds sprung up in 2000, including Cheyne, founded by two famous convertible fund managers from Morgan Stanley, Jonathan Lourie and Stuart Fiertz. Not surprisingly, given J.P. Morgan's role in the invention of credit derivatives, the same year saw several significant launches from that firm's alumni. Blue Crest had started life as an in-house fixed-income fund at the bank and was spun out under the management of its founders Michael Platt and William Reeves. Other J.P. Morgan people launched new funds from scratch that year, including Jeremy Herrmann, the former world fly-fishing champion, who named his convertible arbitrage fund Ferox after the predatory trout, and the bank's co-head of European credit arbitrage Hugh Willis and in 2001 his colleague Mark Poole launched BlueBay.

Uncertain markets in 2001 and the terrorist attack on the World Trade Center in September of that year caused a slowdown in launches, but not for long. As we have seen, central banks slashed interest rates to keep the global economy on track and there was a rush of new hedge fund launches in 2002. Martin Finegold and Bob Kramer, who had traded asset-backed securities at Goldman Sachs, launched Cambridge Place, a structured credit fund. J.P. Morgan spun out another of its in-house fixed-income funds, London Diversified Fund Management, under the leadership of David Gorton, Rob Standing and Mark

Corbett. Alexander Jackson, a convertibles expert who had run the London office of Highbridge, got together with Reade Griffith, his counterpart at another big US hedge fund, Citadel, and Paddy Dear, a hedge fund specialist at UBS, to form Polygon Investment Partners. Fifteen of the sixteen fixed-income specialists identified above had worked for US institutions, and the name J.P. Morgan, the firm that had invented credit default swaps, featured on eight of their résumés.

Between 2003 and 2007 the equity and fixed-income streams in London's hedge fund world converged into a movement of scale and significance. Emboldened and motivated by the success of the early firms over 200 start-ups appeared, dozens more American hedge funds opened up London offices, and the first generation of British funds added new funds for investors. The industry took on more of a corporate feel as it matured. The UK bank Barclays quietly became one of the world's biggest hedge fund managers through its computer-based investment management arm Barclays Global Investors. It became increasingly common for the larger hedge funds to appoint a full-time chief executive, often recruited from outside, to run the business. GLG was one of the first to do this when in 2005 it persuaded a Goldman Sachs managing director, Manny Roman, to be its chief executive, and other firms followed suit.

Hedge fund partners took the opportunity to cash in – monetising their business, they called it – by listing on a stock exchange or selling stakes in the business. RAB Capital, a London hedge fund founded in 1999, listed on the London Stock Exchange's junior market AIM in March 2004. Boussard & Gavaudan, a multi-strategy hedge fund founded by two former Goldman Sachs bankers based in Paris and London, was the first London hedge fund to appear on one of Europe's main markets when it listed on Euronext in 2006. BlueBay Asset Management, the credit fund founded in 2001 by Hugh Willis and Mark Poole, was floated on the London Stock Exchange in November 2006, valuing it at £570 million at the time. In the middle of 2007 GLG, at the time London's second largest hedge fund with more than $17 billion under management, listed on the New York Stock Exchange by folding itself into a US shell company.

Some hedge funds listed only certain funds rather than the entire business. In December 2006, Marshall Wace listed its MW TOPS – Trade Optimised Portfolio System, an automated system that filters brokers' recommendations for the best trading ideas – fund on the Euronext Stock Exchange in Amsterdam, raising €1.6 billion from outside investors. Brevan Howard, another of London's elite hedge fund managers, raised €770 million in the spring of 2007 by listing its BH Macro fund on the London Stock Exchange, the first hedge fund to be listed on the exchange's main market. By the time Brevan Howard launched another fund, BH Global, in London a year later, the number of listed London hedge funds was about thirty.[16]

The first decade of the 21st century also saw investment banks and other financial institutions take stakes in some of London's hedge funds. Investment banks were the incubators of many hedge funds but had to spin them out or park them in their asset management divisions in order to satisfy conflict-of-interest issues. Often their hands were forced when the staff running hedge fund money for the banks handed in their notice to start up on their own. The investment banks were anxious to keep a toehold in the sector, and J.P. Morgan's high-profile purchase of the large US hedge fund Highbridge in 2006 sparked its competitors into a wave of stake buying that washed over into Europe. Lehman bought stakes in a number of hedge funds in the US and UK, including Spinnaker and Marble Bar in London. Morgan Stanley splashed out on a number of US hedge funds and took a 19 per cent stake in Lansdowne. European institutions entered the field in 2007, when Swiss Re acquired a minority stake in Brevan Howard, attracted by 'one of the fastest growing sectors' in asset management.[17]

As private partnerships, hedge funds could afford to be secretive. Websites gave little away and were often password protected. Hedge fund principals generally declined to be interviewed and disliked being photographed. But as they expanded and became listed they had to give up some of their cherished privacy. In 2006 there was a flurry of excitement in the UK about the activities of private equity firms and criticism washed over to the hedge funds. Trade unions noted the increased role that buyout and activist hedge funds were playing in the UK corporate sector and demanded more transparency. London's Alternative Investment Management Association issued sixty-five pages of recommendations to members and its US counterpart the Managed Funds Association updated its sound practices guide.[18] Fourteen leading UK hedge funds formed the Hedge Fund Working Group and, chaired by Sir Andrew Large, former Bank of England deputy governor, produced a set of voluntary standards to which hedge funds were invited to sign up. The FSA would not monitor compliance but pointed out that a signatory hedge fund would be in breach of FSA rules if it did not live up to claims that it was meeting the standards. The London group maintained contact with the US president's hedge fund working party and other groups working on similar issues in America.

An article in the *Financial Times* by Paul Marshall, chairman of Marshall Wace, showed how the hedge fund industry was being forced into the mainstream by its own success. Referring to concerns about financial stability, market integrity and investor protection, Marshall conceded, 'All these are legitimate concerns and it is incumbent on the industry to address them. This does not come easily. Ours is an industry that has always placed a high value on privacy both to respect the confidentiality of our clients and to preserve our own commercial and investment edge. There will be those who argue that public engagement of any kind goes against the grain of the maverick commercialism that is at the heart of the industry's success. But such a position is becoming increasingly untenable.'[19]

In part, growing institutional investor interest in the sector drove this openness. Whereas in 1996 62 per cent of hedge fund assets came from individual investors, by 2006 the majority of funds came from institutional investors. Some 25 per cent of alternative assets under management came from funds of funds, organisations that pooled investors' money and spread it across a range of hedge funds. Funds of funds and other institutional investors answered to boards and trustees for whom governance mattered, and if the hedge funds wanted to manage their money, they had to play by their rules.

HOW HEDGE FUNDS CHANGED THE CITY

Hedge funds took the rewards generated in the UK's financial services industry to completely new levels. In the mid-1990s the £19 million earned by Crispin Odey from his hedge fund business attracted startled press comment; a decade later such pay was noted as a matter of fact. An *Evening Standard* article in May 2005 was not as interested in how much they earned – 'The pay-offs for individual fund managers are large, routinely seven figures, often double digit millions, and in some cases small teams sharing payouts of more than £100 million' – but in who they were.[20]

Investment banking, which had previously set the pace in compensation levels in the City, was suddenly the poor relation. Throughout the 1990s the American investment banks had been the top payers, and Goldman Sachs, as befitted the industry leader, had paid better than most. Its partners and managing directors were the aristocracy of the City's wealth league at the end of the century, but by 2007 they had been surpassed by the hedge fund managers. Goldman had created so many multimillionaires in the UK that it was given its own section in the 2008 *Sunday Times* Rich List, which included a table of the firm's twelve past and present partners with personal assets of £80 million or more. It was an impressive statement of Goldman's wealth-generating abilities yet not one of the twelve would have made it into the top twenty hedge fund managers list published on the same page, for whom a personal fortune of £220 million was the minimum entry requirement.[21]

All this wealth inevitably led to spending on a stunning scale. Few City people in the 1990s had private planes; they became commonplace in the hedge fund world. In 2007 I was given a business card with six telephone numbers on it including the owner's mobiles for his limousine and private helicopter. Spending reached new levels with rock stars playing at hedge fund birthday parties and enormous bills being run up in restaurants, including one by a man who spent £36,000 in a single evening, including a £3,000 tip for the startled waitress.[22]

Although the level of spending was far higher than in the 1980s and 1990s, the hedge fund generation were less ostentatious and less brash than their yuppie predecessors. High-profile occasions such as the networking event Hedgestock, a recreation of the hippies' Woodstock festival of 1969 in the grounds of Knebworth House, Hertfordshire, and the 'hedge fund fight night', at which adrenalin-charged traders let off steam before a braying audience, were attended more by the hedge fund industry's service providers than by big-name fund managers.

Where the top hedge fund managers do come out is for the annual dinner organised by the charity Absolute Return for Kids (ARK). The 2008 event was attended by 1,100 people paying £10,000 per ticket to mingle with stars such as Liz Hurley and Bob Geldof, hear a speech by former Prime Minister Tony Blair and bid for prizes that included a role in the next Uma Thurman movie and a Damien Hirst painting. Huge sums are raised – £26.8 million in 2007 – but despite the copious quantities of fine wine on offer, these are not drunken thrashes. Someone who attends regularly but who wishes to remain anonymous describes the mood as follows: 'The hedge fund managers stay sober and go back to check out the markets when the dinner is over. But as the evening goes on and the auction begins it develops into an arm-wrestling match. They can't bear to come second. The issue, the cause, is lost in the razzmatazz and the competition. They don't care how much they have to pay to win the right to tea with a movie star, or where the money goes. Once the bidding starts, they just have to win.'

Hedge fund philanthropy transformed the fortunes of many good causes and also did a lot for the industry's profile. It became harder to criticise an industry that was so generous with its money, and its benevolence helped to stifle hostility in 2007 when its tax avoidance schemes came under fire. Whilst there is no suggestion that hedge fund philanthropy had ulterior motives, its generosity and support for pet government schemes gave it a voice in Westminster that it would otherwise have lacked.

The arrival of the hedge funds came in the nick of time for the investment banks. For two years after the dot.com bubble burst in 2000, share-trading volumes were depressed, few companies raised equity capital and new IPO share issues were rare. Brokers claimed that equity and bond trading for investors was no longer a profitable business as traditional asset managers squeezed commissions and demanded ever-keener prices from market makers. The boom days of the 1990s seemed long ago, and the business model that had enabled the investment banks to make the most of those market conditions had been curbed by new rules that attempted to control conflict of interest by restricting the role that analysts could play in corporate finance work.

And then along came the hedge funds. Whereas the long-only industry had squeezed banks and brokers because every basis point – one hundredth of one per cent – counted in a business defined by relative performance, hedge funds were different. They were seeking the greatest absolute return possible and they were prepared to pay for good-quality information delivered early. They traded their portfolios much more often than long-only managers and were prepared to use derivatives much more. They were open to innovative suggestions from the investment banks, and their mandates were often broader, enabling them to invest in unusual asset classes such as low-grade debt, commodities and exotic emerging markets. It was an exciting opportunity for the investment banks and brokers, and they set up special systems and departments to deal with the hedge funds. Industry sources suggest that the 3,000 hedge fund managers in London were matched by an equal number of brokers and support staff serving them at the investment banks. The sums generated neatly filled the hole where the dot.com revenues had been. One leading hedge fund in London paid investment banks $300 million every year for trading, advisory and support services. Industry estimates suggest that hedge funds accounted for up to 20 per cent of investment banking trading and advisory revenues in 2006.

The hedge funds had an equally dramatic effect on the asset management industry. As we shall see in a later chapter, hedge fund growth came at a time when this industry was under fire from its clients for poor performance. Hedge funds appeared to be delivering better returns and pension funds wanted to know why. Consulting firms, such as Mercer and Watson Wyatt, published research on alternative investments, welcoming funds of funds as a means of reducing the risk in pension fund portfolios. Traditional asset managers like Schroders, which had turned their backs on hedge funds in the late 1990s, were forced to change their minds. Schroders bought the small hedge fund Beaumont in 2001 in order to secure the services of Michael Dobson as chief executive, and in 2006 paid over $100 million to buy NewFinance Capital, a fund of funds hedge fund manager.

The rise of action-oriented hedge funds prepared to do anything within the bounds of the law to achieve performance added a sharp edge to London's capital markets. It is perhaps simplistic to say that the success of the hedge funds and their obsession with alpha persuaded executives in other financial institutions, for example banks, to be equally gung-ho but their influence was considerable. Three techniques in particular are associated with hedge funds: short selling, leverage and activism, and they had a significant effect on the UK corporate scene.

The idea of short selling is to profit from a fall in the price of a traded asset. In the case of equities, this can be achieved by borrowing shares and selling them in the hope that the price will fall before the borrowed shares have to be returned to the lender. The same effect can be achieved by the use of derivatives called contracts for difference.

Shorting as a risk-management tool, as practised by the founding father of the hedge fund movement Alfred Winslow Jones and legions of modern-day funds, is uncontentious. It involves taking short positions in a basket of stocks so that the portfolio is protected against a drop in the market. Short selling as an active investment strategy is more controversial, especially if aggressive short selling squeezes the market by creating an artificial volume of selling pressure. It was generally believed that this was how the currency speculators of the 1990s smashed sterling and the Asian currencies, and in the 21st century short-selling hedge funds became the usual suspects whenever equity prices fell suddenly.

Short selling is at the heart of many alternative investment strategies, and many of the early hedge funds in London such as Egerton, Gartmore and Lansdowne were long-short equity funds. Short selling first became an issue in UK equities in 2002. During the volatile markets in the summer of 2002, David Varney, chairman of the mobile phone company mmO$_2$, criticised short selling and the hedge funds that did it.[23] David Prosser, chief executive of the insurer Legal & General, suggested a regulatory review of the impact of hedge funds on stock markets. He called for more 'grit in the system' to work against short selling and said a new tax should be introduced to stop hedge funds selling short.[24]

Such ideas were swiftly dismissed by the FSA. In July 2002, speaking in Manchester, FSA chairman Howard Davies described short selling as a 'necessary and desirable underpinning to the liquidity of the London market',[25] and two months later at the FSA's industry round table Davies said, 'The FSA views short selling just like any other investment activity and not as an abusive activity unless used as part of an abusive strategy. We have not so far seen a persuasive case for restrictions, or a prohibition, on short selling.'[26]

The FSA's green light in 2002 opened the way for short selling to become accepted practice in the UK. Many conventional asset managers launched '130–30' funds, which are mandated to go short by up to 30 per cent of assets under management provided that the risk is matched by long positions of 130 per cent. The City became the short-selling capital of the world by 2006 with in relative terms twice as many shares held by short sellers (10 per cent of the FTSE 250) compared to the US (5 per cent of the S&P 500), and this at a time when the global short selling of equities increased fourfold in the three years to 2006 to an annual value of $5 billion.[27]

The second technique that the hedge funds helped to make common practice in London was leverage. Leverage – investing with borrowed money – was a favourite technique of the US buyout funds and it worked if the cost of borrowing was below the returns generated by the funds. Low and stable global interest rates, the Greenspan Put and the development of credit default swaps as a corporate bond insurance policy created these conditions in the years leading up to 2007. As we saw earlier in this chapter, in the opening years of the 21st century there was a surge in fixed-income and other credit funds that depended on leverage, and this was facilitated by the investment banks, which were able to offer them loans to leverage their capital.

During the credit boom at the beginning of the 21st century there were so many hedge funds chasing high-yield opportunities that the price of asset-backed securities went up and their yield came down. The easiest way for hedge funds to make more money was to increase leverage, and globally hedge fund leverage rose from 115 per cent in 2001 to 160 per cent in 2006.[28] No large hedge funds reached the apocalyptic gearing levels of Long Term Capital Management, which had borrowed more than $100 billion, twenty times its assets, but it was standard practice for fixed-income funds to borrow between five and ten times their assets under management. London's hedge funds participated fully in this practice. Although the FSA reported in 2005 that 'leverage by hedge funds remains quite low', individual hedge funds were highly geared and became more so in 2006.[29] By October 2007, FSA figures showed that British hedge funds were nearly two times geared.[30]

The third practice that the hedge funds promulgated in the City was shareholder activism – 21st-century style. This was different to the non-confrontational engagements between companies and their shareholders that had defined activism in the 1970s and 1980s. In those days, following the example of some big US financial institutions, notably the teaching profession's pension fund TIAA-CREF and Calpers, the giant state pension fund of California, a few large British pension funds and investment managers had opened up dialogues with the management of companies in which they held shares. The Prudential and the pension funds of the UK's nationalised industries, such as the Post Office and Telephone (Postel), British Gas, the Electricity Council and British Airways, led this movement. They were long-term investors but were prepared to nudge management into change and to engineer the removal of executives they thought to be incompetent. Later these arrangements were formalised. Hermes, the successor company to Postel, launched a special fund, First Focus, which targeted investment returns by improving corporate governance and strategy,[31] and Legal & General, the insurance company that owned nearly 5 per cent of the UK stock market and usually ranks amongst the three largest investors in any listed British company, formed a special team dedicated to governance and active investing issues.[32]

Whereas these pension funds intended to be long-term investors in the companies they targeted, most hedge fund activists were interested in immediate value creation. As usual the origins lay in the US. In the 1980s corporate raiders such as Ronald Perelman, Boone Pickens, Carl Icahn and Nelson Peltz, backed by huge sums of borrowed money, initiated corporate change at many of America's biggest companies. The old raiders of the 1980s later formed hedge funds and began to use activism as a value-creating tool. Carl Icahn reportedly banked $100 million in 2006 from an active investment in the Korean tobacco group KT&G and the following year built up a 2.9 per cent stake in Motorola and agitated for a seat on the board. A new wave of US hedge fund activists appeared on the scene such as Daniel Loeb, whose hedge fund Third Point had about $4.5 billion under management and for a time returned 30 per cent a year to investors. The new generation had sharp tongues. Irik Sevin, chief executive of Star Gas, a US energy company, stepped down in 2005 soon after Loeb wrote, 'A review of your record reveals years of value destruction and strategic blunders, which have led us to dub you one of the most dangerous and incompetent executives in America.'[33]

In the 21st century the new wave of US activist hedge funds turned their attention to the UK, attracted by the tradition of laissez-faire, non-interventionist government and well-developed equity markets. In 2007 New York-based Sherborne Investors triggered a change of chairman and boardroom upheaval at Spirent, a UK telecommunications company. In 2004 the famous activist US hedge fund manager Eric Knight used a stake of just 0.03 per cent to persuade Royal Dutch Shell to abandon its dual British–Dutch corporate structure. Three years later he chose to attack another large international business with British connections, HSBC, criticising the composition and structure of the board, corporate pay policies and the performance and positioning of some of the bank's global businesses. At the time he launched his initiative, his firm Knight Vinke owned just 35.2 million shares and options, equivalent to about 0.3 per cent of HSBC's total share capital.[34]

In March 2007 it was revealed that Trian Fund Management, an investment fund run by the activist US investor Nelson Peltz, had bought a 3 per cent stake in Cadbury Schweppes. Two days later Cadbury Schweppes announced that it intended to spin off its beverage operations in a direct reversal of its previous comments on the subject.[35] But Trian was still not satisfied, and in December, by which time Peltz's fund had increased its stake to 4.5 per cent, it wrote to Cadbury Schweppes threatening to become 'significantly more active in evaluating all of our alternatives as a large shareholder'.[36]

London's entrepreneurial alternative asset funds soon joined the US hedge fund activists operating in the UK. One such fund was Hanover Investors, formed in 2002 by Matthew Peacock, a former Credit Suisse and BZW investment banker who had become a corporate turnaround specialist in the 1990s. Hanover triggered shake-ups at several companies including Elementis, a specialist chemicals group, and SMG, the Scottish media group. Another was Laxey Partners, formed in 1999 by Colin Kingsnorth and Andrew Pegge, two fund managers with long City experience. With headquarters on the Isle of Man tax haven and offices in Mayfair, it tackled several investment trusts trading at below net asset value including Baring Emerging Europe, Intrinsic Value and Private Equity Investors. In 2002 it used a 3 per cent stake to agitate for change at British Land, walking away with a large profit, and over the next three years was involved in over seventy deals including a high-profile battle with Wyevale, the UK's largest garden centres group.[37] By 2007 Laxey and other activist hedge funds had crossed over into the private equity space, holding stakes in target companies and working with management to improve performance.

The Children's Investment Fund, run by Christopher Hohn, went for even bigger targets. In 2005 it led a campaign to prevent the Deutsche Börse from proceeding with a bid for the London Stock Exchange. TCIF was a big shareholder in Deutsche Börse, at one time owning 9 per cent of the company, and along with some other shareholders was unhappy with the management team led by Werner Seifert. Deutsche Börse was forced to drop its interest in the LSE, make a capital repayment to shareholders and Seifert stood down.[38] TCIF played a role in another big event in the financial sector in 2007 when it called for an end to the acquisition-led strategy of the Dutch bank ABN AMRO and demanded its break-up. This had the effect of putting ABN into play, and led to its eventual takeover by a European consortium led by the Belgian bank Fortis and including Royal Bank of Scotland and Banco Santander, a deal that was to prove disastrous.

Hedge funds were not without their critics. There was much debate about whether they worked. The hedge fund universe's performance numbers showed slender gains over equity and bond indices, and the figures were flattered by the method of calculation. Hedge funds that closed during the year were excluded from the indices, and critics said that this introduced survivorship bias into the methodology because it was the underperforming funds that were most likely to fold. Many index compilers permitted 'backfilling', allowing hedge funds to include histories of performance from their incubation stage. Again, critics said that this flattered the numbers because it was difficult to audit and evaluate such returns. It was said that the best performing hedge funds were simply those lucky enough to have the style of investing that was currently in vogue, and all of this was said against a backdrop of resentment about the fees hedge funds charged.

Other criticisms related to their effect on markets and corporate governance. Cadbury Schweppes's abrupt sale of its beverage division when confronted by an activist investor prompted Anthony Bolton, one of Britain's leading fund managers, who had influenced many companies through his position at Fidelity, to call this one of the 'events that change the investment landscape – an episode that alters the relationship between shareholders and the companies in which they invest'. Bolton argued that 'what happened at Cadbury Schweppes could represent a come-on to every corporate raider or activist investor. It suggests they need to buy only a very small stake to be the catalyst for a significant change of strategy.' Bolton contrasted this with the approach taken at Fidelity: 'it would be rare for us to try to influence a company's policy with only a 3 per cent stake unless there was broad agreement with other shareholders about a change of direction'.[39]

Corporate governance was also threatened by other hedge fund tactics. University of Texas professors Henry T. C. Hu and Bernard Black showed that short selling, which gave financial institutions an economic interest in a stock even though they did not actually own it, could have damaging consequences for corporate governance. They pointed out that where stock has been borrowed to cover a short position, the shorter wants the share price to go down. But the voting rights go with the borrowed stock and in certain circumstances the shorter can use the vote to block a corporate event that would drive the share price up.[40]

The changed relationship between a company and its shareholders was summed up by John Sunderland when he was president of the Confederation of British Industry and chairman of Cadbury Schweppes. He told the UK Investor Relations Society, 'It may be old-fashioned but I view a shareholder as a shareholder; someone whose interests in the success and prospects of the company lasts more than three weeks . . . I have real concerns about promoting the use of my company's stock as hedge fund plays; just as I would if they were chips in a casino.'[41]

Other concerns included the risk that the failure of one or more of the hedge funds' trading partners known as counterparties would bring the financial system down. The Financial Stability Forum, an organisation established in 1999 by the G7 finance ministers and central bank governors in the aftermath of Long Term Capital Management, laid out the issue: 'A small number of core intermediaries have come to play an increasingly important role in some key areas of wholesale financial markets, such as over-the-counter derivatives dealing and securities financing, clearing and settlement. The relationships between these core intermediaries and hedge funds, through prime broking and counterparty relationships, have thus become more central to the robustness of the financial system.'[42] The report urged industry supervisors and regulators to focus on the role of counterparties as protection against what it regarded as an emerging systemic risk.[43]

The problem was that no one knew precisely what the hedge funds were up to. Richard Davies, an investor relations executive in the City with twenty years experience, says, 'Hedge funds are very private organisations, and this has introduced an opaque culture at a time when the rest of the City was under pressure to be more transparent.'[44] European politicians and regulators took a hostile view. French president Nicolas Sarkozy attacked 'predator' hedge funds and called for a European tax on 'speculative movements' by financial groups.[45] Angela Merkel, Germany's chancellor, urged increased regulation for alternative investors, and Franz Müntefering, the man who had denounced hedge funds as 'a swarm of locusts' and 'a danger to our democracy' became vice chancellor and labour minister.[46] German proposals to force hedge funds to register all holdings on an international database – thus giving regulators more information on the risks they were running – were withdrawn in the face of British and American opposition.[47]

It was partly the economic power of the hedge funds that made the British more tolerant of them but also the way their growth-oriented culture had infiltrated corporate and institutional life to such a degree that their values seemed natural. Alpha at all costs, leverage and pressure on incumbent management became standard practice in the UK and the hedge funds were accepted into the club. This was demonstrated by the legion of British establishment figures who took positions with hedge funds, including former FSA chief Sir Howard Davies and Treasury report author Paul Myners at GLG; former SIB chief Sir Andrew Large at Marshall Wace; former Royal Bank of Scotland chairman Sir George Mathewson at Toscafund; and former Bank of England deputy governor Ian Plenderleith and former cabinet secretary Sir Andrew Turnbull at Brevan Howard. The willingness of these heavyweights to take such positions appeared to give hedge funds the seal of approval and confirm their importance as permanent features of the 21st-century City scene. Subsequent events would, of course, cause some of these opinions to be re-examined.

5

ASSET MANAGEMENT

The recovery of the UK asset management industry under the Labour governments was less dramatic than the rise of the hedge funds but it helped to complete the picture of a City in apparently rude health. It was stimulated in part by the hedge funds but was also driven by necessity. Tough new rules for pension funds and a change in conditions in the world's stock and bond markets meant that the industry's poor performance in the 1980s and 1990s could no longer be tolerated. Clients demanded a new approach, and the existing players and a host of new arrivals responded to the challenge, redrawing the landscape of the UK's investment management industry.

Fund management was an industry of national significance. It managed £2 trillion of assets in the UK (£3 trillion, 2006) and contributed over £3 billion to gross domestic product.[1] Its dealings in the capital markets gave the City critical mass and its investment decisions determined the future prosperity of Britain's savers, retirees and other investors.[2]

But despite its economic and national importance and the huge sums it managed, it was a narrowly based industry at the beginning of the period. There were fewer than 5,000 people actually managing money; equities were by far and away the dominant asset; and the UK was the principal source and destination of the funds invested. Hedge funds were rare and considered somewhat risqué, and many traditional funds were prohibited from using derivatives and short selling. It was not yet a global industry, and its business practices appeared to look back to the 1980s rather than forward to the 21st century.

Industry leadership came from the pension funds, but as we saw in Chapter 2 this sector was not in good shape. Its reputation was suffering from poor investment performance, an issue that later culminated in the Unilever Pension Fund's High Court case against Mercury Asset Management, and from operational mismanagement of the kind exhibited at Deutsche Morgan Grenfell in the Nicola Horlick and Peter Young incidents. It was a worrying situation because the failure of the industry could jeopardise one of the UK's advantages in the highly competitive global economy.

For in 1997 the UK was in the minority of countries where most private sector workers – over 85 per cent in its case – had fully funded pension schemes.[3] These occupational pension schemes were paid for by the contributions of employers (also known as plan sponsors) and employees. Actuaries calculated the pension funds' future liabilities based on the age and life expectancy of members and determined the required contribution rates. Managers appointed by the pension fund trustees invested these contributions. In 1997 most of these schemes still offered pensioners defined benefits where the pension was determined by a formula involving the pensioner's salary at or near retirement and number of years of service. Pensioners could rely on these payouts (often indexed or partly indexed for inflation) provided the pension fund remained solvent.

Demographics made pension provision an urgent issue. The ageing of the post-war baby boom generation would create a grey-haired population bubble in the 21st century, a bubble further inflated by changes in working patterns and better healthcare. When I was born in 1951 the average British retiree's age was sixty-five and their average age of death was seventy-two; as I write today, the average retiree's age has fallen to fifty-seven and their age of death has risen to eighty-three. By the late 20th century it was clear that there would be an enormous increase in the number of people drawing pensions in the second and third decades of the next century.

In contrast to many European countries including France, Germany and Spain, the UK appeared in a good position to meet this challenge. Britain's funded occupational pension schemes, it was said, would give the UK an economic advantage when the time came for other countries to support an ageing population out of current earnings. Whether this advantage was in fact realised would be determined by the accuracy of the actuaries' calculations and the ability of the fund management industry to invest pension assets effectively.

At the end of the 20th century this largely depended on the prospects for equities, where 75 per cent of pension fund assets were invested.[4] Pension fund managers were still disciples of George Ross Goobey, the manager of the Imperial Pension Fund, who in 1953 turned conventional wisdom on its head by stating that the rising dividends paid out by companies to equity shareholders were a better match for pension fund liabilities than fixed-income bonds.[5] Ross Goobey moved the tobacco company's pension assets out of gilts – fixed-income bonds issued by the UK government – into equities, and after initial opposition from the actuarial profession, including a public row between Ross Goobey and Britain's most senior actuary, other pension funds followed Imperial's lead.

The rush of pension funds into equities in the second half of the 20th century established the London Stock Exchange as a liquid market and gave the modern City its distinctive equities culture. Equities ruled supreme for four decades, and by and large they delivered. Despite fund managers' inability to meet the benchmarks set for them, rising equity markets bailed out the pension funds, which regularly performed better than inflation.[6] Markets were so strong during the long equity bull run that began in 1982 that the actuarial valuations revealed enormous 'surpluses' in company pension plans. Encouraged by tax rules that penalised companies for adding to such surpluses, most corporate sponsors either reduced the level of contributions into their schemes or cut them out altogether. The rising tide of equity markets had lifted all boats. The fund managers' underperformance compared to the overall growth of the stock market was a minor irritant for pension fund trustees but not yet a fatal flaw.

However, this rosy situation changed in the second half of the 1990s and beyond. New legislation and tougher accounting standards put more onus on pension fund sponsors to support their pension funds, and volatile markets rapidly converted the surpluses of the 1980s and early 1990s into deficits. This meant that pensions would become a looming problem for Britain's corporate sector, forcing pension fund sponsors and trustees to be less tolerant of underperformance and to look again at their pension fund management arrangements.

AN INDUSTRY IN TURMOIL

The laws and accounting standards in question were the Conservative government's 1995 Pensions Act, 2002's accounting standard known as FRS 17 and a new Pensions Act of 2004. The 1995 act defined sponsors' responsibility for keeping pension funds solvent and FRS 17 required them to account for pension fund assets and liabilities on the parent company's balance sheet. The act of 2004 put sponsors even more firmly on the spot, requiring trustees of defined benefit plans in deficit to get sponsors to increase funding whenever funds moved into the red. The two acts and the new accounting standard, which were intended to increase the security of pensioners' funds, caused sponsors to look again at their offer to employees.

By the time the new rules bit, adverse movements in the world's stock and bond markets had left many pension plans in deficit. When bond yields fell dramatically in the late 1990s and early 21st century, plan sponsors had to set aside more money to keep their promises because actuaries had to assume that there would be a lower long term yield on investments. Then in 2000 the long-running bull market in equities came to a juddering halt when the dot.com bubble burst. The bear market that followed lasted for three years; equity holdings plummeted in value; and UK pension funds swung from surplus to deficit.

Underperforming fund managers, rigorous legislation and regulation, and hostile markets left plan sponsors, fund trustees and investment consultants buffeted from all sides. British Airways, whose principal pension fund moved into deficit in 1999, became known as a pension fund with an airline attached. Mergers were abandoned, in the case of a mooted bid for Sainsbury's, or renegotiated, in the case of the takeover of Alliance Boots, once bidders understood the pension fund liabilities they might be facing.

Sponsors did what they could to reduce their exposure. Defined-benefit schemes that guaranteed employees an inflation-linked pension based on their final salary and numbers of years of service were closed to new employees. Instead newcomers were offered defined-contribution schemes into which employers and employees paid as before but with the final pension to be determined by the fund's performance rather than by the salary formula. In other cases the terms of existing employees were changed. In 2006 British Airways, which three years earlier had topped up its pension fund and followed the example of many sponsors by closing its defined-benefit scheme to new employees, made a further payment of £550 million into its pension fund and introduced a range of measures to cut the remaining deficit. These included increasing the retirement age for staff, giving less pension for each year of service and capping inflationary increases. Some trustees outsourced their pension commitments to specialist providers such as Paternoster and the big insurance companies like the Prudential and Legal & General.

However, trustees did not sit back while plan sponsors and scheme members took the pain. Pension funds sold equities and increased bond holdings to reduce volatility, and looked again at their fund management arrangements. In the early days of occupational pension schemes, many of the larger sponsors had managed their own employees' pension funds through their in-house investment departments such as that run by George Ross Goobey at Imperial. In the 1970s and 1980s most of these were wound down and pension fund management was outsourced. By 1997, Gartmore, Mercury, PDFM and Schroders were established as the big four pension fund managers and Deutsche Morgan Grenfell was pushing hard to join them. Smaller pension funds joined pooled funds run by these and other managers while larger funds were managed on a stand-alone basis.

Pension funds tended to make simple choices when appointing fund managers, selecting just one or two management firms to look after their whole fund. This system was known as balanced fund management, and by the 1990s it was coming under fire. It left too much responsibility for asset allocation in the hands of the fund managers and led to them replicating their own institutional biases onto the fund. Paul Myners' review of the institutional investment market reported: 'growing dissatisfaction with the investment performance of a number of leading balanced managers; analysis by investment consultants cast doubt on the ability of fund managers consistently to add value in asset allocation; and within the field of stock selection, it was questioned whether a single fund manager could be expected to have market-beating expertise in all markets.'[7]

Rising pension fund deficits and the sponsors' increased exposure to such deficits put the skids under balanced fund management. Consultants and trustees questioned whether generalist fund managers had the expertise to outperform in all markets. More and more funds therefore decided to set their own asset allocation strategies and parcel out their funds to different managers. The 'core and satellite' model replaced balanced fund management. At the core were low-cost computer-driven funds designed to track beta, the term for market performance, and round the outside were specialist funds given the job of chasing alpha, above-average performance.

Fund management firms had to adapt to this new structure. As the core grew, tracking markets using computer models – known as indexation or passive management – took a bigger share of the pension fund market. Firms such as Legal & General, BGI and the US fund manager State Street swept up assets to manage passively and developed products that promised to give a performance boost to indexation. The satellite funds specialised in chosen areas such as emerging equity markets, bonds, alternative investments and quantitative funds that based investment decisions on computer models. Some pension fund managers bought fixed-income derivatives as a long-term hedge against inflation and interest rate risks. Matching pension funds' assets with their liabilities in this way is known as liability-driven investing, and by 2006 it accounted for over 6 per cent of the UK's pension fund assets, led by investment managers such as Insight, the fund management arm of the UK bank HBOS.[8]

As a result of the new rules pension funds switched from maximising returns to matching assets with liabilities. They set fund managers absolute return targets, usually 2–4 per cent over an agreed benchmark (for example, inflation or a specified investment index), and this replaced the old objective of beating a peer group. Hedge funds were used to working in this way and their influence permeated the pension fund industry. Although direct investment in hedge funds was slow to take off, pension funds were big buyers of funds of funds, and the traditional long-only managers adopted hedge fund techniques, including short selling in 130–30 funds, which could go short of up to 30 per cent of the fund's value and add the proceeds of the sale to existing assets creating a long position of 130 per cent of the fund's value.

The industry's pricing structure changed to reflect the new product architecture. Whereas the balanced business typically earned a management fee of between a quarter and a half per cent, indexation was available for as little as 10 basis points. But there were opportunities too, for the margins on the specialised mandates were much higher at between 1 and 2 per cent, and performance fees crept in as long-only industry fund managers traded off a lower management fee in return for a share of the upside.

The consequence of these changes was that in a very short period the pension fund management industry moved from being a commodity business focused on UK equities into a segmented high-value-added and globally diversified industry. In the year 2000 48 per cent of assets were in UK equities; seven years later that percentage had halved.[9] Between 1993 and 2003, balanced fund managers' share of the UK pooled pension fund market fell from over 40 per cent to below 10 per cent.[10] The specialist mandates that replaced them accounted for 72 per cent of total institutional assets managed in the UK by 2006.[11]

The overall impact can be summed up by the fund management arrangements at one multi-billion-pound UK pension fund that opened its books to me on a no-names basis. Its funds had traditionally been equities-dominated but at the time of writing its assets were split equally between gilts, corporate bonds, UK equities and overseas equities, with just a small property portfolio. Nine separate specialist managers now run the fund, replacing the two managers that had run it between them on a balanced basis in the 1990s. Some 40 per cent of the fund's assets including equities and bonds are managed passively by Legal & General. Three specialist fund management houses manage the equity portfolio by region and three different firms do the same for bonds. The global equities portfolio is divided between a large US fund manager and a specialist quantitative fund manager. Three of the nine fund managers are American-owned, one is Asian, three are British and two are European. Three of the managers have performance fees built into their agreements.

HOW THE FIRMS RESPONDED

This fluid scenario produced three important changes between the mid-1990s and the present day. The first was the reform and regeneration of old firms as they sought to respond to the changed market circumstances. The second was the growth of investment management boutiques started up by fund managers leaving the bigger firms. The third was a major restructuring of the UK asset management industry as existing players merged and new entrants from overseas arrived to grab the opportunities they saw.

The firms with the most to lose were the big four pension fund managers of the 1990s, and the year 1997 was particularly difficult for them. The generally accepted measure of a balanced fund management house was the performance of its pool of small pension funds. In 1997 the pooled funds managed by the big four undershot the FT All Share Index by a staggering 10 percentage points.[12] One reason for this horrendous underperformance was their investing style.

There are two broad styles of investment: growth and value. Growth stocks – companies believed to have exciting growth prospects – are usually found in the new technology and media sectors and were all the rage in the world's stock markets in the second half of the 1990s. Value stocks – companies characterised by their financial solidity and dividend paying potential – had their supporters in the late 20th century but underperformed growth stocks. Examples of both types of investor could be found in Britain and the US in the 1990s, but portfolios managed by UK managers tended to have a value bias whilst US portfolios had a growth bias.

The big four UK pension fund managers were all value investors, particularly PDFM, a subsidiary of UBS, which at its peak in 1998 was running UK pension fund portfolios worth £46 billion. PDFM's chief investment officer was Tony Dye, and he took a firm stand against what he believed to be the overvaluation of US technology companies, which was driving markets in the late 1990s. The dot.com bubble saw the US NASDAQ market that specialised in such stocks quadruple in value between 1995 and 1999, and the fever spread to Europe. Rory Cellan-Jones was the BBC's Internet correspondent and recalled that 'for a short period, roughly stretching from September 1999 to May 2000, Britain had been in the grip of an extraordinary wave of enthusiasm about the potential of the Internet economy to create new wealth. It was a time of energy and optimism that promised to change the way the nation looked at itself.'[13] Britain's first major Internet IPO, Freeserve, had occurred in July 1999, and for the best part of nine months the UK went dot.com crazy as companies such as clickmango.com, an online health products retailer, and boo.com, an online retailer of designer sports gear, made spectacular stock market debuts.

Dye looked on aghast. Lastminute.com, an online bookings agency that had never made a profit and had been formed only two years before, launched on the London Stock Market on 14 March 2000. Investors were entranced by the vision of Brent Hoberman and twenty-seven-year-old Martha Lane Fox, lastminute.com's founders, who were regarded as the next generation of entrepreneurs, which simply got all this stuff. Lastminute.com was oversubscribed by forty-seven times; the Stock Market valued it at £832 million on the first day of dealings; and Ms Lane Fox had her photograph on the front page of the next day's *Daily Telegraph*. Dye's scepticism put him in good company, for over three years earlier Alan Greenspan, chairman of America's Federal Reserve, posed the question, 'How do we know when irrational exuberance has unduly escalated asset values?' in a speech at the American Enterprise Institute's annual dinner.[14] But whereas Greenspan was a central banker trying to cool the excitement in financial markets who could err on the side of caution, Dye was in charge of one of Britain's largest pension fund managers and could afford no such luxury.

As technology stocks soared, PDFM got left behind, underperforming its peer group by 10 percentage points in 1999. Prestigious pension fund clients such as Marks & Spencer deserted PDFM as the high-technology growth stocks of the kind that Dye considered expensive continued their scorching run.

Dye must have endured an excruciating few years. He was nicknamed 'Dr Doom' and later admitted, 'I felt like tearing my hair out. It was terrifying. There was this belief that everything to do with telecoms, media, software was going to be the next Microsoft. And everybody felt they had to join in.'[15] The dot.com bubble was a hot news topic and Dye was every journalist's counterpoint to the story in countless articles about the rise of NASDAQ.

In the end the inevitable happened: Dye was sacked at the bottom of the cycle. The merger of PDFM's owner, UBS, with another Swiss bank, SBC in 2000 brought together two large-value investors, PDFM and SBC's Brinson Partners. These businesses were consolidated into UBS Asset Management, and senior management used this as the opportunity to oust Dye just days before the NASDAQ crashed and all his prophecies came true. Boo.com went through nearly £100 million in a matter of months; the share price of lastminute.com collapsed from nearly six pounds to little over a pound during the month of April 2000; and clickmango.com, in which the actress Joanna Lumley had been an investor and a public face, announced its impending closure in July.

Tony Dye died in 2008, and his *Financial Times* obituary provided a fitting epitaph to Dr Doom and one of the UK's leading balanced-fund management firms: 'The increasingly agitated Swiss bosses of UBS, PDFM's parent company, in Zurich, eventually ejected Tony Dye at the beginning of March 2000, merging the London operations of PDFM into a global structure. Just two weeks later the global equity market finally peaked, then plunged. PDFM's value style began to outperform again quite strongly as technology stocks crashed.'[16]

Mercury also disappeared into the clutches of a bigger firm when, believing it needed more capital, it was sold to the American investment bank Merrill Lynch for over £3 billion in 1997.[17] Mercury's history is one of remarkable value creation since the day in 1979 when, on being appointed chairman, Peter Stormonth Darling was told by the legendary Siegmund Warburg, 'Your first task, Peter, is to get rid of it. I don't care what you get for it. You can give it away.'[18]

Under the leadership of Stormonth Darling and then the triumvirate of Hugh Stevenson, Carol Galley and Stephen Zimmerman, Mercury caught the rising tide of institutional investment in the UK quite brilliantly. It had a more individualistic style than its closest competitors, giving fund managers, particularly those in its famous special situations team, more leeway to back their own judgement. By 1997 it had over 900 pension fund clients, 90,000 clients in unit trusts and personal equity plans, and foreign-sourced assets accounting for 20 per cent of the total £100 billion funds under management. Yet, for all its success, Mercury suffered from its peer group's malaise in the late 1990s. On one occasion it was caught out by a decision to underweight the biggest stocks listed on the London Stock Exchange, and in 1997 the ten largest UK stocks gave a total return of 46 per cent compared with 23 per cent for the next ninety and just 11 per cent for mid-cap medium-sized stocks. Mercury's performance suffered, and critics said that it needed fresh impetus as well as more capital.

The purchase of Mercury by Merrill Lynch proved problematic. Merrill had paid a top-of-the-market price for Mercury but then began to question its own strategy in asset management, in 2006 merging its entire asset management division with the US firm BlackRock in return for a 49.8% stake in the business. According to reports, Merrill had not been happy with the acquisition of Mercury: 'Senior Merrill executives say it overpaid wildly for a business where it failed to identify management and systems weaknesses. Critics blame mismanagement and culture clashes for a flood of defections and a prolonged period of underperformance.'[19]

At the time of writing only two of the big four pension fund managers of the 1990s, Schroders and Gartmore, remain as standalone units, but both are unrecognisable from their balanced-fund management days. By the time Gartmore was sold by Royal Bank of Scotland to the US fund manager Nationwide Mutual in 2000, its chairman Paul Myners had seen the business change hands four times in eleven years, each time for a higher price. At its peak Gartmore had managed £80 billion but by the end of 2000 the total was down to £54 billion as balanced pension funds ebbed away and the company repositioned itself as a specialist house. Its top fund manager was Roger Guy, who joined Gartmore in 1993 five years after graduating in economics from Sussex University. In 1999 his success as a fund manager persuaded one of Gartmore's clients to give him part of its money to be run as a long-short hedge fund. By this time alternative investing was taking off in London and after eight successful months, the idea was hatched to open Guy's hedge fund to new investors. The fund was named AlphaGen Capella and rapidly became one of the industry's star performers. By 2006 it had grown to $2.3 billion and produced a return of 187 per cent.[20] Gartmore used AlphaGen's success to build a hedge fund business as part of its strategy of developing high-margin active fund management. By 2006 it was running over £5 billion of hedge fund assets in nineteen separate funds, nearly a quarter of the firm's total assets under management.[21]

However, ownership problems continued to afflict Gartmore. Nationwide Mutual, one of America's largest life insurance groups, had bought Gartmore at close to the top of the dot.com bull market in 2000 for £1.03 billion, and having written down the value of its investment to £600 million in 2002, it decided to sell. Following a series of internal reorganisations and discussions with possible buyers, there was a £500 million management buyout in 2006 in which the US private equity firm Hellman & Friedman took a 51 per cent stake, leaving the management and staff with a substantial holding.

By this time the commitment of Roger Guy and his colleague Guillaume Rambourg, who managed the largest and highest-margin part of the funds, was crucial. Schroders had made an audacious bid to recruit Guy in 2005, prompting Gartmore into negotiating a new contract with him, but clearly a new deal would now be required if the buyout was to be viable. According to reports, Guy employed his own advisers, cut his share of the fees on the funds he managed in return for equity in the new business, and converted his equity in the old business into equity in the new business.[22] He agreed to become a director on condition that the board meetings he would have to attend would be held after market hours.[23]

In a short period around the turn of the century Gartmore had moved from being an unwanted and outdated business within a large financial institution to becoming an independent, entrepreneurially run and high-performing firm. Funds under management fell further to £25 billion around the time of the buyout, but the business was highly profitable, earning nearly £50 million in 2005.[24] However, Gartmore would not be Gartmore without ongoing debate about its future ownership.

Hellman & Friedman refinanced the deal in April 2007 on advantageous terms before conditions in the credit markets got tough, but as a private equity firm they will eventually be looking for an exit strategy.[25] Speaking in May 2006, Gartmore's Jeff Meyer, who led the buyout, believed that the shares would in due course be listed on the Stock Market once again: 'We selected Hellman & Friedman because they have a long holding period, but if we had to guide, the most likely exit for the business would be an initial public offering in three to five years.'[26]

In terms of continuity of ownership, Gartmore's contrast with Schroders Investment Management, where the Schroder family retains a controlling stake, could not have been greater. But Schroders encountered similar structural problems to those facing the other big pension fund managers and found it no easier to deliver performance. A series of high-profile fund managers came and went; performance in 1998 and 1999 was poor; profits for the year 2000 fell sharply; and in 2001 David Salisbury, the company's chief executive officer and a veteran of twenty-seven years standing, paid the price with his job. Schroders had a tradition of promoting from within but this time the board decided that a new broom was required. It turned to Michael Dobson, one of its non-executive directors, who had been on the board for less than a year.

Dobson was a graduate of Trinity College, Cambridge; had been at Morgan Grenfell, where he became chief executive of the asset management division; and sat on Deutsche Bank's main board, only the second non-German to do so. In 2000 he left to set up his own investment management boutique, Beaumont Capital Management, which by the time Schroders approached him had $275 million under management. Although Schroders did not like paying fancy prices for people businesses, at this particular moment the company balance sheet was full of cash following the sale of its investment bank to Citigroup in 2000, and the need for new management was urgent. After several weeks of negotiation they agreed to buy Beaumont outright for £33.5 million in cash and shares, and in November 2001 recruited Dobson on an annual package of over £3 million.

As was usual in the asset management industry, profits reflected earlier years' investment performance and financial results would inevitably be slow to show through, but Dobson had three things going his way at Schroders. Performance in fund management was beginning to turn round following the sharp downturns in 1998 and 1999, and the years 2000 and 2001 were good.[27] In addition the staff at Schroders were up for recovery and wanted to see change. Jonathan Asquith, who had worked with Dobson at Morgan Grenfell and was his first hire at Schroders as finance director, said, 'Moving things on at Schroders was a question of pushing at an open door. There was tremendous pent-up demand for reasonably decisive action from inside the organisation. This was a company that had made £230 million in 2000 and an £8 million loss in 2001. It was very jarring for a bunch of successful professionals who suddenly see the world derailed. So they were very keen to get back on track.'[28] The final advantage Dobson had was the firm's culture, stretching from the boardroom to the dealing room, something he was quick to acknowledge: 'I had a great admiration for the continuity of the firm – the long-term view they took developing their business and the stability through the family shareholding . . . People are proud to work here.'[29]

However there were also some serious issues facing the firm. It employed too many people spread across thirty-five offices in twenty-five different countries. Schroders' country heads were inclined to act as autonomous regional barons, creating what Dobson described as 'firms within firms'.[30] The business mix was wrong for the future, being over-dependent on balanced pension fund management and under-represented in emerging markets, the US, fixed income and the rapidly growing area of alternative investments.

Dobson's first meeting with the staff en masse was in December 2001 at the firm's Christmas party. It was not a particularly festive occasion. The staff wanted to know what the new man was like and hoped that there would be action to address the problems that had been widely discussed throughout the firm for years. They were not disappointed. Dobson introduced himself and spoke of his excitement at the potential for the firm. But he warned employees of tough times ahead and told them that they should expect cost cutting that could include office closures.[31] In the event the global office network proved harder to tackle than Dobson and Asquith might have believed, but other changes were made including outsourcing back-office functions and administration, and reorganising investment, sales, marketing and distribution, human resources and technology along global lines.[32] The headcount was cut from 2,900 to 2,300 within three years.

Selected outside appointments were made to sharpen up the investment process. Richard Horlick joined from Fidelity in 2002 to head up investments, and he was replaced in 2005 by an even more high-profile hire in the form of Alan Brown, former chief investment officer of the US firm State Street Advisors.[33] Existing businesses, such as private banking and a collection of businesses cobbled together from leftovers after the sale of the investment bank, were turned round into profit.[34] Specialist fund management was developed to compensate for the over-dependence on pension funds, and in 2006 Schroders paid up to $142 million for NewFinance Capital, a fund of funds alternative investments manager based in London.[35] The results were dramatic. At the end of 2006 balanced pension fund management accounted for less than £10 billion out of total assets under management of

£128.5 billion. Margins on the new specialist pension and retail funds were nearly a third higher than on the old businesses.[36]

The changes described in this chapter brought about a revolution in the UK's pension fund management industry. Two of the big four managers of the 1990s, Mercury and PDFM, disappeared into financial behemoths whilst Schroders and Gartmore reinvented themselves as specialists. In all four cases the focus on domestic equities was replaced by a global approach spanning several asset classes, and the reliance on low-margin defined-benefit pension funds was replaced by value adding products for the defined contribution, retail and high-net-worth markets.

These changes also brought opportunities for the other sectors of the UK fund management industry, insurance and retail. The top pension fund managers had won their leading positions by their performance over many years and it had been difficult for competitors to break in. It was a big decision for trustees to switch an entire fund over, but once they realised that they could try out new fund managers by giving them specialist mandates, the market became more fluid: 'Market share flattened as fund managers had the opportunity to win some business on the basis of performance in one asset class or lose it on performance in another, rather than winning or losing the whole fund.'[37]

With £1.2 trillion of assets under management, insurance was the largest sector, and it was ideally placed to expand into the pension fund market.[38] Life insurance grew up in the 19th century, when insurance companies realised that it was possible to predict mortality and offered life policies as a protection against the financial risk of death.[39] This developed into a savings business, with policies paying out at a fixed point in time rather than on death, and by the late 20th century the life companies had their own investment departments to manage these assets.

During the 1990s the life insurance industry went through a period of consolidation and, in the case of many former mutual societies, demutualisation. New accounting rules and FSA regulations required life insurance companies to recalculate their future liabilities and to reorganise their portfolios. Faced with this more stringent solvency regime, institutions such as Standard Life (2006) converted to public companies and listed on the stock exchange in order to access the capital markets. Senior management was now answerable to shareholders and looked for new profit centres in the race for earnings. Growing their investment departments into external-facing businesses was the obvious way to go, particularly since their life insurance products could offer tax advantages in the rapidly expanding defined-contribution pensions market.

Faced with these opportunities, the life companies expanded their investment departments and marketing teams and went in search of new pensions and retail clients. By the end of 2006 Legal & General was the largest manager of assets in the UK, with £233 billion under its control.[40] The company was quick to develop the huge demand for passive fund management and to enter new segments such as hedge funds and the bulk annuity market – in which companies with defined-benefit pension schemes buy annuities in order to supply their retirees with guaranteed pensions.

The Prudential, the UK's fourth largest investor at the end of 2006, bought M&G, the UK's pioneer of unit trusts, in 1999 to fill a gap in its retail products and later rolled its entire investment management activities into M&G. M&G's chief executive became one of the Prudential's highest-paid directors and the investment arm contributed nearly a fifth of the insurer's operating profits in 2005.[41] For several years Aviva, the insurance company formed out of a series of mergers involving CU, General Accident and Norwich Union, branded its investment business under the name of Morley Fund Management, a boutique bought by CU in 1990, and by the end of 2006 was the UK's fifth largest investor.

These changes transformed the insurance sector's involvement in the UK's fund management industry. At one level it became more commercial and more involved. Robin Angus has been observing the investment scene in Edinburgh, the life industry's financial capital, for over thirty years as a broker and fund manager. At the beginning of his career the investment departments of the life companies had a reputation for being sleepy and slow to act. Not any more: 'There is much less difference between an insurance company and a retail fund now. Previously life company officials were like old-fashioned civil servants. They were rather lordly. They managed what they had. Nowadays the pressure is on. They are open to more scrutiny and they are more like client-hungry retail or pension fund managers.'[42]

However, at another level the insurance industry lost influence. In the last decade of the 20th century, the insurance companies owned a quarter of UK industry. Its investment portfolios consisted mainly of domestic equities and the industry was known to exercise discreet influence on underperforming company managements. But in the 21st century the industry has switched its portfolio out of equities into bonds to improve its capital adequacy reserves and diversified its remaining equities into foreign shares. The increase in the shareholdings in British companies by overseas investors, mutual funds and hedge funds meant that, according to Peter Montagnon, the director of investment affairs at the Association of British Insurers, 'We are no longer in control of UK plc.'[43]

Retail funds – pooled investments available to the public in various legal entities such as unit trusts, open-ended investment companies and investment trusts – account for about a fifth of the institutional investment management industry.[44] Britain's army of independent financial advisers (IFAs) account for 75–80 per cent of sales to the public, with the remainder split between investment companies' own sales forces, tied agents and direct sales via the media and Internet. Savings schemes with tax breaks such as personal equity plans (PEPs) and individual savings accounts (ISAs) account for a fifth of the total with products forming part of defined-contribution pension plans taking a rising share. Funds of funds have been growing particularly strongly in recent years and represent a quarter of new sales.

Over three quarters of UK retail investments are in equities, and unlike the pension fund market there has been no significant movement into bonds. Since 1997 UK equity holdings have dropped from 50 per cent of portfolios to 40 per cent, and there has been an increasing use of derivatives and hedge funds since the European investment directive UCITS3 gave retail fund managers progressive freedom to invest more adventurously from 2003. Sales of new retail products tend to reflect underlying movements in equity markets: the peak year was 2000 when net sales were over £17 billion; by 2004 that figure had fallen to £4 billion.[45] A third of the retail money run by UK fund managers is domiciled outside the UK in tax havens such as Jersey and Guernsey, and most of this comes from European investors.

The market is fragmented with the top ten having less than a quarter share and the sector leader Invesco Perpetual, part of the Atlanta-based Invesco global fund management group, having only 3 per cent. Fidelity International, the huge privately owned American fund management firm, is number two in the market, and Threadneedle, part of Ameriprise Financial, completed the trio of US-owned firms in 2007's retail top ten. Reflecting the diversification strategies outlined earlier in this chapter, insurance companies such as Scottish Widows, Standard Life and Legal & General also have big positions, as does Schroders.

Largest UK retail fund managers[46]

Company	UK funds under management £ billion
Invesco Perpetual	25.2
Fidelity	21.2
Jupiter	13.7
M&G	11.9
SWIP	11.4
New Star	11.0
Legal & General	10.2
Schroders	10.2
Threadneedle	10.0
Artemis	9.0

The most remarkable feature of the retail sector is the presence of three relatively new firms in the top ten. Jupiter, New Star and Artemis were able to exploit the underperformance of the industry leaders, the opportunities in the defined-contribution pensions market and the market access that the IFAs facilitated to build substantial businesses.

In 1997 four rising fund managers at Ivory & Sime – Mark Tyndall, John Dodd, Derek Stuart and Lindsay Whitelaw – saw an opportunity to form an active investment management house specialising in managing the money of retail investors. They called their new firm Artemis, the goddess of the hunt. They believed in straightforward active fund management with individual managers taking responsibility for the management of named funds. They wanted to avoid bureaucracy, believing, according to Tyndall, that 'fund management is a business that can very easily be over-managed'. They were equally dismissive of management by committee, a practice that Tyndall believed led to mediocre investment decisions. 'We like products where one person can manage that portfolio. We consult but there's no such thing as a team decision. The fund manager is the guy with whom the buck stops.'[47] Using a combination of good investment performance and aggressive billboard advertising, Artemis rapidly built a good reputation and in 2002 received an approach from the Dutch bank ABN AMRO. ABN took a 58 per cent stake, appointed Mark Tyndall chief executive and gave Artemis full operational independence as well as its own UK retail funds to manage.[48]

The cult of the individual that enables firms like Artemis to make their mark is best illustrated by New Star Asset Management, the creation of one of the City's real characters, John Duffield. Duffield founded his first investment management boutique, Jupiter, in 1985, and built it into a business with £12.2 billion under management before selling it for £680 million to the German Commerzbank ten years later. Old Harrovian Duffield, seventy years old in 2009, is an outspoken individual, and relations with the bank were difficult. It was reported that on one occasion, in a row about how much Commerzbank would pay for the 25 per cent of Jupiter retained by staff, he told three of the bank's top executives that they were Nazis, and it was inevitable that he would leave.

His next fund management vehicle was New Star, which by the middle of 2007 had built up assets under management of £25 billion. Duffield's method was to create an environment where individual fund managers could flourish, and a reward structure that got them to join in the first place. Every member of staff owned shares in Duffield's business, and he had a ready eye on the value-creating event – trade sale in the case of Jupiter, stock market listing in the case of New Star. These two events created, according to Duffield, a total of 250 millionaires – 150 at Jupiter and another hundred when New Star was listed on the stock exchange in November 2005.[49]

The firm Duffield left behind, Jupiter, is the third of the boutique firms to appear in 2007's top ten retail funds. Jupiter is run by Edward Bonham Carter, brother of the actress Helen and like Duffield a Harrovian. Rivalry between Jupiter and New Star is intense, especially after New Star poached a number of Jupiter fund managers soon after it set up. Commerzbank tried to sell Jupiter in 2002 and when it failed proposed to list it on the Stock Market. But Jupiter's senior management insisted on buying the firm themselves. The stand-off lasted a year, in which Commerzbank stated many times that they wanted to float the business and Bonham Carter and colleagues held out for a management buyout. They teamed up with TA Associates, a private equity firm, and bought it out for £740 million in 2007, a figure some estimates put at about half what Commerzbank could have achieved from a public listing. But Bonham Carter and the other managers held all the cards in a personal franchise business such as retail fund management. They claimed not to want to run their business in the spotlight of public markets and forced the Germans' hand, ending up with six representatives on a nine-person board and a 60 per cent stake in the business, which Bonham Carter points out is essential currency for attracting stars to the business.[50]

The recovery of the asset management industry from the problems of the late 1990s was not serene. In 2001 the City was rocked by what became known as the split-cap investment trust scandal. Investment trusts are listed companies that invest their shareholders' capital. Shareholders receive income in the form of dividends and capital growth if the share price responds to growth in the investment portfolio. Split-cap trusts offered investors enhanced dividends at the expense of capital growth or enhanced growth at the expense of dividend payments. During the 1990s bull market, some investment trust managers became so confident of rising prices that they borrowed money to leverage their returns. Cross-holdings between trusts became common, leading to accusations of a magic circle of insiders working together to prop up each other's share prices.

However, in 2000 the Stock Market crashed and, amplified by the effect of leverage, the investment trusts' share prices fell away, so that when it became time to wind up the trusts they proved worthless. The FSA launched an investigation, and on Christmas Eve 2004, after months of negotiations, eighteen split-cap firms agreed to pay £194 million into a compensation fund. Eventually 25,000 small shareholders received 40 per cent of their money back, having been the victims of mis-selling.

Aberdeen Asset Management was the UK's biggest split-capital investment manager with responsibility for nineteen split-capital funds.

The man in charge of Aberdeen's split-cap funds was investment director Christopher Fishwick, who resigned from the firm and was barred from holding a senior position in the industry for a period of seven years. Aberdeen's chief executive, Martin Gilbert, has described the firm's involvement in the split-cap affair as a 'near-death experience' after it came up against banking covenants on the high levels of debt it took to leverage its investments. But the firm's recovery is a metaphor for the fund management industry's rebirth, for Aberdeen became one of the UK's biggest fund managers and bought the UK arm of Deutsche Asset Management – Morgan Grenfell's former owner!

By the summer of 2007 the recovery of the UK's asset management industry appeared to be a good example of free-market economics at work. New rules and regulations, competition from hedge funds and the industry's previously abject performance combined to create customer demand for change. In what looked like a classic free-market response, a fresh generation of boutiques sprang up and, faced with customer demand and increased competition, the existing players reworked themselves from being suppliers of a commodity service into value-added service providers. The industry recovered its reputation, but the next eighteen months were to reveal that the rising tide of markets had flattered its achievements. In the excitement costs had been allowed to run away with themselves, and an opportunity to reform the business model was missed. The industry would be forced to address this issue in the months and years ahead.

6

PRIVATE EQUITY

The dog walkers and joggers on Clapham Common on a quiet Sunday morning in May 2006 thought the circus had come to town. A group of people, some garishly dressed, carrying placards and preceded by a small camel, wended their way across the common towards Holy Trinity, a famous church where the anti-slavery campaigner William Wilberforce had once worshipped. A few photographers were there to capture the moment and the passers-by, perhaps wondering what time the circus started, stopped to read what was written on the placards.

The words were a quotation from Matthew 19.24: 'Again I tell you, it is easier for a camel to go through the eye of a needle than for a rich man to enter the kingdom of God.' The camel and one or two of the group were draped in banners bearing the letters GMB, but there was no mention of a circus for this was the launch of a campaign by one of Britain's biggest trade unions against the private equity industry, which it alleged was enriching itself at the expense of the employees and customers of some of Britain's biggest companies. The immediate object of their attention was a forty-two-year-old man named Damon Buffini, the boss of Permira, one of Britain's largest private equity companies, who along with other members of his family attended Holy Trinity.[1]

It was not that the GMB regarded Buffini as an especially bad man. In fact, as someone of mixed race who had grown up on a Leicester council estate and fought his way up through the state education system to Harvard and a senior position in a business not noted for ethnic diversity, Buffini might be regarded as a role model for the equal-opportunity world that the trade unions advocated. But as head of one of the biggest firms in the UK in an industry that was occupying a controversial and increasingly important place in the British economy, he was an obvious target for a union with a point to make.

Private equity – also known as buyout – firms specialise in buying and turning round other companies, and it was Permira's purchase of the Automobile Association, the AA, that became a symbol of the union's campaign. The AA had been a mutual organisation owned by its members until the energy firm Centrica bought it in 1999 and then, in the biggest buyout of 2004, sold it to Permira and another private equity firm, CVC Capital Partners, for £1.8 billion.

The organisation's history reflected the passing times. The AA man ready to help members in trouble at the roadside had been an enduring feature of British motoring since the 1950s. Motorists of a certain age remembered him as reassuring and resourceful. Originally AA men had saluted every car they came across that displayed the association's yellow and black, ceramic and chrome badge. Those days had long gone. Privatisation offered new opportunities for management and a £240 windfall for members, and the AA became much more commercial, diversifying into related activities and taking a more businesslike approach.

When Permira took over the pace was stepped up. The new owners got to work on running the business even more efficiently. They closed down loss-making operations, invested in new equipment for AA vans and introduced more flexible working practices. They swiftly doubled profits but the consequences, according to the GMB, were disastrous for the AA's members and employees. The GMB claimed that since the private equity people took over in 2004 they had laid off approximately 3,300 of the 10,000 staff delivering services to motorists, leaving less then 2,400 patrol staff to deal with 11,000 breakdowns per day. The AA fell from first to third in *Which* magazine's survey of fastest response times. The GMB said call-centre staff were subject to constant oppressive surveillance and monitoring, and were required to sell extra cover and spare parts to motorists. 'Patrol staff', as the roadside AA men were now called, were required to cruise the highways looking for broken down motorists to sell AA membership to. Failure to reach targets to sell cover or spare parts led to a drop in pay or disciplinary action or targeting for the sack. The GMB made a formal complaint to the Disability Rights Commission, alleging that the AA picked on disabled and sick employees for dismissal. Paul Maloney, GMB's senior organiser responsible for the AA, said, 'These venture capitalists have opened up a nightmare world for AA staff. In 2004 they borrowed £1.3 billion from banks to buy the AA. After installing a regime to "sweat" the workforce and fleece the public they now leak the plan to borrow a further £500 million to pay themselves £500 million "special profits" leaving AA "in hock" to the banks to the tune of £1.8 billion.'[2]

AA executives disputed much of what the GMB said and attributed its claims to trade union politics, but the campaign struck a chord. Until the credit crunch of 2007 knocked it off the front page, private equity was the main financial story in the UK for most of 2006–7. The *Financial Times* website carried 4,000 references to private equity for 2003 and 2004; for 2005 the total rose to 5,106, then 6,541 for 2006 and 9,723 for 2007. There was a similar pattern in other publications including *The Economist*, which mentioned private equity over 300 times in 2007 compared to just over 100 in 2004, and the tabloids also made an issue of private equity, focusing on 'fat cats' and buyouts gone wrong with headlines such as FOCUS DIY BOSS: I BODGED IT UP.[3]

In November 2006 the FSA issued a discussion paper on private equity, in response to 'concerns about a perceived lack of understanding amongst public policy makers, potential future investors and commentators with respect to the nature of private equity business models and their inherent risk.'[4] The regulator examined various issues including the lack of transparency in buyouts, conflicts of interest and excessive leverage. Thirteen banks responded to an FSA survey on leverage and reported an increase in their exposure to leveraged buyouts from €58 billion to €68 billion in the twelve months to June 2006, and their total exposure was much greater than this as a result of the distribution of debt to hedge funds and other financial institutions. The FSA described private equity as a 'compelling business model' but warned that: 'Given current leverage levels and recent developments in the economic/credit cycle, the default of a large private equity backed company or a cluster of smaller private equity backed companies seems inevitable.'[5]

Public pressure was such that in March 2007 the industry's trade association, the British Venture Capital Association (BVCA), announced the formation of a working party under the chairmanship of Sir David Walker, a former deputy governor of the Bank of England, with a view to improving disclosure in this extremely private industry. The same month, the Treasury dropped hints that it would be addressing public criticism of the generous tax treatment of private equity. In June Nicholas Ferguson, chairman of SVG Capital, a leading listed investor in private equity, told the *Financial Times*, 'Any commonsense person would say that a highly paid private executive paying less tax than a cleaning lady or other low paid worker . . . can't be right.'[6] And then on three days in June and July 2007 the Parliamentary Treasury Select Committee, a cross-party group responsible for scrutinising Britain's economic affairs, took witness statements on private equity from practitioners, academics, trade unionists, regulators and other experts.[7]

First up before the Treasury Committee on 12 June 2007 were three executives from the BVCA: Peter Linthwaite, chief executive, Wol Kolade, chairman and Jeremy Hand, deputy chairman. Having worked out of the public eye, the men were not prepared for the public grilling that select committees habitually hand out. The *Financial Times* reported, 'Labour MPs on the Treasury select committee were visibly exasperated and angered . . . during a fraught hour-long session of evidence.' Labour MP Sion Simon accused the BVCA men of 'irritating semantics' and his colleague Angela Eagle rejected the BVCA's suggestion that the industry was a creator of jobs with the comment 'It's not objective, it's not transparent – which is the problem with you.'[8] Linthwaite, a City veteran of fifteen years, including time as a director of Royal London Private Equity, resigned two days later, and the Treasury Select Committee licked its lips waiting for its next session on 20 June.

This time it was the heavyweights' turn to do battle, and they had been in training. Damon Buffini, Philip Yea, chief executive of 3i, Britain's first ever private equity organisation, and senior executives from two of the largest American private equity firms, Dominic Murphy of KKR and Robert Easton of Carlyle Group, prepared for the interview by answering mock questions from their own staff and by reading the transcript of the previous session. They came determined to show their industry in a better light, working in examples of its philanthropy and transparency and, in the words of Dominic Murphy, portraying it as 'a patient, involved, long-term investor'. Despite the last-minute absence of David Blitzer, senior managing director of another US private equity giant, Blackstone, it was a much better display, summed up by the headline: DEPLETED PRINCES LEAVE WITH THEIR HONOUR INTACT.[9]

Blitzer did make his appearance at the committee's final session of evidence on 3 July, along with three other private equity executives, on the same bill as Sir David Walker, by this time midway through his review, and Hector Sants, at that time in charge of Wholesale and Institutional Markets at the FSA. The element of surprise had gone, but the Treasury Select Committee and others stayed on the attack, and on the day of the final hearing. Jack Dromey, a senior official with Unite, Britain's biggest union, who had already given evidence to the committee, called for 'specific new legal protections for workers in private equity deals'.[10]

The millions of British people who saw reports of the GMB campaign and the select committee hearings on television and in their newspapers must have wondered what sort of world had crept up on them. Overnight, private equity had moved from being a little-known industry, a remote corner of the financial world that mattered only to its practitioners, to becoming headline news – on account, it seemed, of its ability to garner huge rewards under the approving eye of the tax man while wrecking the lives of employees and destroying customer experience.

There were elements of truth in this picture, but private equity funds covered a wide range of skills and practices. One authoritative study concluded that 'private equity backed companies maintain comparable levels of cutting edge research' to other companies.[11] In many cases private equity supplied energetic and focused management and improved the underlying earnings potential of portfolio companies to the advantage of customers, employees and other stakeholders. But in other cases profits were improved by less sustainable means as companies were denied long-term investment and saddled with debt, leaving them vulnerable to economic downturn and tighter credit conditions.

Private equity originated in Britain and America as venture capital – funding for new business. In 1945 a British government-sponsored agency, the Industrial and Commercial Finance Corporation (ICFC), was formed to make loans to small businesses, and the following year the American Research and Development Corporation was founded across the Atlantic by a group of academics to invest in businesses set up by returning Second World War veterans. ICFC concentrated on financing start-ups and early- and middle-stage businesses for much of its life, and this defined the place of private equity in British industry for a long time. As late as 2001 the Myners report on institutional investment appeared to envisage a restricted role for Britain's private equity industry: 'Private equity capital has a distinctive role to play, particularly for smaller and younger companies, combining strong financial incentives for growth with mentoring and networking support to investee companies.'[12]

But in the US private equity had taken on a different meaning altogether. The US venture capital industry remained an important backer of early- and middle-stage companies, but the really explosive growth came in non-venture private equity with the first big-ticket buyouts in the 1980s. Innovative financing, especially junk bonds – securities issued by companies regarded as below investment grade – enabled entrepreneurs to borrow huge sums to fund leveraged buyouts. Initially the big players were opportunistic corporate raiders such as Carl Icahn and Ronald Perelman, whose 1985 buyouts of the airline TWA and the healthcare and beauty products group Revlon helped to trigger off an avalanche of debt-financed deals.

The raiders usually operated through holding companies, but an alternative vehicle was emerging in the form of private partnerships between principals and outside investors. These private equity firms were pioneered by men such as the cousins Henry Kravis and George Roberts of KKR and the brothers Theodore and Nick Forstmann and Brian D. Little of Forstmann Little & Co., and these two firms went head to head in the most famous buyout of all time, the $25 billion 'barbarians at the gate', battle for the US tobacco giant RJR Nabisco in 1988.[13] Institutional investors, particularly the state employee pension funds such as Calpers in California, developed an appetite for private equity, and between 1981 and 1988 over 1,500 US companies went private.[14] Leverage brought previously untouchable targets within range. The junk bond experts Michael Milken and his employers Drexel Burnham Lambert became the kings of Wall Street and admirers proclaimed a new business paradigm.

However, at the end of the 1980s rising interest rates and a tightening economy undid the sums on which many leveraged buyouts had been based. Evidence of market manipulation emerged; Milken went to jail and Drexel Burnham Lambert went bust. Many leveraged buyouts, including the Revlon and TWA deals mentioned earlier, struggled to raise the cash to support their debt, and KKR had to pump in $1.7 billion of new equity into RJR Nabisco.

Leveraged buyouts were a synonym for dodgy deals for much of the 1990s. Once-bitten-twice-shy lenders were more cautious, and although private equity continued to grow, the deals done were not on the same scale as in the previous decade.[15] That changed in 2003 after the Federal Reserve cut interest rates to 1 per cent. Cheap money was in plentiful supply, and between 2003 and the first half of 2007 private equity went ballistic. The size and scope of the deals done in the US were astonishing. In 2006–7 at the peak of the wave the utility giant TXU went private for $44.4 billion; Equity Office Properties, America's largest office landlord, cost its private equity buyers $37.7 billion; HCA, the largest private operator of healthcare facilities in the world, was sold for $32.1 billion; Enron spin-off Kinder Morgan sold itself for $27.5 billion; casino operator Harrah's Entertainment was bought out for $27.4 billion; Clear Channel, the biggest radio owner in America with 1,200 stations, was sold for $26.7 billion; and in the technology sector Freescale Semiconductor went for $17.5 billion.[16]

The top four private equity firms in the US – Blackstone, Texas Pacific, Carlyle and KKR – joined the ranks of the world's most powerful financial institutions. When Blackstone listed on the New York Stock Exchange in 2007 it was valued at $32 billion, making founder Stephen Schwarzman's personal holding worth $7.5 billion at the time. The credit crunch of 2007 caused KKR to postpone its own listing but by then it had made a total of over 160 transactions with an enterprise value of $410 billion and its $39 billion of capital invested had an equity value of $86 billion.[17] The influence of the Carlyle Group, a company that according to one authoritative study operates within a powerful and profitable world known as the Iron Triangle, 'the place where the world's mightiest military intersects with high-powered politics and big business'[18] appeared to know no bounds. Its chairman Lou Gerstner was the former boss of IBM and Nabisco; its advisers included former US president George Bush Senior and former British prime minister John Major; and since it was founded in 1987 it had invested $43 billion.[19] Texas Pacific was founded five years later. In a single year, 2006, it was involved in deals that totalled a record-breaking $101 billion and won a string of 'business of the year' awards.

At first the UK was slow to catch on to what was happening in America, and for a long time private equity in Britain meant venture capital. In the early 1980s British venture capital houses such as the investment trusts Electra and Candover and the US-style partnership Advent Venture Partners did small buyouts, but it was not until 1986 that investments in buyouts exceeded those in venture capital for the first time. Even then, the targets were usually small-scale manufacturing businesses; the average deal size was only just over £10 million; and the biggest management buyout of the year, the privatisation of the shipbuilder VSEL cost only £100 million.[20]

It was small beer compared to what was happening in the US, but in the second half of the 1980s the ripples from America's corporate raiding and leveraged buyout boom reached the UK. American raiders and buyout firms got involved in contested takeovers such as the battle between Ernest Saunders' Guinness and Sir James Gulliver's Argyle for Distillers in 1986 and the bids for the Gateway food retail group in 1989. Publicly listed industrial conglomerates such as Hanson and BTR used private equity techniques in taking over underperforming companies, cutting costs and selling them on. There was a mini-boom in private-equity-backed management buyouts in 1988 and 1989 involving companies such as the home improvement specialist Magnet, Sir James Gulliver's leveraged buyout of the carpet retailer Harris Queensway and the holiday firm International Leisure Group,[21] but in the 1990–1 recession several of these deals – including those named above – collapsed as they struggled to service their debts.

Despite this setback, in the 1990s US-style private equity partnerships became more active in the UK. One of the leading firms was Apax, formed by Ronald Cohen and three partners in 1971. Originally an advisory business, it linked up with Alan Patricof, one of America's early venture capitalists in 1977, and moved into private equity soon afterwards. Permira's predecessor company Schroder Ventures was founded in the UK and Europe by a Schroders' director, Nick Ferguson, in 1984, and was soon doing deals there. Another private equity partnership, BCG, also started life at one of the old-style merchant banks, Barings in this case.

The private equity arms of US and other foreign banks had set up in London, including Goldman Sachs Private Equity, CVC (formerly Citibank Venture Capital) and Nomura's Principal Finance Group (later bought out and renamed Terra Firma under the leadership of Guy Hands). The syndicate of British banks that owned the Industrial and Commercial Finance Corporation sold out in 1987 and, as an investment trust named 3i, the organisation added private equity to its venture capital activities. Executives with private equity experience started their own firms, such as Doughty Hanson and Alchemy. Pension funds, banks and insurance companies owned or partly owned funds such as Cinven, previously the National Coal Board Pension Fund's Venture Capital arm, Barclays Ventures and the in-house private equity team at Legal & General.

Immediately after the failures of the early 1990s investors and lenders were more cautious, but in the second half of the decade deal sizes started to climb and then took off in the 21st century. In 1997 the biggest private equity deal in the UK was the buyout of the betting chain William Hill for £700 million, organised by Cinven and CVC Capital Partners. By 2000 the biggest deal size had risen to £3.5 billion – for the property company MEPC, taken private in a deal co-led by Hermes, manager of the BT pension funds, and an American partner. Britain's high street became a private equity battleground. The fashion chain Arcadia, demerged out of Burtons and listed on the stock market in 1998, was bought out by the retail entrepreneur Philip Green for £775 million in 2002 and refinanced in 2005 with the help of £1 billion of bank debt. Debenhams, another Burtons' spin-out listed on the Stock Market in 1998, went private in 2003 for an equity investment of £600 million and re-floated three years later at treble that price, generating a profit of over £1 billion for the private equity backers.

For eighteen months in 2006 and the first half of 2007 the financial press was full of actual or rumoured buyouts, and the deals came thick and fast. In 2006, AWG, the Anglian water group, was taken private for £2.2 billion by a private equity consortium including 3i.

Another consortium including Goldman Sachs and a government of Singapore investment fund bought out Associated British Ports for £2.8 billion. Singapore appeared in another big deal at the end of the year, when BAA, the operator of Britain's airports, was bought for over £10 billion by a private equity consortium led by Grupo Ferrovial. In February 2007 Britain's third largest supermarket group J Sainsbury nearly fell into private equity hands in the form of a CVC-led consortium, to be saved in the end by its founding family shareholders.[22] Then, in the summer of 2007, KKR, the firm behind the 'barbarians at the gate' deal nearly twenty years before, bought out Alliance Boots in a £11 billion transaction.

In a very short period of time the private equity industry had come from nowhere to become a significant factor in everyday life in Britain. By 2007 one in twenty British people worked for private-equity-backed companies,[23] consumers spent millions of pounds every week in private-equity-owned stores, pubs and restaurants and nearly 10 per cent of government tax receipts came from private-equity-owned businesses.[24] The industry was also making a significant contribution to the City's reputation as a global financial services centre. Over half of Europe's private equity business was done out of London;[25] most of the money raised by UK buyout funds was invested overseas;[26] and London was acknowledged to be Europe's private equity capital. This cemented the City's position as the European headquarters of the big investment banks, for which the UK is second only to the US in terms of global private equity revenues.[27]

The dynamism of private equity helped to keep the rest of the City at work. With over 6,000 professionals working in the sector, it rivalled public equity fund management as a direct employer. As a voracious user of professional services it sustained the equivalent of a further 12,000 full-time jobs in financial services and related professions, generating £5.4 billion in revenue for them in 2006. Lawyers, accountants and consultants as well as investment banks thrived on the back of this business, forging new relationships and setting up specialist teams to work with the buyout firms.

In 1997 private equity was a slightly mysterious closed world as far as the rest of the City was concerned. It brought the occasional medium-sized IPO but was playing a different game to what was going on in the public markets. But over the next ten years, with a gathering force that appeared irresistible in 2006–7, private equity moved into the mainstream and stands alongside hedge funds as a driver of the City's renaissance. The hyperbole of Wol Kolade, chairman of the BVCA, was understandable: 'In just one generation, the venture capital and private equity industry has grown to become a dynamo for growth, innovation and enterprise.'[28] Where did this growth come from and why were the GMB, the Treasury Select Committee and others so upset?

The underlying cause of the global private equity boom was a change in mindset in corporate and government circles in the 1980s. Free-market thinking in Britain and America ushered in the era of deregulation, privatisation and non-intervention. The invisible hand of the market replaced the dead hand of government as the force that shaped industry. Investment bankers fanned the flames, telling corporate chief executives that shareholder value could be created by mergers or selling off subsidiaries, and offering financing packages and introductions to private equity investors to get the deals done. This led to an 'anything goes' philosophy, and the ensuing mayhem of corporate restructuring had a galvanising effect on previously conservative business leaders. Soon after setting up Schroder Ventures in 1984 Nick Ferguson and colleagues began looking for buyout candidates in Europe. He recalls 'going to talk to the CEO at Siemens, whose initial response was "We at Siemens never sell anything." But globalisation was in the air and some years later they had a whole lot of away weekends to discuss what to do about it. He came back to me and said, "Unless I change this company with its 5,000 divisions, we are not going to get anywhere. We have got to concentrate on a few key areas." And so he started to restructure, and we eventually bought two divisions including his entire dental equipment business.'[29]

Industry in Britain and Europe was behind the curve and ready for restructuring, a point made to Ferguson on another visit, this time to Harvard Business School in 1990. 'They said, "Look here. The number of battery makers in America is four, average return on equity 17 per cent. The number of battery makers in Japan is three, average return on equity 15 per cent. The number in Europe is twenty-seven, average return on equity minus 5 per cent. They told me this will not last. Some of them are going to die, somebody is going to sort this out and this is the opportunity for you." And this was the picture in countless industries all over Europe and for a while in Britain too.'[30]

The application of hard-nosed American business thinking to continental Europe's fragmented corporate sector and to British industry – only midway through its Thatcher-inspired shock treatment – led to a raft of opportunities for private equity. Making the most of those opportunities required operational rigour involving, according to Lord Hollick, who joined the buyout firm KKR after a successful career in the corporate sector, three stages: 'First find a good company, add talented management and then implement a bold plan.'[31] At this time, March 2007, cheap credit was still in plentiful supply and was evidently taken for granted.

Buyout experts say that finding a good company is the product of diligent research: 'It is down to the number of people and the hours of effort. We might have fifteen people studying one company for nine months. We look at every angle. The state of the competition, customer behaviour, pricing trends in key markets, cost factors as well as the financials.'[32] If a deal can be done, bold plans such as KKR's 'first hundred days' come into play.[33] According to a World Economic Forum study, public-to-private buyouts usually involve management changes: 'When a company goes private . . . the board size and presence of outside directors are drastically reduced.'[34] A new chief executive is often appointed and senior managers are required to invest in the business to align management's interests with other shareholders.[35]

The ability to focus on a smaller stakeholder group is vital to the success of the buyout. A private equity fund might typically have 150 limited partners compared to FTSE 100 companies, which have an average of 150,000 shareholders.[36] Those that work closely with the industry such as chartered accountants have no doubt about the effects of this: 'a publicly listed company . . . will invest significant time and money in communicating with shareholders, investor relations and periodic reporting. By contrast, management of a private equity backed company has more opportunity to focus on strategy.'[37]

The results of the application of private equity techniques to a receptive corporate sector appeared impressive. For the decade up to the middle of 2007 the average annual earnings before interest payments, tax and depreciation on European-leveraged buyouts ranged between 12 and 14 per cent per annum, slightly ahead of the returns achieved by public listed companies. Crucially, this was a much better rate of return than the cost of borrowing, which fluctuated between 3 and 7 per cent over the same period. The average private equity fund could therefore expect a handsome return on any money it borrowed, especially during the industry's boom years of 2003–6, when the gap between the cost of money and the return from private equity was a juicy 10 percentage points.

Not surprisingly against this background, it was easy for private equity firms to attract funding. The benign economic conditions of the late 20th and early 21st centuries meant that the world's pension schemes, foundations and banks were cash rich and looking for places to invest. The US state pension funds were the biggest investors; European charitable foundations, family trusts and private banks and sovereign wealth funds in Asia also poured money into buyout funds. But British institutions were cautious. Some 79 per cent of the money raised by the UK's largest private equity groups between 2004 and 2006 came from outside the UK.[38] And even in 2006, by which time private equity had a high profile in Britain and investment conditions were at their most favourable, UK sources provided only a quarter of the money raised by British buyout funds.[39]

The revolution in banking practices completed a virtuous circle in funding. In the typical private equity deal investment capital provides only a third of the acquisition costs, the remainder being bank debt. From the mid-1990s the new banking model, originate and distribute, enabled the banks to expand their loan books. As we have already noted, banks no longer kept debt on their balance sheet until it matured; it was repackaged and distributed as structured product to hedge funds, investment banks, pension funds and insurance companies. The FSA calculated that on average banks distributed 81 per cent of their loans to the biggest buyouts within 120 days of them being made. In theory this left the banks with only a fraction of the risk.[40] The new arrangements had another advantage, for under banking regulations banks had to set aside less capital to cover traded debt than for conventional debt. Freed from restrictive regulatory constraints, and insulated, they thought, from credit defaults by the derivatives they were using, they competed to lend money to the private equity sector. Veteran bankers shook their heads in amazement as credit rules were eased on 'covenant-lite' loans, and in a shocking snub to the tradition of prudent banking, lending officers were given market share targets.

Thus globalisation, free-market theories, disciplined management, low interest rates, institutional liquidity and the new banking model came together to create the buyout movement, but why did activity gravitate to London? The explanation can be found in conventional cluster analysis: the City had all the right skills. Nick Ferguson regards this as a major reason for the ability of his own and other early buyout firms to achieve lift-off in the 1980s and 1990s:

You can't do private equity without other professional services. We used hundreds of thousands of hours over the years of management consultants' time. Before you go and spend several hundred million buying Siemens dental equipment or any other large business you have got to know everything there is to know about some very esoteric markets. You need to know about healthcare policies in different countries, manufacturing costs, the opportunities for consolidating manufacturing, the connections with suppliers and how you make a margin through that. You need to understand the different buying patterns that prevail, and you need to understand the competition. The consulting firms responded famously. Also you need really good legal advice – you can imagine the number of agreements that you have to analyse and understand. To sell a huge tool machine business that we bought in Germany with multiple contracts to the auto industry we needed to understand the liabilities for late delivery, the warranties we were liable for and a host of other things. So before you go ahead you need packs of lawyers and you need to structure the deals. And then the banks were important. The first borrowings were all from Americans such as Citigroup, but then Royal Bank of Scotland and Bank of Scotland in particular were fast to get into the buyout business.[41]

New Labour also made its contribution to the City's private equity industry. Chancellor Gordon Brown believed that Britain's long-term future required strong technology and life-science industries, and one of his objectives in setting up the Myners review of institutional fund management was to facilitate venture capital investment. But by the time the report came out in 2001 he had already inadvertently provided the entire private equity industry, including venture capital, with a shot in the arm.

Private equity firms receive an annual management fee of about 1.5 per cent of the assets they manage and 20 per cent of any profits from selling portfolio companies above an agreed hurdle rate – usually 8 per cent per annum. This 20 per cent share is known as carried interest. The fee income is taxed as ordinary income, but reforms introduced by Gordon Brown in his 1998 budget enabled private equity partners to take advantage of an extraordinarily generous tax concession on their carried interest.

This was taper relief, introduced primarily to encourage new business ventures, but also benefiting private equity partners. Taper relief applied to the capital gains tax on business assets, which was so defined as to include private equity carried interest. The tax was reduced from 40 to 10 per cent, provided that the assets were held for ten years. This holding period was reduced to four years in 2000 and to two in 2002.[42] Private equity partners could scarcely believe their luck. This unexpected and unsought change was the equivalent of a 50 per cent increase in their after-tax pay. When considered alongside other British tax rules that allowed interest to be treated as a business expense[43] and permitted non-domiciles to work in the UK but pay almost no tax, it is easy to see why London became the location of choice for private equity partnerships.

But as we saw at the beginning of this chapter, by 2006 the growth of private equity had become highly controversial, leading to select committee inquiries, the high-profile union campaign, hundreds of newspaper articles and the resignation of the chief executive of the industry's trade association.

The trigger was 2006 and the first half of 2007, when the barbarians really did seem to be at the gates of corporate UK. Interest rates were low; easy credit was available; and no target seemed out of range of the buyout firms. Half-understood lessons from American business history, including the leveraged buyout and junk bond tags, had given US-style private equity a bad name, and when it seemed as though this method of business would sweep the UK it was easy to mobilise opposition.

The high profile of some buyout targets increased public interest in what was happening. Early this century, in addition to the big deals already mentioned in this chapter familiar businesses such as Bird's Eye frozen foods, Yell, Halfords, Kwik-Fit and MFI were bought out. In 2007 the Alliance Boots deal and the possible buyout of J Sainsbury aroused particular concern about the 'anything goes' City. Sainsbury's was Britain's third largest food retailer; the founding family remained big shareholders and for some the company remained a rare and welcome symbol of paternalist capitalism. Alliance Boots, itself the product of a merger a year before, was the first member of the FTSE 100 index of leading shares to be taken private. Boots was one of Britain's oldest and best-known companies, a bastion of the British high street and a company that retained family values, regional roots and a reputation as a good employer. Critics said that it had been auctioned off unsentimentally to a new buyer with no background in the UK and no interest in customers and employees other than as a means to an end.

Employment was the raw nerve. The sharp end of private equity can be very sharp indeed, and if aggressive action is required to sort out a company that they have acquired, buyout firms are prepared to take action and to take it fast. This was frightening for those involved, and the unions did everything they could to protect their members by whipping up public opinion.

Private equity's record in employment is hotly debated. The industry rebuffs criticism that it is a job cutter, and backs its claims with research saying that during the five year period to 2006–7, UK private equity backed companies increased staff levels by 8% per annum, significantly more than quoted companies.[44]

But other research reveals a more mixed picture, particularly for private-equity-backed buy-ins as opposed to management-initiated buyouts.[45] In an effort to reach a definitive answer, the World Economic Forum commissioned an in-depth study from a panel of academic experts led by Josh Lerner, a finance professor at Harvard. The employment study examined virtually all private-equity-backed companies in the US from 1980 to 2005 and matched them against comparable firms and establishments in terms of industry, age and size. The study revealed that in the first two years of private equity ownership, employment declined by 7 per cent more in the private-equity-backed group of companies before stabilising and performing in line with the peer group. UK firms were not included in Lerner's work, but it can be taken as a reasonable proxy for what happens in Britain, and the unions and other private equity critics found plenty of examples to support their case.[46]

Financial engineering was another contentious matter. The levels of debt used in buyouts became a potential public interest issue as the scale and number of buyouts in Britain rose. As the UK had seen after the recession of 1990–1, highly leveraged companies can struggle to meet their interest payments, with nasty consequences for employees, suppliers and pension funds.[47] The new legislation that pinned responsibility for pension fund solvency on the plan sponsors meant that the pension fund issue could be particularly tricky in leveraged buyouts, and pension fund trustees found themselves in an unaccustomed limelight. The obduracy of the pension fund trustees helped to scupper private equity interest in J Sainsbury; KKR had to put in £418 million to plug a gap in the Alliance Boots pension fund; and I spoke to a trustee of another company pension fund whose private equity bidder demanded his removal 'for being too difficult'. In fact, leverage in private equity deals in the UK never breached the US norm of 70 per cent of total capital, and although leverage rose from a norm of 50 to 60 per cent during the buyout boom of 2006–7, we shall see that it was leverage in the banking sector not in private equity that posed the biggest systemic risk.[48]

Accusations of financial engineering also extended to the private equity technique of refinancing, which critics regarded as sleight of hand. Refinancing involves private-equity-backed companies borrowing from the banks or selling assets and paying out all or part of the money raised as a special dividend. This enables the buyout funds to withdraw large amounts of capital, leaving the company itself saddled with an increased amount of debt. When interest rates were low and the banks were falling over themselves to lend to private equity, the annual value of private equity refinancing in the UK rose from just over £2 billion to more than £12 billion between 2003 and 2005.[49] Strong cash-generative companies were able to service this increased debt and, as discussed above, leverage in the UK did not get out of hand. But there were cases of refinancing that exposed the private equity firms to accusations of profiteering and greed.

One example concerned the management buyout at Debenhams backed by the private equity groups CVC Capital partners, TPG Capital and Merrill Lynch Private Equity in 2003. The backers had put up £606 million in equity and £1.1 million of debt was raised on Debenhams balance sheet. By remortgaging some of the stores and raising £325 million from the bond markets, the company was able to pay its new owners £130 million by way of a special dividend within months of the takeover. This perfectly routine piece of financial engineering would have attracted no attention except that soon after the business was listed on the Stock Market in May 2006 profits and the share price collapsed. Angry shareholders complained that the private equity investors, who had nearly doubled their money within two years, had enriched themselves while under-investing in the company's stores and infrastructure.[50]

Complaints about refinancing also surfaced in June 2007 when Duke Street Capital, a mid-market private equity firm, and Apax sold Focus DIY to Cerberus, a US hedge fund, for a nominal sum. Focus had not been able to generate enough cash to service its £248 million of debt, and its bond holders were paid only 40 pence in the pound upon the sale. The original private equity investors, on the other hand, had done very well out of the struggling debt-laden business because, despite receiving only £1 for their shareholding, they had already sold the Wickes division of Focus for £950 million and taken money out of the business as a dividend.[51] Bond holders complained that the proceeds of the sale of Wickes should have been used to bring down Focus's debt.

News of the profits made on private equity deals enraged the public. When Charterhouse, CVC and Permira agreed to merge Saga and the AA in 2007, they revealed that they had made a combined profit of £2.4 billion from the deal and paid themselves a £2 billion dividend.[52] The GMB's Paul Maloney was quick to make the obvious point: 'This money was made on the back of 3,500 sacked workers, cuts in the pay of call-centre staff, the elongation of the working day for the patrols and a decline in the service to the customers.'[53]

The industry's reputation was not helped by the low taxes it paid. The personal taxes paid by private equity partners contrasted starkly with the fate of employees of their portfolio companies and with the general level of taxation in the UK. By the time Nick Ferguson intervened with his comparison of the tax paid by his private equity friends and his cleaner, the issue was already attracting attention, and hard-nosed private equity executives lined up behind him. Sir Ronald Cohen, co-founder of Apax, one of the elder statesmen of the industry said, 'Maybe the 10 per cent rate needs to be raised to something more reasonable'.[54] Jon Moulton, founder of the Alchemy private equity group, conceded, 'I don't think we pay quite enough tax.'[55] A leader in the *Financial Times* summed up the growing consensus in rejecting the arguments that private equity carry – the partners' share of any profits once they have paid back investors – should be taxed as a capital gain: 'That might make sense if the equity partners were earning gains exclusively on their own invested capital, but carried interest is mostly a payment for managing other people's money. It is a performance bonus and should be taxed as income.'[56]

By the time of the Labour Party conference in September 2007, Treasury officials were confirming that work was going on to look at the tax position of private equity. The issue was becoming a hot topic, and in response to questions prime minister Gordon Brown told an audience of party members, 'Private equity will be dealt with in the pre-Budget report. I can assure you that we will do so.'[57] Soon after-wards capital gains tax was raised from ten per cent to eighteen per cent and taper relief was abolished.

As evidence emerged of aggressive management, low taxes, refinancing and huge profits, the private equity industry's lack of transparency became an issue. Buyout firms were private partnerships and so were not obliged to reveal much about the performance of the companies they owned or how they made their money. Secrecy led to suspicions that something untoward was going on and that employees and suppliers were being subjected to undue risks. Opponents argued that private equity was now such a force in the UK economy that public interest considerations required fuller disclosure, and in a conciliatory gesture the industry set up the Walker Working Party to see what could be done to improve transparency.

Critics had picked out four issues alleging secrecy, lack of account-ability, brutal management and leverage. They were concerned that these issues put employees, customers and perhaps the whole economy at risk. The fuss reached a crescendo during the summer of 2007, but then the credit crunch happened, liquidity dried up and buyouts were off the agenda. With hindsight, the furore was out of proportion to private equity's actual role in the economy. As we have shown, private-equity-backed companies were significant employers and taxpayers but still represented under 10 per cent of the national economy. It was their rate of growth and their potential rather than their actual importance that led to the private equity panic of 2006–7. The credit crunch would test the industry's operating model to the full and throw further light on its credibility as a method of corporate governance.

7

INVESTMENT BANKING

It was 24 April 2007 and London was enjoying its warmest April since records had begun. As the directors of Schroders plc gathered for their annual general meeting at the firm's gleaming new headquarters in Gresham Street in the heart of the City of London, their mood matched the peerless weather.

Two board members in particular had reason to be pleased. They were Bruno Schroder and his brother-in-law George Mallinckrodt, heads of the family that controlled the company. Their judgement in selling Schroders' investment bank back in 2000 in order to focus on investment management was paying off. The businesses they had kept were turning round under the leadership of Michael Dobson, and the part they had sold in January 2000 was flourishing under Citigroup's ownership.

Whilst their prime interest was in Schroders, the success of the investment bank they used to own was important to them, for these were decent men who wanted to do the right thing for their clients and employees. Both Bruno Schroder and George Mallinckrodt were up for re-election at the 2007 annual general meeting, a purely routine matter given their family's shareholding and the company's success. A shareholder speaking from the floor briefly spoiled the bonhomie by complaining about the firm's slow progress, but if the board were troubled by this they need not have worried for help was at hand.

Robert Swannell, a suave and distinguished corporate financier who had joined Schroders thirty years before and transferred to Citigroup after the change in ownership, got to his feet. He recalled a conversation some eight years before on the night that the sale of the investment bank was agreed when he had assured Bruno Schroder that selling it was the right thing to do, a decision that now appeared to have been vindicated. He praised the firm's glorious 200-year history and looked forward to what he hoped would be an equally successful future.

It was an assured performance from an assured corporate financier. It nipped any dissent in the bud and chimed well with accepted wisdom about investment banking in the City. Whilst there had been worries in the 1990s that American ownership of the UK's investment banking sector would lead to an era of fast finance, snuff out London's unique culture and jeopardise its standing as an independent financial centre, in 2007 these fears seemed groundless.

THE AMERICANS

Indeed in the spring of 2007 the City's investment bankers were enjoying unprecedented wealth and influence. Hedge funds might be the new game in town, the place where fund managers and traders went to try to make really serious money, but life was still very good for the investment banking crowd. Business in Europe was booming and London was firmly established as the industry's regional capital. Profits were at record levels and City workers had just been awarded the most generous bonuses ever in the January compensation round. Freed from the embarrassment of working for failing firms, senior investment bankers were in their pomp. The City's contribution to the national economy gave them the ear of government, and they strutted in and out of Downing Street and the Treasury summoned by politicians and civil servants to discuss an ever-broadening agenda.

American banks like Citigroup that had bought or built their way into London found that they had struck gold. At the turn of the century European capital markets were still immature compared to those in the UK, but as free-market ideas spread – helped by the missionary zeal of self-interested investment bankers – equity and debt financing and investing took off on the continent. Europe became an important profit centre for the US investment banks. One senior American investment banker told me, 'When I came to Europe in

1999, 85 per cent of all revenues and 115 per cent of all profits came from the US. Today we see a completely different dynamic with under 50 per cent of revenues being done in the US, and in profits international has moved from loss to now accounting for half the profits. During that time our US revenues and profits grew dramatically; it's just that international, well, it exploded.'[1] By 2007 Europe accounted for over a third of global investment banking revenues; over a quarter of this business was originated by institutions based in the UK; and over half of European turnover passed through London.[2]

As the importance of Europe grew, the American investment banks placed key executives in London. Goldman Sachs shifted leadership of one of its major global functions to London when Edward Forst, its chief administrative officer, moved there.[3] It became common for the investment banks to appoint co-heads to run their big divisions and to place one in New York and the other in London. Some of the leading American US investment bankers, such as John Thornton at Goldman Sachs and John Studzinski at Morgan Stanley, spent twenty years or more in London and built their reputations there. Others moved seamlessly between the two capitals. After Citigroup bought Schroders, Robert Swannell found himself reporting to Michael Klein, who had joined Salomon Brothers in 1985 after graduating from Wharton Business School. Klein later moved to London, became head of European investment banking and co-head of global investment banking for Citigroup, and in 2001 was named investment banker of the year by the influential magazine *Investment Dealers' Digest* and one of *Fortune* magazine's twenty-five global leaders to watch.

London prospered, and the British economy seemed to thrive on the medicine of hard-edged capitalism administered by investment banks. As we saw in the chapters on hedge funds, private equity and asset management, the financial services industry made the judgements that determined the survival of the fittest in the corporate sector, and the investment banks were orchestrating the action. They initiated and advised on hostile takeovers of underperforming businesses, provided the funding for such deals and influenced the institutions that determined their outcome. Lip service in the form of support for education, skills and the venture capital industry was paid to the need for long-term investment in people and products, but by and large the free market was left to its own devices. Sentiment and tradition went out of the window; anything was up for sale; and the invigor-ating breeze of open-market competition was seen as an essential component of Britain's economic revival.

This then was the world as seen from the towers in Canary Wharf and Manhattan, the offices in Whitehall and the cabinet rooms in Westminster in the spring and early summer of 2007. It had evolved after the Big Bang financial services deregulation of 1986, but not until the 21st century, after the home-grown institutions had fallen by the wayside, could the investment banks operating in London be described as successful.

It was the equity bull market that ran from 1982 until 2000 that was the making of the US investment banks and the breaking of their UK counterparts. The value of the world's stock markets rose from under $3 trillion to over $30 trillion; there was a record-breaking wave of mergers and acquisitions; and the size and number of IPOs reached unprecedented heights, culminating in the dot.com bubble of the late 1990s. Annual profits in the US securities industry trebled to $21 billion between 1995 and 2000 and the top investment banks established themselves as global leviathans.

London's banks and brokers might have expected to flourish in these booming markets, but in the second half of the 1990s the US investment banks saw an opportunity in Europe and squeezed them out. They used their super-profits from Wall Street to cross-subsidise the development of their businesses in London, paying top dollar for talent and tolerating several years of losses. The UK firms had no such cash cow, lacked the management skills to draw up an alternative agenda to the US business model and were unable to compete. The story of the sudden capitulation of the City's independent investment banks and brokers – Warburg, Barings, Kleinwort and Smith New Court in 1995; NatWest Markets and Barclays' equivalent investment banking division BZW in 1997; and Schroders and Fleming in 2000 – has been told elsewhere,[4] but what of the institutions that replaced them?

The 'bulge bracket', the term used to describe the leading US invest-ment banks, set the pace. The pre-eminent investment bank in London, as it was in the rest of the world, was Goldman Sachs. It had been building up its operations in London since before Big Bang in 1986 and accelerated its presence steadily from the mid-1990s onwards. It preferred recruitment to acquisition and was careful and highly selective in choosing the people it hired. It had set up its offices in Peterborough Court just off Fleet Street, handy enough for the City but a long way from the emerging financial services centre further east at Canary Wharf. Luckily for Goldman, the hedge fund industry that emerged as the driving force in the City in the 21st century located itself in London's West End, leaving Goldman perfectly placed between the City's old and new centres.

To begin with, Goldman's entry into Europe was focused on corporate finance. John Thornton, who came to London from New York in 1984, led the drive, building superb connections in corporate and government circles, and Goldman Sachs appeared regularly at the top of the investment banking league tables. This was combined with the aggressive use of capital for customer and proprietary trading, leading-edge risk management and a determination to make the most of the firm's wide range of financial disciplines and connections. It was the prime example of an American investment bank at the top of its game. One insider described the model: 'Trading, investment banking and capital markets became totally integrated in the drive to succeed. Traditional merger and acquisition and IPO work was supplemented by new ideas like hedging, risk management products for clients and corporate buybacks. Business from high-net-worth individuals would come from hedging their equity stakes in their companies, tax planning and corporate finance advice. It gushed billions of dollars.'[5]

Goldman's great rival in global investment banking was Morgan Stanley. It had also been in London for a long time and pursued a similar strategy of organic growth. It was one of the first banks to move out to Canary Wharf, and in the 1990s and the early years of the 21st century established a reputation as a blue-chip, discreet and deliberately understated operation, its reputation matching its slogan of doing 'first class business in a first class way'.

The ousting in 2005 of Philip Purcell, Morgan Stanley's global chief executive after a public spat with a group of disaffected former employees and shareholders – ironically given the way things turned out, the dissidents wanted Morgan Stanley to take more risk in its business – had little effect on this reputation in Europe. By then a small group of bankers had driven Morgan Stanley up the league tables. Among them was John Studzinski, an American who came to

London in 1984 and was said to handle forty client relationships personally including top corporate names such as BP, Unilever and Reed Elsevier. If it lacked the trading clout of a Goldman and the cutting edge of some of the European derivatives specialists, it still stood up there as an industry all-rounder of the very highest quality.[6]

The third member of the élite group at the head of bulge bracket, Merrill Lynch, supplemented organic growth with an acquisition, taking over the UK broker Smith New Court in 1995 and using it as a building block for its European business. Other bulge bracket US banks and investment banks also stepped up the pace in London. Lehman expanded rapidly, staff numbers rising from 1,000 in 1999 to 4,000 by December 2005, when it moved into new offices in Canary Wharf. Credit Suisse was troubled by global regulatory and cost issues but remained a member of the group of leading investment banks and based its European business around BZW's equities and corporate finance teams. Citigroup had a presence in London through its acquisitions of Salomon Brothers and Smith Barney in 1997, and the purchase of Schroders, which we have already discussed, added broadly based corporate connections in UK boardrooms.

The dark horse amongst the US investment banks in London between 1997 and 2007 was J. P. Morgan, an institution that in the mid-1990s had not quite lived up to the reputation of its eponymous founder, who a hundred years before had rearranged corporate America and rescued the US banking system on two separate occasions. But in the 1990s the bank's global derivatives team working out of London and New York came up with a series of ideas that restored J. P. Morgan's reputation and transformed the world's banking system. The ideas in question related to credit derivatives – financial instruments that enable lenders to insure themselves against borrowers defaulting.

According to the *Financial Times* capital markets editor Gillian Tett, who was the first mainstream journalist to home in on this area, a young British banker named Robert Reoch working for J. P. Morgan in London sold one of the first of these products on a basket of bonds to a client in 1994. If one of the bonds defaulted, the client would reimburse J. P. Morgan; if the bonds carried on to maturity, the client would keep the fee it had received for writing the insurance. Other banks copied J. P. Morgan's idea and the credit default swaps (CDS) market was born.

Three years later J. P. Morgan's transatlantic derivatives team was at it again. The Asian currency crisis of 1997 had left the bank needing to sell down part of its credit risk by the year end in order to stay within its regulatory limits. An American named Bill Demchak and Blythe Masters, a young British woman who had moved over to New York, came up with the idea of parcelling up these loans in a package known as a collaterised debt obligation (CDO) and placing them in an off-balance-sheet entity which would issue interest-paying securities to investors. The device was known as a special investment vehicle (SIV) and was to be at the heart of originate-and-distribute banking over the next ten years.

The marketability of the SIV's bonds relied on them being awarded a high grade by credit rating agencies such as Standard & Poor's and Fitch. The agencies liked what they saw and gave them the highest possible grading of AAA. Lenders and investors appeared to be in a win-win situation. Investors such as pension funds had to keep a certain proportion of their assets in investment-grade bonds. CDOs had such a rating and offered an income premium over other AAA bonds, a crucial advantage for yield-hungry investors. The win-win for lenders such as J. P. Morgan came from the profit from arranging the deals and a regulatory bonus. Under international banking rules, banks have to hold a certain level of reserves to protect themselves against their loans defaulting. Since J. P. Morgan had passed on the risk of default to a third party – the SIV – they were able to argue that they did not need to hold capital reserves against these loans.[7]

Credit derivatives were the growth story of the decade and J. P. Morgan's CDOs and CDSs were the ideas that made it all happen. Competitors copied and modified J. P. Morgan's product, and the market increased from $180 billion to over $20 trillion between 1996 and 2006. London was central to this development. In addition to the key role played in the invention of the products by members of the J. P. Morgan team, nearly 40 per cent of the business being done in credit derivatives was booked in London on account of its light-touch regulation and lenient tax regime.

For J. P. Morgan the effect was sensational. By the time it merged with Chase Manhattan in 2000 it had a strong position in debt and derivatives markets and became the new group's investment banking arm. It expanded into equities and corporate finance and in 2004 linked up with one of the City's most famous names when it formed a joint venture with Cazenove, a blue-blooded stockbroker and investment bank. Cazenove had long been regarded as invincible, untouchable and epitomising old-style City values. Its joint venture with J. P. Morgan set the seal on the Americans' domination of the City.

Aside from the Americans, several European banks were determined to have an investment banking presence in London. UBS, created by the merger of Union Bank of Switzerland and Swiss Bank Corporation, took on the Americans, scaling up in Europe and buying the US broker Paine Webber. Deutsche Bank reworked itself from an inward-looking German bank into a global corporate and investment bank run from London, and paid $10 billion for the US investment bank Bankers Trust to help its ambitions. French banks BNP Paribas and Société Générale built significant derivatives-based businesses out of London, a strategy they may now regret but which before the credit crunch won a string of accolades including the latter's equity derivatives bank of the year awards from *Risk* and other magazines.[8]

The replacement of the City's domestically managed institutions with anonymous global behemoths led to fears that UK interests would be damaged. Would British investment bankers become mere servants of their American masters? Would they be able to adapt to new business methods and a harder work ethic? Would American managers live down their hire and fire reputation? Would the integrated business model operate against client interests? Would the increased capital committed through leverage and trading positions jeopardise the financial system? Would the lack of substantial domestically managed institutions result in a structural weakness to the UK economy?

Between 1997 and 2007 most of these fears appeared misplaced. The top positions at the US investment banks were occupied by Americans who had been with their firms a long time and it was unrealistic to expect newly acquired British talent to jump straight into the chief executive's suite. Whilst the proportion of British people in senior management positions at the investment banks was less than London's share of their global business, fears that there would be an American monopoly were not borne out.

At divisional level British investment bankers did make an impact. As already mentioned, Roger Nagioff, who had started his working life as a trader in London with firms such as Smith New Court and

NatWest Markets, became co-head of global equities and then global head of fixed income at Lehman, where Jeremy Isaacs, another Smith alumnus, ran the company's European business. Other Brits close to the top of investment banks included Nagioff's boss at Smith, Michael Marks, who went on to become head of Merrill Lynch's European business and its first executive vice president outside the US. At Goldman Sachs north Londoner, Michael Sherwood, who had joined the firm straight from the University of Manchester in 1986, became the head of the European fixed-income division and was then promoted to co-head of the bank's international business alongside the UK-based American investment banker Scott Kapnick. Blythe Masters, the most senior British woman on Wall Street, became chief financial officer of J.P. Morgan's investment bank in 2004 and global head of the bank's currency and commodity business in 2006. The European banks were more recent creations than their US rivals so there were fewer career bankers striving for the top positions, and this opened the way for more British people to get to the top, the most notable example being Huw Jenkins, an affable Welshman with an equities background who was appointed to head up investment banking at UBS in 2005.

One of the reasons for these promotions was that British bankers and traders were able to adapt to new business practices and work ethics and were in fact energised by them. One senior British investment banker who moved to a top US bank after a career with British institutions told me, 'There was a different culture of boldness, a determination to become a major player, a willingness to invest. This "one team, one dream" stuff was mainly hype but it was very invigorating. The attitude was let's find a way to do it.'⁹ Americans were bemused by the longer holidays in Britain and Europe, but the City had long ago moved on from boozy lunches and half-days on Fridays. Traditional City-style corporate financiers were happy to commit to investment banking US style, including the integration of many different financial services into one firm, the cross-selling of these services and client relationships that are assumed to carry no commitment from either side beyond the duration of the transaction being worked on. These practices contrasted with London's traditions of independent advice, separation of business lines and long-standing client relationships that would see a bank stand down from a deal if two of its clients were in conflict. But corporate finance people I have spoken to found it easy to adjust. The old traditions had been crumbling for years; clients knew what to expect; and many old-school City bankers were happy to throw in the towel and do things the American way. One veteran banker told me that it was like having a complete deck of cards to offer clients whereas previously he could show them only the joker.

The Americans' hire and fire reputation had been earned in the decade after Big Bang. Tempted by impending deregulation, many American banks had made ill-judged forays into London. Examples include Citibank, which bought Scrimgeour Kemp Gee, one of London's premier brokers, ruined it and closed it within five years, and a West Coast bank named Security Pacific, which fared little better with another top broker, Hoare Govett. The habit of expanding when times were good and cutting back when markets became difficult persisted through the late 1980s and early 1990s. As late as 1994 the mighty Goldman Sachs responded to a crash in the bond markets by laying off salespeople, traders and analysts in its London equities business.

City people, the author included, were therefore sceptical that the relentless expansion in London in the second half of the 1990s would be sustained, but for several years we were wrong. The recently expanded investment banks enjoyed vintage years in both America and Europe until 2000. The dot.com bubble saw the US NASDAQ market that specialised in such stocks quadruple in value between 1995 and 1999, and the fever spread to Europe. Britain's first major Internet IPO, Freeserve, took place in July 1999 and the UK went dot.com crazy. Share turnover soared, corporate financiers burned the midnight oil working on new deals and the investment banks even lost a few of their best people to Internet start-ups, at the time a rare example of the City ceasing to be the career of choice for talented British graduates. Those that stayed in investment banking were too busy to notice or care about the change in ownership and business model of the company they were working for.

But then in the middle of March 2000 the bubble burst. By the end of the year NASDAQ had halved, the stock prices of bellwether Internet stocks such as Yahoo collapsed and a host of hot new issues went bust. New-wave technology companies in the UK were equally affected: 'the wave of selling . . . spread instantly across the Atlantic . . . by the end of the year there was only a handful of dot.coms of any size still in British ownership'.[10] It was worrying news for those who had jumped ship from the City to dot.coms – they nervously joked that B2B, the acronym for the business-to-business Internet companies, now stood for 'back to banking' – and also for all those who had stayed behind. Would the American investment banks in London revert to type and treat their overseas offices as dispensable luxuries?

The anxiety lasted three years. Stock markets were depressed, corporate finance activity was muted and scandal on Wall Street threatened the investment banks' business model after New York state attorney general Eliot Spitzer exposed malpractice in IPO research and stock allocations. These were exactly the circumstances in which redundancies and office closures might have been expected, but a recovery in equity-related areas from 2003 and an ongoing boom in another part of the investment banking industry, fixed income, currencies and commodities (FICC), saved them from the worst.

There were three driving forces behind this boom, all tied together by securitisation. First, globalisation of business and investing led to a massive increase in foreign exchange flows, and currency dealing became a huge business. Second, the rapid expansion of the BRIC (Brazil, Russia, India and China) economies created huge demand for raw materials. Traded markets in base metals, oil and other commodities grew to epic scale. Third and most important, following the dot.com crash in 2000 and the terrorist attacks on the World Trade Center in 2001 the US Federal Reserve slashed interest rates to head off the risk of recession. US interest rates were pegged at little over 1 per cent for 2002, 2003 and 2004, and traders were able to borrow money in the US, put it on deposit overseas and hedge the currency risk. This is the carry trade. It was money for old rope, and the investment banks and hedge funds geared up massively to exploit the opportunity.

Strong underlying demand in all three parts of the FICC business was converted into a bonanza by securitisation, the technique that enabled US banks and investment banks to shift assets off their balance sheets. There was a convergence between the two as a result of legislative changes in America. Between 1933 and the late 1990s US deposit-taking banks were prevented from large-scale dealing in securities by the Glass-Steagall Act passed in the aftermath of Wall

Street's Great Crash of 1929. In the era of neo-liberal economics in the last quarter of the 20th century the banking industry lobbied for the repeal of Glass-Steagall, eager to expand its investment banking business. Restrictions were gradually eased in the 1990s and finally removed in 1999 with the passage of the Gramm-Leach-Bliley Act.

New rules on capital ratios set by global banking regulators in the Basel Accord of 1998 encouraged banks to get as many loans as possible off their balance sheets, and now that they were free to deal in securities, they turned to securitisation. Using the model pioneered by J. P. Morgan in 1997, they set up SIVs to facilitate securitisation of debt and lent wildly to a wide range of borrowers such as mortgage brokers, real estate developers, hedge funds and private equity firms in the apparently safe knowledge that they would be able to sell on the risk. The capital deployed in the US securities industry grew from $92 billion to $190 billion between 1997 and 2005, half of which was debt, and there were billions more off balance sheet.[11] By 2007, aggressive investment banks such as Bear Stearns and Lehman were running leveraged positions of over thirty times their own capital and more conservative firms such as Goldman Sachs and Morgan Stanley were over twenty times leveraged.

For six golden years, from 2001 to 2007, booming underlying business in all three components of the FICC business was amplified by leverage; FICC divisions reported record results and this shielded the big investment banks from the downturn in equities. The combined value of IPOs and mergers and acquisitions, the barometers for equity-related investment banking, in a three-year period, 2001, 2002 and 2003, did not match the business done in a single year, 2000, yet the major US investment banks hardly blinked. After dipping at the beginning of the dot.com crash, margins were back at record levels by 2003, and profits bounded ahead over the next three years.

The US investment banks took the opportunity of the equity bear market to downsize their over-expanded businesses in London. The recruitment firm Heidrick & Struggles estimated that 35,000 of the City's 300,000 jobs were cut in 2001–2.[12] '3X3' bonuses for equity specialists and corporate financiers – annual pay of $3 million guaranteed for three years – became a thing of the past. But the retrenchment was tough rather than savage, and it was proportionate to what was going on in New York, where 17 per cent of securities industry jobs were cut in these years. It seemed to be a vindication of the American business model and a laying to rest of old fears. Fixed income and equities had proved complementary to each other, the American gunslingers had not eliminated droves of British investment bankers when they took over and after a short downturn hiring and bonuses resumed at their previous levels.

Fears that the integrated model of investment banking would work against client interests were more difficult to shake off. The American model saw investment banks combine trading for themselves with trading for clients, and combine advising investors who bought securities with advising corporates who issued them. The latter was more controversial, although in the UK the former was probably more significant. The controversy was caused by evidence that some analysts in the US had shamelessly promoted the stock prices of investment banking clients even though they believed them to be overvalued.

Personal experience tells me that it was increasingly common for chief executives in the British corporate sector to threaten to withhold investment-banking business from firms whose analysts were judged 'unsupportive', and as a result few if any analysts made sell recommendations about corporate clients. My impression is that this kind of thing became more common in the 1990s but that analysts stopped short of brazen promotion of overvalued corporate stocks. In a global settlement of 2003, the leading investment banks agreed to pay fines and apply new regulations designed to curb the involvement of analysts in corporate finance work. The FSA said that it expected investment banks operating in the UK to observe these rules but could find no evidence of the egregious misbehaviour seen in the US.

Proprietary trading in securities was an accepted part of the investment banks' business. A rare public example of proprietary trading working against market interests came in August 2004 when a Citigroup trader sold €11 billion of Eurozone government bonds in just two minutes and bought them back lower down, having fooled other traders and crashed the trading system. Suspicion that information routinely leaked in investment banks was supported by the frequency with which share prices moved in advance of takeover bids, but proof of insider dealing was never forthcoming.

The changing nature of client relationships and the potential for conflict of interest under the investment banking model were illustrated by Goldman Sachs's London-based principal investing activities run by Richard Sharp. In 2004 Sharp's team committed £800 million to an unsuccessful bid by the retail entrepreneur Philip Green for Marks & Spencer, appearing to reverse Goldman's policy of not investing in hostile bids. Corporate clients such as J Sainsbury and BSkyB feared that Goldman might turn against them and appointed new advisers. Matters came to a head in 2006 when, having offered to advise BAA against a hostile bid from Ferrovial, Goldman put together its own bidding consortium for BAA. The furore this aroused resulted in the firm's then senior partner, Hank Poulson, stating that Goldman would not invest as a principal in the takeover of a public company without a board recommendation.[13]

It was feared that American business practices would increase risk in the global financial system, but until 2007 most investment bankers and central banks believed that the opposite had occurred as a result of originate-and-distribute banking. Far from destabilising the system, bankers argued that transferring risk from banks to investors in this way made it more robust since the risk was spread across many holders. They cited the opinion of Federal Reserve chairman Greenspan who had for a long time believed that 'if risk is properly dispersed, shocks to the overall economic system will be better absorbed and less likely to create cascading failures that could threaten financial stability.'*

There were some signs at the beginning of 2007 that this might not be the case. Central bankers including by this time Greenspan, warned that risk was being underpriced in markets. The previous October the widely respected financial journalist Barry Riley had predicted that 'there will inevitably be a crunch in at least part of the financial sector in order to restore prudence and risk awareness'.[14]

In January 2007 the FSA warned of challenging conditions with a rising probability of 'those conditions unwinding in a disorderly fashion.'[15] Residential mortgages underpinned many securitisation deals and a downturn in the US housing market at the end of 2006 caused HSBC to write down its book of sub-prime mortgage loans

---

*Remarks by Chairman Alan Greenspan at Lancaster House

by $10.6 billion. US housebuilders warned of sub-prime losses; the price of CDSs crept up; and the ratings agencies looked again at the AAA ratings on sub-prime debt. But in the opening months of 2007 these concerns reflected slight anxiety rather than fundamental doubts. Originate and distribute still ruled supreme and critics could not yet pin a single charge on the new system.

The City appeared to have done particularly well out of the new system. Not only had it made a lot of money out of the FICC boom but the nature of the business now being done enabled some British banks to address a structural weakness in their businesses. The arrival of the Americans and the disappearance of so many UK-owned and -managed banks and brokers had been expected to mark the end of British investment banking, leaving the country's biggest banks with a strategic gap. However, the boom in securitisation, bonds, foreign exchange and commodities trading reopened the door to investment banking, encouraging some banks to rebuild investment banks and persuading others to use originate and distribute to expand their assets. As we now know, this was not the panacea they had expected.

THE BRITISH

One of the apparent curiosities of the 1990s was that Barclays, HSBC and NatWest were perceived to have failed at investment banking despite reporting respectable profits in their markets divisions. In 1993 the Barclays investment banking arm, BZW, reported profits of over £500 million, a return on capital of over 40 per cent.[16] In 1996, the year before it exited equities, NatWest's equivalent business contributed over 40 per cent of the £1 billion of the bank's profits, and HSBC's made over $1 billion in 1998 dealing in foreign exchange, securities, derivatives and other market instruments.

The problem for the British firms seeking to build reputations to challenge the likes of Goldman Sachs, Morgan Stanley and Merrill Lynch was that shareholders and customers judged investment banks by their performance in equities. It was evident to observers that when it came to IPOs, advising on mergers and acquisitions and competing in the global market for advice and equity financing, the bulge bracket banks were winning hands down. What the British banks described as investment banking profits mainly came from foreign exchange, interest-rate derivatives and debt securities, activities that were taken for granted in the 1990s. One number sums this up: a paltry 1 per cent of HSBC's $1 billion of dealing profits in 1998 came from equities.

But soon after Barclays and NatWest pulled out of equity-related activities in 1997 the boom in fixed-income trading changed the nature of the investment banking market in a way that was very helpful to the British clearing banks. Through their corporate lending side, they had always enjoyed good relations with corporate treasurers, and they did substantial interest-rate trading and foreign exchange dealing for them. The growth of the swaps market in the 1990s – derivative trans-actions enabling clients and proprietary traders to trade between debt products of different maturity and credit quality and between different currencies – meant that this became very profitable. Credit derivatives were a natural extension of this business, and as that market expanded the clearing banks were able to lever their way into broader investment banking business, escalating their relationships up the corporate ladder from treasurer to finance director and eventually to chief executive.

Barclays had kept its debt and currency trading businesses out of the sale of the rest of the investment bank in 1997, and it had a good man to run these retained businesses. In 1996 it had recruited a forty-five-year-old American named Bob Diamond to head up debt trading. Diamond was a big hitter in the bond world. He had run European and Asian fixed-income trading for Morgan Stanley and became global head of fixed income and foreign exchange at Credit Suisse.[17] Barclays' retreat from equities had not been planned when Diamond was hired, but he shrugged off any doubts he may have had about the bank's commitment to markets and pressed on with developing the business.

The markets division of Barclays was immediately renamed Barclays Capital – BarCap for short. Diamond's US style of management contrasted with Barclays' more gentlemanly tradition, and initially things did not go well. Diamond was a gym-going hard-working American big shot and there was a culture clash. Resentment was aroused by the arrival of a string of high-profile and expensive recruits, and a number of BZW veterans left including one quoted by Martin

Vander Weyer in his book about Barclays: 'The place was suddenly filling up with these million-dollar fruit-eating bond people.'[18]

In the summer of 1998 the Russian debt crisis caught Barclays holding £340 million of Russian debt and securities, mostly within BarCap. In the first week of September Barclays warned that it would have to make a charge of £250 million to cover potential losses and warned of a further £75 million of trading losses. Later that month Barclays contributed $300 million to the bail-out of the failed US hedge fund Long Term Capital Management, and there was a storm of press and investor criticism of the firm's strategy, dragging down the share price by more than 50 per cent in six months.[19] At a board meeting in New York in October 1998 Barclays' chief executive Martin Taylor floated the idea of de-merging the bank's entire corporate banking business including BarCap, but the idea found little support at board level and eight weeks later he resigned.[20]

After the debacle of 1998, BarCap caught the rising tide of markets, and profits grew rapidly at a rate of 25 per cent a year between 2000 and 2007, based on areas such as underwriting bond issues, hedging commodity exposures, principal investments and private equity, securitisation and equity derivatives. Diamond became one of the most powerful and written-about people in the City. Stories circulated that after he lost out to John Varley in a battle for the chief executive's job in 2003, Diamond made BarCap a no-go area for the rest of the group and that he had made enemies in the traditional banking side of the business.[21] However he was appointed to the bank's main board in 2005, was paid nearly £23 million in 2007 and widely acclaimed for rebuilding Barclays' presence in investment banking. Very few people inside or outside Barclays questioned the wisdom of the bank's growing dependence on securitisation for a proportion of its profits and funding.

BarCap's apogee came on a fine summer evening in June 2006. In a glittering ceremony in the grounds of the Honourable Artillery Company it was named European bond house of the decade by the British magazine *Financial News*, which said:

When Barclays Capital was forged from the ashes of Barclays de Zoete Wedd more than eight years ago, few expected it to wield much clout. But the bank has proved the doubters wrong and joined the top table in the debt capital markets . . . Unlike many of its rivals the bank does not offer equity underwriting or M&A advisory services, but the bank makes no apologies and instead can point to record profitability to support its model. Barclays Capital has upped its equity derivatives trading and commodities revenues in that pursuit, and revenue diversity has become a mantra for the bank.[22]

The same evening the contribution of BarCap's chairman Hans-Joerg Rudloff was also recognised when he was inducted into the *Financial News* hall of fame. He was described as 'a pivotal figure in the success of the debt-focused investment bank over the past decade, cementing a reputation as one of the legendary figures in the evolution of the Euromarkets'.[23]

Barclays' great competitor in British banking in the 1990s, NatWest, had made similar and equally unpopular attempts to build an investment bank after Big Bang. Financial losses and a rigged rights issue for its client Blue Arrow gave the investment bank County NatWest a bad reputation, but under new management and rebranded NatWest Markets in the 1990s it was making progress. In 1996 it paid £385 million to Long Term Credit Bank of Japan for the American firm Greenwich Capital, an underwriter and dealer in US Treasury bonds, mortgages and other asset-backed securities. But shortly after agreeing the Greenwich deal, a £90 million black hole was discovered in NatWest Markets' options books, and management came under pressure from shareholders to scale back its investment banking ambitions. The equities and corporate finance businesses were sold, but shareholders remained very wary of any grand plans from NatWest. When a merger with Legal & General was agreed in 1999 in what would have been the UK's first banking and insurance group, shareholders revolted, the plan was dropped and NatWest was taken over by Royal Bank of Scotland (RBS) for £21 billion.

RBS had kept well away from experiments in broad scale investment banking in the 1980s and 1990s, focusing instead on corporate lending, interest-rate trading and foreign exchange dealing. When RBS acquired NatWest, Greenwich was about to be sold as part of NatWest's plans to return cash to shareholders. RBS cancelled the sale and embarked on what it described as a careful plan for its Global Banking and Markets division (GBM): 'The strategy for GBM . . . was to start in the UK and cement our position in the UK capital markets, in sterling bonds for example in particular, then go into Europe and the Eurocurrency and build our position in loans and bonds in Europe, then to start in America again to build our position in loans and bonds and finally Asia.'[24]

RBS used its position as a large commercial lender to sell other services to clients and to broaden its geographical reach. The UK was obviously its strongest area but it built up its operations in France and Germany by lending to private equity groups, becoming the biggest player in European leveraged finance. In the US Greenwich gave RBS critical mass in important sectors such as US Treasury bonds and asset-backed securities, and the product range was broadened by senior recruits in areas such as investment-grade corporate bonds and asset-backed trading. When considered alongside its leveraged finance business, RBS was building a large exposure to the activities that were to be at the heart of the global banking crisis of 2007–8.

Despite having a relatively small position in some other fast growing sectors of the market such as equity derivatives and commodities, RBS's expansion into these debt and currency products enabled its markets division to average growth of over 17 per cent per annum in the six years to 2006. The division was led by a well-connected Oxford graduate named Johnny Cameron, who had joined RBS in 1998 from the investment bank Dresdner Kleinwort Benson. Cameron appeared more like the traditional British clearing banker than the dynamic Bob Diamond at Barclays but appearances can be deceptive. RBS was playing a very similar game to Barclays in aggressively building a global debt trading business. Analysts and shareholders liked what they saw and few seemed concerned by the bank's growing dependence on debt trading to fund its lending and boost its profits. Instead they admired its resolute avoidance of equity underwriting and mergers and acquisitions, activities that Cameron believed would have led to cultural problems: 'Having worked in an investment bank, I know it is hard for the fighter pilots of M&A to work with the less glamorous bomber pilots of commercial banking.'[25]

Cameron downplayed RBS's ambitions. He told *The Banker* magazine, 'If we're in the race to be the best provider of debt finance for corporates and financial institutions worldwide, then we are one of the few runners and our chances of winning are high. Another race is trying to be the best universal bank or investment bank. We are not in that race.'[26] In March 2007, at which point GBM accounted for 40 per cent of group profits, Cameron was able to boast of its success and take a sly dig at old rivals: 'That is a huge number. It is bigger than Coca-Cola's profits! Compared to other banks it is, for example, twice the size of BarCap – we make more or less twice as much money as BarCap with just over half as many people.'[27]

The credit crunch ripped apart RBS's investment banking strategy but at least it had been consistent. This contrasted strongly with HSBC, a bank that for twenty years had periodic rushes of enthusiasm for investment banking and then retrenched when management priorities changed. HSBC had scooped the pool in equity broking at the time of Big Bang, buying the leading firm of the day James Capel, but it never came to terms with the financial commitment needed to build a big investment bank. Equities never gelled with HSBC's currency and debt-trading businesses nor with corporate banking, and in 1990 HSBC sent one of its top managers from Hong Kong to London to run the broker with a mission of damage limitation. He was told, 'We don't care about James Capel', a sentiment that for several years seemed to apply equally to the entire investment bank.

There was a flurry of excitement in the second half of the 1990s when there was a renewed attempt to build up equities and corporate finance, but this soon died down until 2003 when HSBC hired John Studzinski from Morgan Stanley to be co-head of investment banking. This was a startling move. Studzinski was one of the world's most highly respected corporate financiers. He is a devout Christian, a generous philanthropist and admired by the HSBC chairman Sir John Bond for the advice he had given HSBC while at Morgan Stanley. Competitors usually provide knocking copy when a senior person changes firm but no one could suggest that Studz, as he was universally known, was past his best or just a cynical mercenary. An HSBC veteran, Stuart Gulliver, who had come up through the foreign exchange trading business, was to be co-head of HSBC's investment bank, and would run trading while Studzinski got to work on the advisory business.

Studzinski led a hiring spree, poaching investment bankers from leading competitors. His silver tongue and HSBC's market reputation and chequebook meant that the bank was able to recruit a roster of able bankers, but just as many others had found when trying to build an investment bank in a hurry, the recruiting is the easy part. Corporate clients take a long time to change their buying habits, especially where a bank has a mixed record of commitment to a product. Why drop Morgan Stanley, clients would think, when HSBC might not even be committed to investment banking in three years?

The consequence was that HSBC rapidly built up a bulge-bracket-size cost base and B-grade revenues. To veteran HSBC watchers, the next step was all too predictable. In 2006 Studzinski left HSBC in order to join the private equity firm Blackstone. Studzinski is known to be a man of high principles, and observers reckoned that he would only have made such a move with good cause. Soon afterwards HSBC indicated that it would be abandoning its efforts to build up a full-scale global investment bank in order to concentrate on its strengths in fixed income and emerging markets, and changed the name of the division from Corporate and Investment Banking and Markets to Global Banking and Markets. The elimination of 'Investment Banking' was symbolic and might prove final, but given HSBC's flirtations with this activity, it would be unwise to bet on it.[28]

Barclays, RBS and HSBC all followed overt investment banking strategies but the British retail banks also used investment banking methods including securitisation to leverage their balance sheets and accumulate dealing profits. HBOS, Lloyds TSB, Northern Rock, Bradford & Bingley, Alliance & Leicester and the smaller mortgage banks made no claims to be building investment banks, but we shall see in a later chapter that they were all involved in investment banking to a greater or lesser degree, through their treasury departments.

As the credit bubble built they were able to ride the markets and use investment-banking techniques to lower funding costs and increase lending. Investors scarcely noticed the development of these subterranean investment banks and paid little attention to the risks involved – until it was too late.

One criticism of the Big Bang generation of City executives was that they mostly allowed themselves to get sucked into the agenda set by the American firms. There was very little evidence of originality, of firms looking to find a different product niche or to offer clients anything different to the integrated investment banking and broking model that the Wall Street investment banks operated. By the time RBS and Barclays had grown investment banking by exploiting their strengths in fixed income and foreign exchange, another UK firm was already well on the way to demonstrating the virtues of setting its own agenda.

In 1986 a thirty-one-year-old stockbroker with a previously undistinguished employment record set up a specialist financial derivatives broking firm in London with a total of four employees. The firm was called Intercapital and grew to become Icap, a member of the FTSE Index of the UK's largest companies, and the man was Michael Spencer, by 2007 one of the UK's richest men with a fortune estimated at £800 million.

Spencer is a public-school- and Oxford-educated son of a colonial civil servant but no stuffed shirt. He was a spirited gambler, winning and losing fortunes in the 1970s and being asked to leave his first City job in 1979 at the broking firm Simon & Coates after running up losses in gold trading. After time at the controversial US firm Drexel Burnham, then in thrall to its high-yield king Michael Milken, and then a spell with a smaller City broker, Spencer left in 1986 to set up his own firm.

It was a brave thing to do at a time when the financial landscape was changing rapidly in the run-up to Big Bang. All eyes were on equities and the integration of merchant banking with broking, and agency dealing with trading. The big banks dominated the markets in government and corporate bonds, and also the interest rate and foreign exchange markets. Derivatives at that time were still an obscure corner of the financial world, consisting mainly of exchange-traded futures and options. But what Spencer had spotted was that the financial services deregulation of 1986 would open up the London market to a variety of new dealers and new products. The business would become more international; dealing costs would fall; and volumes would explode. The emerging trends in high-yield securities and the use of leverage and derivatives that Spencer had seen during his time at Drexel Burnham would, he expected, come to London.

The business that Spencer set up concentrated on inter-dealer broking, an activity that involved acting as a discreet agent for investment banks wishing to offload the positions they had built up in their everyday trading activities. The product range was extended from the original area of interest rate swaps to include derivatives, fixed-income securities, money market products, foreign exchange, energy, credit and equity derivatives. The business has been transformed by new technology. By 2007 its 3,700 staff were spread across thirty-two of the world's cities including 600 people in ten offices across Asia-Pacific, where it claimed to be the largest inter-dealer broker.

With a remarkable 32 per cent share of global inter-dealer broking, much of it executed electronically, Icap became a model of careful growth achieved through a mixture of acquisition and organic methods. It retained a fleet-footed approach despite its size and broadening spread of products and geographies. It stayed ahead of new technologies and avoided using large amounts of capital, defying conventional wisdom that said it was impossible to succeed in the modern financial services industry without access to a big balance sheet.[29]

Michael Spencer was not the only man in London who could see a way past the bulge bracket investment banking model. Groups of brokers got together to form mini-investment banks such as Numis (of which Spencer is non-executive chairman) and Oriel Securities. Both of these companies provided sales, research and dealing services to institutions, focusing on small companies, often acting as their corporate broker and with a particular interest in bringing new companies to AIM, the London Stock Exchange's market for listing smaller companies. Agency broking was revived by Nick Finegold, who left Deutsche Bank in 1999, where he had been head of European sales trading, to set up Execution Limited in a disused brewery just off Brick Lane in London's East End.

Out of this cluster of smaller broking start-ups, one firm, Collins Stewart, rose to be a business of some scale. It started out as a conventional sales, trading and research house and wealth manager, and listed on the stock market in 2000. It bought the inter-dealer business of Tullett & Tokyo in 2003 for £250 million and added the complementary business Prebon in 2004 before spinning them both off in 2006 and returning £300 million to shareholders. Terry Smith, the forthright former analyst who had built up Collins Stewart, became chief executive of Tullett Prebon and non-executive chairman of Collins Stewart.

As the financial landscape changed, new niches emerged. Turmoil in the pension fund market as new accounting rules and market volatility swung funds from surplus to deficit in the twinkling of an eye posed problems for trustees and pension scheme sponsors. Pensions experts such as the former chief of Prudential's UK business who set up Paternoster, an insurance company that took responsibility for the risks associated with final salary pension schemes, were quick to see new opportunities.[30] Two former Lazard bankers formed Penfida, to advise pension fund trustees who as a result of new pension fund regulations found themselves in the spotlight during changes in corporate control. The trustees of the J Sainsbury pension fund, for example, at the time a private equity bid was in the air, pointed out that any new owners would face a £3 billion pension fund deficit.[31] The bid was withdrawn, which some commentators attributed to the pension fund issue.

In corporate finance, the demand for independent advice and the desire of a few senior investment bankers to get out of the large-scale institutional environment led to several successful start-ups. One of the most surprising events occurred when Simon Robertson, the old-Etonian former president of Goldman Sachs Europe and perhaps the City's pre-eminent corporate financier, set up his own boutique to give high-level independent advice. Robertson undertook to work for only one client in each sector to avoid conflict of interest and to charge annual retainers rather than success fees in order to establish his objectivity. Robertson said, 'Boards of directors like the idea there's someone who doesn't get paid depending on what he says.'[32]

Robertson's remark could be taken as a barbed comment on the American investment banking model that had swept London, but if so, it was a minority view at the time. Investment banks were riding high; the new model had weathered a storm in equities; customers were not complaining; and employees like Robert Swannell, whose comments opened this chapter, were happy. There were a few clouds on the horizon in credit markets but most people sided with Chuck Prince, Swannell's ultimate boss as Citigroup chief executive, who in July 2007 told the *Financial Times*, 'When the music stops, in terms of liquidity, things will be complicated. But as long as the music is playing, you've got to get up and dance. We're still dancing.'[33] Little did anyone know that Prince had inadvertently called the top of the market, that he would be out of his job by the end of the year and that the investment banking strategies of the leading American and British banks would be shown to have been flawed.

8

THE MANSION HOUSE
DINNER 2007

Wednesday 20 June was the date of the 2007 Mansion House Dinner and a big occasion for Gordon Brown. Tony Blair had finally agreed to stand down and in less than a fortnight Brown would achieve his long-standing ambition of becoming prime minister. He had been the longest-serving Chancellor in British history and one of its most successful. Ten years earlier Brown and his henchmen had briefly unsettled the audience by breaking the dress code, but by now the lord mayor and his guests were accustomed to seeing their principal speaker in a lounge suit, and the Mansion House dinner of 2007 provided a harmonious and apparently fitting end to his chancellorship. Britain had enjoyed continuous prosperity in the intervening years and much of the credit was given to Brown for his prudent management of the economy. But the Bank of England by its adept use of monetary independence and the City by plugging the UK into the global economy had also been involved, and with all three parties in the room the stage was set for an end-of-term celebration.

Brown was in no mood to miss the moment, and when he got to his feet he looked back 'over the ten years that I have had the privilege of addressing you as Chancellor' and believed that this would be 'an era that history will record as the beginning of a new golden age for the City of London.' Many of those present could remember his Mansion House speech the previous year when he had·delivered a eulogy to globalisation, free markets and the British economy. On that occasion he had worked in a reference to Adam Smith, the 18th-century Scottish philosopher whose treatise on free trade was the market economists' bible, and name-dropped Alan Greenspan, the US central banker most closely identified with globalisation. As a result of following free market principles and prioritising monetary and fiscal stability through an independent Bank of England, Brown had been able to boast, 'Government debt in Britain is lower than France, Germany, Italy, America and Japan,' and that growth in Britain was 'expected to be stronger this year than last and stronger next year than this'.[1]

It had been a revealing summary of New Labour's economic philosophy. Globalisation was good and free markets were better. Taxation was a competitive weapon, not just a means of raising revenue. Light-touch regulation was as much a way of making progress as a means of prudential supervision. On that occasion Brown had reminded his audience that 'ten years ago there were nine separate regulatory bodies for financial services. To meet the challenge of global markets we created a single unified FSA.' He had been in the mood for gloating: 'In 2003, just at the time of a previous Mansion House speech, the Worldcom accounting scandal broke. And I will be honest with you, many who advised me, including not a few newspapers, favoured a regulatory crackdown. I believe that we were right not to go down that road which in the United States led to Sarbanes-Oxley, and we were right to build upon our light-touch system through the leadership of Sir Callum McCarthy – fair, proportionate, predictable and increasingly risk based.'

The 2007 speech was equally positive and Chancellor Brown had the bankers purring in the aisles as he lavished them with praise. They were told that 'the City of London has risen by your efforts, ingenuity and creativity to become a new world leader.' The statistics rolled off his tongue: over 40 per cent of the world's foreign equities were traded in London, more than New York; the City's share of global currency trading was over 30 per cent, more than New York and Tokyo combined and in a recent study of the world's top fifty financial cities, the City had come first. Brown saluted their achievements: 'The financial services sector in Britain and the City of London at the centre of it, is a great example of a highly skilled, high value added, talent driven industry that shows how we can excel in a world of global competition. Britain needs more of the vigour, ingenuity and aspiration that you already demonstrate.'

It was a remarkably upbeat speech and it is easy to understand Brown's smugness. He probably believed that he had given the lie to his favourite joke that there were two types of Chancellor, those who fail and those who get out in time. The economy appeared to be set fair, and the City had delivered. During his time in office its contribution to the economy and global standing had gone from strength to strength, and its embarrassing institutional weaknesses had been ironed out. The ailing industries of the 1990s, investment banking and asset management, had restored themselves to health, and two newer industries, hedge funds and private equity, had burst onto the scene. Not only had his overall support for free markets and globalisation created a welcoming environment in which financial institutions could do business, Brown's own reforms in the field of regulation and taxation had contributed directly to this success.

The doubters appeared to be wrong. For Gordon Brown and his audience the arrival of the American investment banks had not destroyed Britain's corporate culture; it had sharpened the country's financial services industry into an internationally competitive asset. Foreign ownership of the country's financial institutions was no longer judged relevant in the age of cross-border shareholdings. The high levels of remuneration in the City that many had criticised as evidence of an unhealthy industry now appeared to be the fuse that lit the whole economy. Tax concessions to entrepreneurs and non-domiciles that were elsewhere seen as being socially divisive were lauded for broadening the City's appeal. Non-intervention and light-touch regulation were not an abdication of responsibility but an adult interpretation of free-market economics.

But as Gordon Brown got ready to become prime minister he would have done well to reflect on the remarks made by the previous speaker at the Mansion House Dinner, Mervyn King, who had taken over from Eddie George as governor of the Bank of England in 2003. King did not spoil the harmony of the evening and congratulated Brown on 'a remarkable decade for the British economy', but he used his speech to sound a note of caution. He appeared to have a much deeper understanding of what had been going on in the City on Brown's watch and began by describing the new banking system: 'Securitisation is transforming banking from the traditional model in which banks originate and retain credit risk on their balance sheets into a new model in which credit risk is distributed around a much wider range of investors. As a result, risks are no longer so concentrated in a small number of regulated institutions but are spread across the financial system.' The governor was familiar with the advantages claimed for originate-and-distribute banking. He described it as 'a positive development because it has reduced the market failure associated with traditional banking – the mismatch between illiquid assets and liquid liabilities – that led Henry Thornton and, later, Walter Bagehot to promote the role of the Bank of England as the "lender of last resort" in a financial crisis.'

But King was not a man to get carried away with the mood of the moment. He knew that his own organisation's biannual *Financial Stability Review* had laid out in chilling detail in its July 2006 edition six potential areas of stress for the UK financial system, and the recent April 2007 edition had warned that easy credit had 'increased the vulnerablity of the system'.[2] King was an academic trained to base his conclusions on evidence, and he knew that elements of the modern financial system were untested in a crisis. Whereas originate and distribute undoubtedly spread certain kinds of risk, the financial instruments that underpinned it carried their own dangers:

New and ever more complex financial instruments create different risks. Exotic instruments are now issued for which the distribution of returns is considerably more complicated than that on the basic loans underlying them. A standard collateralised debt obligation divides the risk and return of a portfolio of bonds, or credit default swaps, into tranches. But what is known as a CDO-squared instrument invests in tranches of CDOs. It has a distribution of returns which is highly sensitive to small changes in the correlations of underlying returns which we do not understand with any great precision. The risk of the entire return being wiped out can be much greater than on simpler instruments. Higher returns come at the expense of higher risk.

The governor left this subject with a question that the hubristic 21st-century bankers in his audience probably regarded as dumb: 'Assessing the effective degree of leverage in an ever-changing financial system is far from straightforward, and the liquidity of the markets in complex instruments, especially in conditions when many players would be trying to reduce the leverage of their portfolios at the same time, is unpredictable. Excessive leverage is the common theme of many financial crises of the past. Are we really so much cleverer than the financiers of the past?' King's rhetorical question would be definitively answered in the months that followed.

PART THREE

THE CREDIT CRUNCH 2007–8

It looks good for long enough
knock 'em out and sell 'em
move on
it's a fast buck
and the race is on
to get in get out
get what you want
get out
it's the short term
the long term can look after itself
unless you happen to be living here

'Ring Road' from the album *Oblivion with Bells*, Underworld

PART THREE

THE CREDIT CRUNCH 2007–8

9

NORTHERN ROCK

If you had been asked in the spring of 2007 to nominate one company that summed up Britain's successful transformation from a manufacturing to a service economy, Northern Rock would have been a reasonable choice. Originating as a self-help movement for artisans in the heavy industrial heartland of north-east England, it became an IT-enabled finance house, filling the vacuum left by that region's industrial decline and offering well-paid jobs in modern air-conditioned offices to 6,000 employees. These children and grandchildren of miners and shipyard workers had learned new skills as members of Britain's financial services army, an industry at the cutting edge of the country's new knowledge economy.

Northern Rock was much admired. After the company was listed on the stock market in 1997 its profits and share price soared, and economic liberals hailed the invigorating effect of market forces on a boring old mutual society. Left-wing critics of demutualisation were placated by Northern Rock's strong regional identity and philanthropic work: its charitable foundation paid out £175 million (5 per cent of pre-tax profits) between 1997 and 2006 to support good causes in the north-east and Cumbria.[1]

The company's success appeared to justify the government's faith in the financial services industry. As readers of its 2005 annual report were told, this was not just a domestic building society located in a remote corner of England: 'Northern Rock is a global company in terms of where it raises funds, a national company in terms of where it lends but a regional company in terms of where it mainly employs people.'² This was exactly how modern finance was meant to work. The wonderful world of Wall Street and the Wharf had enabled Northern Rock to transform itself and help regenerate a moribund regional economy. The benefits were there for all to enjoy including rich pickings for those at the top, cheap mortgages for customers and secure employment in a safe environment for the workforce.

NEWCASTLE UPON TYNE

The history of Northern Rock was a remarkable story. Back in the 18th century small groups of artisans had formed mutual societies to help each other build and buy houses. Originally these associations dissolved once all the members were housed, but during the 19th century they became permanent building societies and took on new members as the founders completed their house purchases. By the end of the 19th century there were 1,700 such organisations in existence, and building societies became a recognised feature of every large town in England. In the 20th century, as Britain moved from a regional to a national economy, the building societies consolidated as they looked for economies of scale. Up in the north-east two of the biggest societies, the Northern Counties Permanent Building Society, established in 1850, and the Rock Building Society, established in 1865, got together in 1965 to form Northern Rock Building Society.

It was a very successful union. Northern Rock became the leading financial institution in the north-east and then took advantage of the collapse in the housing market in the early 1990s to pick off its rivals including two large societies, Lancastrian and Surrey. These deals took it out of its original geographical base but it was still recognisable as a regionally based mutual society that looked after its members. Whereas some banks and other commercial financial institutions were quick to repossess properties if mortgage holders fell into arrears with their repayments, Northern Rock was careful who it lent to and repossessed only as a last resort. But it was no soft touch. By 1997 Northern Rock was in the top ten of British building societies with nearly a million members, half of whom lived in the north-east, and 2,500 employees, most of whom worked at the corporate headquarters near Newcastle. It was well regarded for combining tight cost control and prudent lending with measured expansion, and as such it was a prime candidate for the gold rush that was gripping the building society movement: a stock market listing.

During the financial services deregulation of the 1980s the building societies had successfully campaigned to be allowed to demutualise and become banks. The attractions of a public listing were obvious. Members would get free shares – 500 in Northern Rock's case, worth £2,260 when dealings began on 1 October 1997 – and management could expect to see the open road ahead with private-sector pay including share options and bonuses. Three years after the first Building Societies Act of 1986, Abbey National demutualised, and a second Building Societies Act in 1997 triggered a wave of demutualizations including Alliance & Leicester, Bristol & West Country, Halifax, the Woolwich and Northern Rock.

Northern Rock stood out as a promising investment. Shortly before dealings began one financial adviser said, 'Northern Rock is a small but well run society which could well prove attractive to a potential buyer over the next few years. It is hard to see it doing so badly that hanging on to the shares is a mistake.'³ Whether Northern Rock lived up to this potential would largely depend on its management. Five months before the flotation Northern Rock's chief executive, Christopher Sharp, died suddenly. It was essential for the success of the issue that he was quickly replaced with a safe pair of hands. The society turned to Leo Finn, who had started his career in 1959 as a clerk with Northern Counties Building Society and worked his way up the organisation. Finn was in his late fifties and let it be known that he would retire in three or four years – long enough, it was felt, for the new company to find its feet and for a successor to emerge. The obvious internal candidates were Adam Applegarth, at that time a thirty-four-year-old graduate of Durham University who had joined Northern Rock as a cashier in 1983 and been appointed to the board in 1996, and forty-nine-year-old Bob Bennett, who had been finance director since 1993.

The race was now on in every sense. As a listed company Northern Rock ceased to be owned by members and run for their benefit, and became a profit machine working in the interests of its outside investors. Analysts wrote reports on it; the press analysed its results; and institutional shareholders developed relationships with the management, nudging them towards making bigger profits and paying higher dividends. Investment bankers made their way up to Newcastle, proposing deals and recommending sophisticated financial products. The directors, particularly chief executive Finn, finance director Bennett and charismatic types like Applegarth, became men with a profile, open to public criticism and carrying the burden of investors' and pundits' expectations. Everything was now stacked up for a dash for growth: demanding shareholders, ambitious management and deal-hungry advisers.

Under these circumstances some companies go to pieces – diversifying recklessly, making unwise acquisitions and taking their eye off costs – but not Northern Rock. After flotation it continued to build its reputation as a lean and mean business, closing branch offices and encouraging customers to use technology for their banking. It blundered in 1998 when it arbitrarily tightened the terms on a range of deposit accounts, triggering an Office of Fair Trading investigation, but it was a rare slip and Northern Rock avoided many of the traps that can befall newly listed companies.

In order to meet the stock market's growth expectations Northern Rock developed a new mortgage product branded Together. It enabled customers to borrow 125 per cent of the value of their home plus up to six times their annual income, thus rolling up their existing debt and mortgage into one package. With interest rates so low in the early years of the 21st century, it was a winner, particularly with young professional couples, and helped Northern Rock raise its share of the residential mortgage market from 6 to nearly 20 per cent over ten years.

The company's loan book grew at a rate of 20 per cent per annum between 1997 and 2007, rising from £16 billion to £101 billion, 85 per cent of which was in residential mortgages. Analysts worried that the bank might be letting its credit standards slip, but Northern Rock's management had grown up in the home loans business and knew all about bad debts. Adam Applegarth, Bob Bennett and their colleagues had been around during the housing market slump of the early 1990s and had seen for themselves the havoc wrought on building societies by borrowers who could not keep up with their payments. Although Northern Rock lent its customers increased multiples of their income, the default rate was only half the industry average and was actually improving in 2006 and the first half of 2007, earning praise from the governor of the Bank of England: 'Most of the staff that worked in Northern Rock on the lending side, all the evidence shows, did an excellent job in appraising the loans that they were making, and that they monitored very carefully and they did not lend money to people who should not be borrowing from them.'[4]

Profits and the share price raced ahead, and Northern Rock became a member of the FTSE 100 index of the UK's largest companies in September 2001. Under the leadership of the newly appointed Adam Applegarth, the second youngest chief executive of a FTSE 100 company, Northern Rock was the epitome of a forward-looking, go-getting financial services company. Over the next five years it did not disappoint, profits more than doubling to £415 million and the share price reaching a heady £12–52 at the beginning of 2007. Just ten years after it had come to the stock market, this little building society from the north had become Britain's eighth largest bank.

What the stock market had not noticed, however, was a major change in Northern Rock's business model. In the early days all the money lent by building societies came from members' deposits, but as they became more commercial the societies discovered a new way to make money for their members. They borrowed cheaply in the wholesale banking markets, marked up the interest rate and lent on to retail borrowers at a nice premium. Provided that they matched the maturity of their assets and liabilities it was money for old rope. Northern Rock was active in this market, and at the time of flotation customers' deposits covered two thirds of its loan book and the other third was borrowed from the wholesale market.[5] All building societies did it, and there was nothing exceptional about the scale of Northern Rock's wholesale borrowing or the ratio between its wholesale borrowing and retail deposits. But in 1999 it changed the structure of its liabilities. Previously it had been holding the loans it made to maturity, the traditional method of banking called originate and hold. In the 1990s, as outlined in previous chapters, banks developed the new originate and distribute model. Instead of holding the loans to maturity, banks originated loans – in Northern Rock's case residential mortgages – and then sold them on to investors through securitisation.

Northern Rock went for securitisation hook, line and sinker. It did its first securitisation deal in 1999, a relatively modest £600 million representing less than 4 per cent of the bank's total loan book. Over the next two years it securitised nearly £5 billion more, and at the end of 2001 Northern Rock had securitised 22 per cent of its £22.8 billion mortgage loan book. Over the next five years the pace accelerated still further with securitisations averaging £10 billion a year, so that at the end of 2006 £60 billion of Northern Rock's £101 billion loan book had been securitised or converted to covered bonds, a form of mortgage-backed securities similar in purpose to securitisation.[6]

The process was complex, but it was a well-trodden road and expert advisers were on hand to show the way. Northern Rock formed an offshore SIV in Jersey, parked its loan book there, parcelled up and repackaged the loans and distributed securitised bonds to investors. Underwriting, funding and distributing the deals and organising AAA ratings for the bonds from the credit agencies was facilitated by blue-chip banks such as Barclays, J. P. Morgan Chase, UBS and Merrill Lynch. Northern Rock was in good company in securitising its assets. It was accepted banking practice; all of Britain's major banks did it and prior to 2007 there was no suggestion that the banking industry was engaging in a reckless strategy. In fact, as we have seen, securitisation as the key to originate and distribute was perceived to have lowered risk in the banking system.

There was nothing extraordinary in the size of each Northern Rock deal but their frequency relative to the company's asset base was unusual. Northern Rock was securitising much faster than it was able to grow its retail deposits, and this led to an unusually large imbalance in its liabilities. Whereas banks such as Alliance & Leicester and Bradford & Bingley funded nearly half their loans from retail deposits, a proportion that passed without comment at the time but would eventually be shown to be dangerous, Northern Rock's retail deposits covered less than a quarter of its loan book. The remainder was funded by securitisation (60 per cent) and short term wholesale banking markets (15 per cent) meaning that Northern Rock was about twice as dependent as its peer group on external funding. With such a large gap between its deposits and loans, and such reliance on securitisation, Northern Rock was an extreme outlier in an industry in which even the more conservative strategies of other banks would shortly be shown to be high risk.

The smooth operation of Northern Rock's new business model

relied on it being able to roll over its borrowing. The average term of the loans it made, assuming they were typical of residential mortgages, was about twenty-five years; the average duration of its own debt was only three years. This meant that during the average life of a loan Northern Rock would have to refinance it eight times, and if credit terms tightened or liquidity dried up, Northern Rock would not be able to refinance enough loans on good enough terms to sustain its business.

According to Adam Applegarth, the board was aware of this risk and 'worked very hard over the previous decade to try and diversify our funding platform by geography and product. That is why we moved to having four funding platforms – retail cash deposits, covered bonds, securitisation and traditional wholesale – and it is why in each of those markets we look to diversify by geography.'[7] But in fact Northern Rock's 'hard work' had achieved very little. It was heavily dependent on continued demand for its securitised bonds, and in 2006 on the other side of the Atlantic events began to unfold that would wipe it out.

AMERICA

Investment bankers sold securitisation as a global product but in reality it was a US-dominated market. American banks were the main issuers of securitised debt; American investors were amongst the main buyers; and the most frequently traded asset was American residential mortgages, of which a total of $6 trillion was securitised, including a fair slice of the US housing market's hottest new product, sub-prime mortgages. This was much appreciated by central bankers, 'Especially important in the US has been the flexibility and size of the secondary mortgage market. Since early 2000 this market has facilitated the large debt-financed extraction of home equity that has in turn been so critical in supporting consumer outlays in the US throughout the recent period of cyclical stress. This market's flexibility has been particularly enhanced by extensive use of interest rate swaps and options to hedge maturity mismatches and prepayment risk.'*

*Remarks by Chairman Alan Greenspan at Lancaster House

In fact the sub-prime loan market started in the 1980s but really took off in 2001 when US interest rates first fell to 1 per cent. The cost of borrowing was so low that families on small incomes could contemplate home ownership for the first time. The American mortgage broking industry saw a big opportunity and went on a door-knocking campaign to tempt first-time buyers into the housing market. Banks and other mortgage lenders were eager to provide funds, knowing that they could get the risk off their balance sheet through securitisation. They used computerised credit scoring models to assess borrowers' ability to pay and dropped their requirements for detailed employment records and financial histories. With the prospect of getting loans in return for minimal documentation (low-doc) or in some cases none at all (no-doc), borrowers bent the truth: so-called liar loans, in which the borrowers gave different figures to the lender than those they showed in their tax returns, amounted to nearly half of all sub-prime mortgages. Lenders stopped insisting on a down payment and the NINJA classes (no income, no job, no assets) flooded into the housing market. Home ownership in the US rose from 65 per cent of households in 1995 to almost 70 per cent by 2006, and by the end of this period one in four new mortgages was sub-prime. Driven by this new demand, house prices rose at close to 10 per cent a year, and with the economy buoyant, home ownership seemed to be a one-way bet for borrowers and lenders alike.[8]

However in 2005 the first problems began to emerge. Sub-prime loans had been pushed hardest in some of the most deprived parts of the US, and these areas proved vulnerable to a slowing economy. In states such as Michigan and Ohio, where job cuts in the auto industry caused widespread pain, sub-prime borrowers missed their payments. Interest rates rose, the housing market began to weaken and a vicious circle developed. The sub-prime failure rate rose from 10 to 20 per cent between 2005 and 2006 as Ben Bernanke, chairman of the US Federal Reserve, observed: 'For these mortgages, the rate of serious delinquencies – corresponding to mortgages in foreclosure or with payments ninety days or more overdue – rose sharply during 2006 and recently stood at about double the recent low seen in mid-2005.'[9] By this time, conditions in the US housing market were at their worst since the time of the Great Depression of the 1930s.

News of mortgage defaults soon spread to the credit market. If borrowers were unable to pay the interest on their loans, the cash flows on mortgage-backed securitised bonds and derivatives would be impaired. Yield-hungry investors would starve and they reacted in an entirely rational way: they dumped mortgage-backed bonds and derivatives. What had formerly been an active two-way market in the nuts and bolts of securitisation – mortgage-backed securities, credit default swaps and CDOs – now became an 'offer only' market. Traders would sell investors such bonds but were unwilling to buy them back. The IMF reported an increase in the cost of insuring against the risk of defaults in mortgage-backed securities, noting 'a pronounced widening in cash and credit default swaps on asset-backed securities and collaterised debt obligations backed by recently originated sub-prime mortgages, beginning in early 2007'.[10]

The effects were not confined to the sub-prime sector. As 2007 wore on, the market began to increase its expectations for non-prime mortgage-related losses, and credit spreads began to rise on many other asset-backed securities, irrespective of whether they were sub-prime. According to the British Bankers' Association, after June 2007 'the impact was no longer confined to the US sub-prime market, but affected the market for all mortgage-backed securities globally and banks who typically securitised their mortgage book found that they either could not do this at all or could only do so on much worse terms than before'.[11]

There had already been some signs of the sub-prime crisis feeding through to the corporate sector. Back in February 2007 a trading statement from HSBC disclosed worsening sub-prime-related credit losses. In April 2007, Countrywide Financial, the largest US mortgage lender, reported a 37 per cent drop in first-quarter earnings and later in the summer announced significant losses from mortgage lending.[12] In July 2007 Wall Street was shocked by news that another big mortgage company, American Home Mortgage Investment, would be delaying dividend and preference-share payments because it needed to conserve cash, and trading in the shares was suspended.[13] By now investors were running scared. Two hedge funds run by the investment bank Bear Stearns were faced with redemption requests and margin calls from investors and counterparties. The funds had borrowed in order to invest in sub-prime mortgage-linked CDOs. Bear Stearns pumped $1.6 billion into one of them but had to admit that there was very little value left in the funds, and they had to be wound down in July.[14]

The contagion spread to continental Europe, and on 7 August German banks organised a rescue for IKB Deutsche Industriebank, sunk by investments in sub-prime CDOs.[15] Two days later, the French investment bank BNP Paribas suspended withdrawals from three of its own sub-prime CDO-based hedge funds.[16]

From late July 2007 onwards conditions in the inter-bank money markets became very difficult. Although there was plenty of money in the system, banks would not lend to each other, needing to conserve capital to shore up their SIVs and other conduits. The SIVs usually funded themselves using a sector of the money market known as asset-backed commercial paper, in which they issued paper on a rolling basis to money market mutual funds and fixed-income investment managers such as BlackRock and Pimco. The collapse of the Bear Stearns funds caused these investors to lose confidence; liquidity in this market dried up; and the SIVs could not fund their business. Banks had to take them back onto their balance sheets, and as Mervyn King, governor of the Bank of England, told the Treasury Committee, 'Faced with the possibility that they would have to finance these vehicles themselves, banks with spare cash hoarded it.' Liquidity shrank and the cost of inter-bank borrowing went through the roof.[17]

LONDON

Northern Rock's share price started weakening in early 2007 once the problems of the US sub-prime sector began to spill over into the wider credit markets. From a peak of 1,252 pence in February, the shares had already fallen to 1,000 pence on 27 June 2007, when the company surprised the City with a trading statement. It admitted to having been 'caught out' by higher funding costs and the share price plunged a further 12 per cent to 834 pence. A month later the company revealed flat first-half profits but made optimistic comments about a positive medium-term outlook and an improving environment for bad consumer debts. The stock market remained doubtful and investors maintained the selling pressure despite Northern Rock's announcement on 20 August that it had sold almost £500 million of its commercial property loan book and that it had no exposure to US sub-prime mortgages.[18]

The market was right to be sceptical for by then Northern Rock's senior management was aware that it was in deep trouble. Its traders reported to senior management a 'dislocation in the market' for its funding on 9 August 2007.[19] It was worrying news because Northern Rock had a big securitisation to do in the middle of September and the market appeared to be seizing up. Matt Ridley, Northern Rock chairman, and Adam Applegarth discussed the problem on Friday 10 August, reflected over the weekend and reported it to the FSA on Monday 13 August. The following day, senior officials from the authorities involved in the tripartite arrangement – Hector Sants, the FSA's new chief executive; Sir John Gieve, deputy governor of the Bank of England; and a Treasury official – met to discuss the matter, informing the governor of the Bank of England about the situation later that day and telling the Chancellor of the Exchequer on 15 August.

Discussions between Northern Rock and the three regulators continued for a month, during which time conditions in the markets tightened considerably. The overnight inter-bank borrowing rate jumped from ten basis points over the official rate to over fifty basis points above; three-month inter-bank rates rose even more.[20] Banks stopped lending to each other and securitisation deals ground to a halt. As the mid-September deadline approached, it became clear that Northern Rock's big securitisation would not get done, and the search for alternative solutions was stepped up.

Northern Rock's advisers were already trying to find a white knight to take the company over. Lloyds TSB showed some interest but wanted the Bank of England to guarantee up to £30 billion of liquidity for up to two years at favourable rates.[21] This was rejected by the Chancellor of the Exchequer on the grounds that it might constitute state aid under European Union competition law and would set a precedent for other banks in trouble. No one else came forward and on 10 September the search for a white knight petered out.

It was now clear that Northern Rock would only survive with some kind of support from the Bank of England but the Old Lady was playing hardball. In August 2007 the British banks asked the Bank of England to provide additional liquidity to the banking system without penalty. Other ideas were for the Bank to lend for longer terms and to increase the range of collateral against which it would lend. Taking a harder line than the European Central Bank, which smoothed the timing of its supply of credit to help the crisis, and the US Federal

Reserve, which cut the interest rate charged to banks and extended the term of inter-bank financing, the Bank of England refused requests for system-wide measures. Mervyn King still believed that the banking system was strong enough to withstand the credit crunch and wanted to allow market forces to re-establish valuations of asset-backed securities. There was also the issue of moral hazard: if central banks were too ready to help in a crisis, commercial banks might assume that they would always be rescued if they got into difficulties, leading to more risk-taking and bringing on the next crisis.[22]

Refusing system-wide support at a time when no single institution was in danger was one thing, but the imminent risk of an individual bank failing was altogether more serious. If Northern Rock was declared insolvent, depositors would be guaranteed only the first £2,000 of their funds and 90 per cent of the next £33,000. There would probably be a bureaucratic logjam before any money was returned to depositors and a total loss of confidence in the UK banking system. Under these circumstances moral hazard would be the least of the authorities' worries, and at a meeting on 3 September 2007 Alistair Darling, Mervyn King and FSA chairman Sir Callum McCarthy agreed to give support to Northern Rock if securitisation and takeover failed.

Ten days later Northern Rock formally requested such help from the Bank of England. Full disclosure to the stock market was required because Northern Rock was a public company, and it was planned to make an announcement on Monday 17 September. But on the afternoon of Thursday 13 September rumours in the market started and the share price fell to a new low of 634 pence. The Court of the Bank of England met that evening; the terms of the funding facility were agreed in the early hours of the following day; and this announcement was made at 7 a.m. on Friday 14 September:

The Chancellor of the Exchequer has today authorised the Bank of England to provide a liquidity support facility to Northern Rock against appropriate collateral and at an interest rate premium. This liquidity facility will be available to help Northern Rock to fund its operations during the current period of turbulence in financial markets while Northern Rock works to secure an orderly transition to its current liquidity problems . . . The FSA judges that Northern Rock is solvent, exceeds its regulatory capital requirement and has a good quality loan book.[23]

However, by the time the announcement was made it was already old news. The BBC's business editor Robert Peston was onto the story and it was first reported at 8.30 p.m. on Thursday 13 September on BBC News 24. A run on the bank started immediately, with Northern Rock's online customers bombarding the company's website as they tried to make withdrawals. The Internet site crashed repeatedly – the company blamed the premature leak for stymieing their plans to increase the available bandwidth – and customers panicked. Queues began forming outside Northern Rock's seventy-two branches but the bank was ill prepared. There were only four branches in London; most of the rest did not normally do much business over the counter; and all were too small to cope with the volume of traffic. Money-laundering regulations and security considerations meant that it took about fifteen minutes to deal with each customer. The queues built up and the panic spread. As Adam Applegarth later admitted, 'I can understand readily the logic of somebody who has their life savings invested in an institution and who sees pictures of people queuing outside the door and they go and join that queue. That is quite a logical reaction.'[24]

The queues persisted over the weekend and on Monday 17 September. The risk of the panic spreading to other banks was growing by the hour, and at 5 p.m. that afternoon the Chancellor of the Exchequer called a press conference to announce that the government would guarantee all the existing deposits in Northern Rock during the current instability in the financial markets. He said, 'This means that people can continue to take their money out of Northern Rock. But if they choose to leave their money in Northern Rock, it will be guaranteed safe and secure.'[25] The announcement had the required effect. Panic subsided and the run on the Rock was over.

ANALYSIS

At the time the fall of Northern Rock was the most dramatic financial event of my thirty-year career. It caused every saver in the UK to wonder whether the bank where they kept their money was safe. The visual images were memorable: queues outside Northern Rock branches, pensioners leaving with their life savings in carrier bags and anxious staff pouring out of the bank's headquarters with uncertain jobs. It was a kick in the teeth for the knowledge economy. It was Britain's first banking crisis of the Internet age, and the Internet failed. Unless you were very early onto Northern Rock's underpowered website, online banking proved to be not up to the job, and worried users had no alternative but to find a branch and join the queues. It caused people to reappraise the pillars of British society. Banks in Britain were meant to be safe, like the fire and ambulance services. Now they joined the likes of the police, the postal service and British Airways as fallen idols.

A drama of this sort would have been hot news at any time but the timing made it more so. The crisis occurred when the UK's financial services industry was in the unusual position of receiving national acclaim. The City of London was perceived as a powerhouse of the global financial services industry. Britain's financial regulators were widely admired as role models for light-touch supervision. New Labour was credited with having created the right environment for finance to flourish and the Conservatives had evidently decided not to make the City a political issue. The combination of the profound shock to previously held assumptions and the realisation that what had formerly been safe ground for the government had now become a political minefield meant that commentators and the opposition parties looked round to apportion blame.

Initially Mervyn King, governor of the Bank of England, took the heat. The Bank was accused of being slow by waiting until after the weekend run on Northern Rock before guaranteeing deposits. Critics said that if this had been done at 7 a.m. on the 14th, the time when the funding facility was announced, the crisis would have been averted. The Bank of England was also criticised for failing to organise a rescue for Northern Rock behind the scenes in the month leading up to the run. It was said that with national interests under threat the Bank should have risked breaching UK takeover and European Union laws. In the early days of the crisis, the Bank of England was under such fire that commentators doubted that Mervyn King would be reappointed when his first term as governor expired in 2008.

Suspicion that the FSA, Northern Rock's lead regulator, had been asleep on duty began to form the day the crisis broke. Commentators wanted to know how regulators could have missed the shift in the pattern of Northern Rock's funding and not been alert to the risks it brought. They wanted to know what the FSA's partners in the tripartite arrangements, the Bank of England and the Treasury, were doing while Northern Rock was busy putting all its chips on red. Gordon Brown had set up the tripartite structure in 1997 soon after he became Chancellor, and the arrangements were revised in 2000. Were the roles and responsibilities of the three authorities adequately defined? Had the senior officials failed to appreciate the gravity of the situation or had each assumed that the others had the final say? The opposition parties said that the buck stopped at the top, and questioned whether Alistair Darling was up to his new job as Chancellor and whether the achievements of his predecessor in the role, Gordon Brown, were all they were cracked up to be.

The City was back on the political agenda and the opposition parties had a field day, but the most telling criticisms were made of Northern Rock's management, particularly its two top executives, chairman Ridley and chief executive Applegarth. Questions were asked as to whether Ridley, an author and businessman in that order, according to the 2006 annual report, and Applegarth, only partly qualified as a banker, were competent to do their jobs. And what of the non-executives? Sir Derek Wanless, a former chief executive of NatWest with extensive experience of financial markets, chaired the risk and audit committees, and Nicola Pease, a former broker and fund manager, was a member of the audit committee. All apparently failed to see the risks inherent in Northern Rock's lopsided business model.

Reading Northern Rock annual reports gives the impression of a company that was a model of corporate governance. There were five executive directors with clear descriptions of their roles, a non-executive chairman, six non-executives with a broad range of experience and a committee structure that complied with best practice. The board and the committees met regularly and the directors were assiduous in attending. What went wrong? Although securitisation started in Leo Finn's time as chief executive, it was during Adam Applegarth's tenure that it grew to dangerous proportions. The race for the chief executive's job had been on since 1997, when it was evident that Finn would be retiring in a few years. Applegarth was a determined and ambitious individual who understood what would impress the City in this newly listed company. His responsibilities included marketing; he became closely identified with Northern Rock's expansion in market share and was an uncontroversial choice as chief executive in 2001.

Northern Rock was no shrinking violet under Finn's leadership but it changed in character once Applegarth took over. Old City hands look carefully at corporate headquarters for signs that ego is out of control. In 2001, the year Applegarth became chief executive, the board decided to extend the bank's head office, spending £30 million on seven new buildings to be named after castles in the area. In 2005 a £20 million, ten-storey semicircular office building was commissioned.[26] Annual reports are another telling indication of a company's style. Immediately after the stock exchange listing Northern Rock's reports were like the company itself: plain, factual and understated. In later years they became glossy and grandiose. Applegarth was a keen sportsman, and Northern Rock sponsored Newcastle's soccer and rugby teams and Durham County Cricket Club; by 2006 the company's annual report was littered with photographs of sports stars and looked more like a marketing brochure for a ticket agency than a bank's financial filing.

Applegarth had the reputation of being 'difficult to challenge'[27] and needed equally strong colleagues on the board to keep him in check. Northern Rock insiders told the journalist Alex Brummer, 'Any rival plan or idea was rejected by those close to him on the basis that "Adam wouldn't like it." He had an iron grip on the company. There was no feedback. He surrounded himself with "yes men" who worked their way up the company and who were dependent on him.'[28] It is easy to imagine that the influence of Bob Bennett, who had overall responsibility for risk, treasury, finance and securitisation, will have been weakened by losing out to Applegarth in 2001 in the chief executive competition. Bennett's early retirement was announced in September 2006, and speaking in 2008 he was critical of the company's subsequent expansion: 'I always advised against that sort of aggressive growth when I was at the bank but I was ignored.'[29] The only other serving executive director to have preceded Applegarth on the board was deputy chief executive David Baker, who ran the operations end of the business but was described by Alex Brummer as 'almost invisible'.[30] Anyone who has seen the workings of a big company board at first hand will know that it would have been extremely unusual for the three remaining executive directors to stand up to the man who appointed them.

With a strong chief executive and a subservient executive board, responsibility for keeping a check on overbearing ambition lay with the non-executives, particularly the chairmen, of whom there were two during Applegarth's reign. Sir John Riddell, 13th Baronet Riddell, chairman during the start of the securitisation binge 2000–4, was an investment banker, having been deputy chairman of the investment bank Credit Suisse First Boston and a senior adviser to ING Barings, the successor company to Barings, the British merchant bank brought down by managerial incompetence and derivatives fraud.[31] CSFB was one of the world's leading structured finance experts and Northern Rock's securitisations were ratcheted up during Riddell's time in the chair.

When Riddell retired he was replaced by Dr Matt Ridley, chairman since 2004. Ridley was an unusual choice to chair a FTSE 100 company. He was an old Etonian with a first-class degree and doctorate from Oxford and like Riddell a member of Northumberland's upper crust. He worked for the free-market magazine *The Economist* between 1983 and 1992 and then became a freelance journalist and writer, selling half a million science books. The career résumé on his website shows no relevant commercial experience but he did have a family connection to Northern Rock as his father, 4th Viscount Ridley, was a previous chairman. Ridley was unqualified to run a major company, let alone one operating at the complex end of the financial services industry, but he is highly intelligent, trained to be a critical thinker, and if he had been more commercially savvy might have been able to use these talents to spot the dangers of Northern Rock's strategy.

Five of the company's six other non-executives had backgrounds in or experience of the financial services industry. Sir Ian Gibson, the company's senior independent director, had been on the board since 2002 and had been a member of the Court of the Bank of England from 1999 to 2004. Nicola Pease, a non-executive since 1999, had the financial services industry in her blood. Her father was chairman of Yorkshire Bank, her husband Crispin Odey was a successful hedge fund manager, her brother-in-law John Varley is chief executive of Barclays and Nicola and her brother are fund managers.[32] Two non-executives were appointed in 2005. Rosemary Radcliffe had previously been chief economist at Northern Rock's accountants, a situation that left her vulnerable to criticism. Michael Queen was director of the private equity group 3i. The non-executive quota included Derek Wanless, appointed to the board in 1999 soon after resigning as chief executive of NatWest during its battle for independence. Wanless chaired the risk committee, which also included Radcliffe, Gibson and the executive directors, and Pease sat on the audit committee, which was also chaired by Wanless.

The financial services background of so many non-executives seems to have worked against the company. They were all far too close to the industry to challenge the executives' key assumptions that financial markets worked and that securitisation was a repeatable process. Riddell rose to the top of an organisation that was in at the start of structured finance. The Bank of England during Gibson's time purred at the growth of a markets economy, and Pease and her relatives made a living from it. Radcliffe had worked for an organisation that lubricated the system and Queen for one that relied on it. Wanless had been chief executive of one of the UK's major players in debt trading.

It was of course a major error of judgment for the board to have allowed the company to become so vulnerable to market liquidity, but I do understand it. They had all grown up in a system that was sweeping all before it. Presidents and prime ministers, regulators and regulated, central bankers and investors, left and right all agreed that markets were the way forward. The investment banks had the resources to employ the best people, the best machines to dream up sophisticated products and an army of talented, persuasive individuals to sell them to customers. The pressure to be part of the trading set was enormous. A whole range of customers, from the treasurer of Orange County, who was sold inappropriate products by Bankers' Trust derivatives salesmen in the 1990s, to the wide-eyed and innocent board of Northern Rock a decade later, were swept away by the current.

The pressure from shareholders to perform, the prevailing wisdom that regarded securitisation as the way forward and the apparent success of what they were doing stopped Northern Rock's board from asking the obvious question: what will happen to us if markets seize up? But why did Northern Rock take securitisation to greater extremes than its peer group? The clue lies in a logo entitled the Virtuous Circle that appears in the company's annual report. At the core is the investors' Holy Grail: 'enhanced earnings per share growth, improved returns, enhanced capital efficiency'. Round the edge of the logo is a circle that shows how Northern Rock intended to achieve this: 'cost control, competitive products, product innovation and transparency, highest quality asset growth'. One surprising omission from the Virtuous Circle was 'risk management', and it is an absence that says a lot about its corporate culture. Risk management analysis was tucked away at the back of the annual report, and it is tempting to believe that was how it was in the day-to-day management of the business. Northern Rock was evidently the type of company that sees the glass as half full in an industry where the most successful companies see it as half empty. It had simply got carried away with its own success and forgot the old adage 'Risk never rests and constantly changes shape.' While the senior management was on top of bad debts, the risk that traditionally haunted building societies, a new risk, a sudden collapse of liquidity, crept up on the company and brought it down.

At the time of Northern Rock's demise, observers regarded it as an exception, a badly managed company that had got out of its depth. Within nine months we knew that it was only an extreme example of a recklessness that had affected the rest of the British banking industry.

10

SEPTEMBER 2007– DECEMBER 2008

Once the British government guaranteed the deposits of Northern Rock savers, the run on that bank subsided, but the credit crunch was only just beginning. It was driven by events in the US, where in a devastating demolition of the theory that originate-and-distribute banking and derivatives had reduced risk to below systemic levels, continued weakness in the housing market caused the global financial system to unravel between September 2007 and October 2008.

AMERICA

It was appropriate that the American investment banks, who had contributed the most to originate-and-distribute banking by pioneering securitisation and leverage, were the first to fall. At the beginning of the 21st century there were ten investment banks that mattered. There were the five largest independent investment banks, Goldman Sachs, Morgan Stanley, Merrill Lynch, Lehman and Bear Stearns, and five financial services conglomerates with embedded investment banks, Credit Suisse, UBS, Deutsche Bank, J. P. Morgan Chase and Citigroup. Collectively known as the bulge bracket, Goldman Sachs, Morgan Stanley, Merrill Lynch, J. P. Morgan and Citigroup made up an elite sub-group nicknamed the 'super-bulge'.

In September 2007 their position seemed secure. They had a strong grip on markets and to all intents and purposes ran the global economy. Yet by the end of October 2008, after the most traumatic period in investment banking history since the Great Crash of 1929, three of the independent investment banks had disappeared, the remaining two had converted to commercial banks and the conglomerates had taken a beating in the form of write-downs, losses and redundancies.

It was an incredible collapse. The decade 1997–2007 had been a typical one for this volatile industry with a three-year slump in the middle sandwiched between periods of great prosperity. After a strong start to the period fed by the technology-stock bull market, the investment banks' profits and reputation suffered when the dot.com bubble burst in 2000. President Bush called for 'an end to the days of cooking the books and shading the truth' on Wall Street, and the investment banks were in the doldrums until 2003. They cleaned up their acts and rebuilt their businesses, riding the credit boom, reporting record profits in 2004, 2005 and 2006. They reinserted themselves into Washington's good books and Henry Paulson, chief executive of Goldman Sachs, was appointed US Treasury secretary in 2006.

Their business model was racy. It depended increasingly on trading rather than the traditional investment banking staple of fee-based advisory work, but risk management techniques such as value at risk, a model widely adopted after heavy losses were sustained in the bond market crash of 1994, appeared to have brought risk under control. It helped that the dice were loaded. The investment banks were permitted to carry out such a wide range of activities that they were able to act simultaneously for buyers, sellers and themselves, and this gave them an information edge over other market players. Their results were so good and their borrowing costs so low that they had the confidence to go out and borrow capital to add to their own to invest in markets. The comparatively conservative Goldman Sachs and Morgan Stanley had leverage ratios of 24:1 and 25:1 respectively whilst leverage ratios at the more daring banks such as Lehman Brothers and Bear Stearns peaked at 32:1 and 33:1. While markets were going up and credit was plentiful, gearing up like this was an easy way to make money and the investment banks' confidence and belief in their invincibility grew.

They looked away from traditional low-margin equity and bond markets for new places to invest their own and borrowed capital. They explored investment opportunities in the emerging capital markets of Asia, South America and eastern Europe, and they invented ever more complex derivatives to play the currency, commodity and real estate markets. The aggressive trading firm Salomon Brothers, later absorbed into Citigroup, was the first to identify mortgage-related securities trading as a major growth area in the 1980s, and the development of structured finance and the housing boom expanded this into a massive industry in the opening years of the 21st century.

The investment banks had such influence over corporates and investors that they lured them into mortgage-based investing. The investment banks' results were so spectacular; credit markets were so benign; and the pressure on chief executives to grow profits was so great that financial institutions of all kinds followed the investment banks into leveraged investing in mortgage-related assets.

The American investment banks and other financial institutions such as hedge funds, banks and insurance companies were involved in the real estate sector in up to four ways. First, they could own mortgage-backed securities directly in their own hedge and proprietary trading funds and special investment vehicles (SIVs). Second, they could lend to and arrange funding for SIVs and vehicles run by other financial institutions. Third, they could buy, sell and hold insurance policies against defaulting bonds and mortgage-backed securities. Fourth, they could lend to investors in mortgage-backed securities and other real estate assets. It added up to a huge bet on a single asset class, and it all depended on US mortgage borrowers continuing to keep up with their interest payments.

The chapter on Northern Rock described the weakness in the US housing market and rising mortgage arrears in 2006 and the first nine months of 2007. The mortgage default rate continued to rise and house prices continued to fall in the final quarter of 2007 and throughout 2008. The flow of interest payments from borrowers on which mortgage-backed securities depended was interrupted; the market value of mortgage-backed securities and derivatives fell; the investment banks wrote down the value of the assets they carried and poured money in to support their struggling SIVs. It turned sour very quickly. Suddenly they needed cash and called in their loans to hedge funds and other borrowers, who then had to sell assets in order to repay them. This wave of selling further depressed mortgage-backed markets. Banks tried to reduce their leverage ratios and stopped lending to each other except on an overnight basis, accepting only blue-chip collateral such as US Treasury securities. This forced mortgage lenders to cut back on loans, further depressing house prices, increasing default rates and weakening the market value of mortgage-related assets. Northern Rock used to describe its funding model as the Virtuous Circle; by the early autumn of 2007 the Vicious Circle would have been a better description of an ailing industry.

Conditions in financial markets deteriorated at a frightening pace, and the monetary authorities became more and more anxious. On 31 July 2007 two hedge funds run by the US investment bank Bear Stearns filed for bankruptcy after they had lost virtually all of their investors' $1.6 billion capital as a result of disastrous mortgage-backed investments. In August 2007 Federal Reserve chairman Ben Bernanke, who had taken over from Alan Greenspan in 2006, tried to calm nerves by promising to intervene in the money markets, and widened the collateral the Fed would accept when making loans to include mortgage-backed securities. On 17 August the Fed held an emergency meeting and cut the discount rate – the price it charged for lending to financial institutions. The benchmark Federal Funds Rate was cut by 50 basis points in September and 25 basis points in October and December 2007, and in January 2008, after poor US economic figures caused a heavy fall in the stock market, it was cut by 75 basis points to 3.5 per cent, the first emergency rate cut since 1982. In March 2008 the Fed, the European Central Bank (ECB) and the Bank of England made a coordinated intervention in markets, and the Fed extended its discount window facility – the preferential rate at which it lent to banks – to investment banks. The Federal Funds Rate was then down to a mere 2.25 per cent, not far above the levels that had set off the credit spree; later it would fall to between zero and 25 basis points..

Despite these and other extraordinary measures, the housing market continued to fall, as did the value of mortgage-related securities and derivatives. America's leading financial institutions had to own up to their difficulties. In October 2007 Stanley O'Neal, chief executive of Merrill Lynch, the 'thundering herd' of Wall Street, revealed that it had lost $7.9 billion on mortgage-backed securities, 75 per cent higher than it had recently disclosed. Under pressure from the bank's board and shareholders, O'Neal retired with a leaving package of $160 million.[1] In November 2007 Citigroup announced a further $11 billion mortgage-related write-down on top of previously announced losses, and the bank's chairman and chief executive Chuck Prince, who only four months before had boasted that it was 'still dancing' in the lever-aged loans market, stepped down. It was, he said, 'the only honourable course'.[2]

In January 2008 Bear Stearns' seventy-three-year-old chief executive Jimmy Cayne left a short time after it had revealed fourth-quarter losses of $850 million and a $1.9 billion write-down on mortgage-related assets.[3] The abrupt departure of three of the top people on Wall Street in such a short space of time was as startling as the size of their leaving packages but there was much more to come.

Financial institutions became wary of doing business with any counterparty perceived to be at risk, and within two months of Cayne's departure Bear Stearns was taken over at a knock-down price by J. P. Morgan and with the help of $29 billion of guarantees from the Fed. In April the Senate Banking Committee called in Christopher Cox, chairman of the Securities and Exchange Commission since 2005, to explain what was going on. His account of the distressed sale of Bear Stearns neatly sums up how the credit crunch crunched Wall Street's investment banks:

What happened to Bear Stearns during the week of March 10th was like-wise unprecedented. For the first time, a major investment bank that was well-capitalized and apparently fully liquid experienced a crisis of confidence that denied it not only unsecured financing, but short-term secured financing, even when the collateral consisted of agency securities with a market value in excess of the funds to be borrowed. Counterparties would not provide securities lending services and clearing services. Prime brokerage clients moved their cash balances elsewhere. These decisions by counterparties, clients, and lenders to no longer transact with Bear Stearns in turn influ-enced other counterparties, clients, and lenders to also reduce their exposure to Bear Stearns. Over the weekend of March 15th and 16th, Bear Stearns faced a choice between filing for bankruptcy on Monday morning, or concluding an acquisition agreement with a larger partner.[4]

By the time Bear Stearns fell in March 2008 US investment banks and brokers had taken a capital hit of $175 billion on mortgage and credit-related issues.[5] Many had survived only by selling stakes on preferential terms to sovereign wealth funds in the Middle East, Singapore, South Korea, China and elsewhere.

The growth of the credit derivatives market had created many sub-sectors that supported it, and as the crisis unfolded victims emerged from dark corners of the financial system. Monoline insurers were specialist insurance companies that underwrote the CDSs against the risk of bonds defaulting. It had been a profitable and steady business during its ten-year history but the credit crunch changed all that. In January the ratings agencies downgraded the monoline insurers and one of the largest companies, MBIA, reported a first-quarter loss of $2.4 billion in 2008. Another leading monoline, FGIC, needed help from the New York insurance superintendent to broker a deal to stave off insolvency.[6] Its rival AMBAC paid Citigroup $850 million to cancel a guarantee it had written on a $1.4 billion collaterised debt obligation.[7]

America's two biggest mortgage finance companies, Fannie Mae and Freddie Mac, were hit heavily by the increase in default rates in the housing market and the rising cost of funding their operations. Their business was to buy up mortgages from lenders and then either hold them to maturity or securitise them. As government-backed companies they increased market share during the crisis as other investors lost confidence in the securitisation deals put together by the investment banks. In February 2008 the US government eased lending restrictions on them and in July 2008 put together a contingency rescue plan. Early in September 2008 the government took control of them after advisers said that Freddie Mac's accounting methods had overstated its capital cushion. The government cancelled common and preferred stock dividends and in an arrangement referred to as 'conservatorship' agreed to invest as much as $100 billion in each company in return for senior preferred stock.

The US authorities hoped that government protection for Fannie Mae and Freddie Mac would restore confidence in the markets but they were disappointed. As September progressed panic kicked in and financial markets went into meltdown. The wholesale funding markets dried up and inter-bank borrowing rates soared. Libor – the London Inter-Bank Offered Rate – is the main interest rate in the wholesale money markets and reflects the supply and demand of money as banks go about their daily business of lending to and borrowing from each other to balance their books. In normal times Libor trades at 10–20 basis points above central-bank interest rates; in the middle of September 2008 it rose to 6.4 per cent – over four percentage points or four hundred basis points above the Fed's official rate of 2 per cent.

The share prices of financial institutions that relied on wholesale markets to fund their businesses plummeted and the price of CDSs on their own bonds, a reliable guide to market confidence, hit record highs. There was persistent selling of the shares of independent investment banks such as Merrill Lynch, Goldman Sachs, Lehman and Morgan Stanley, and of AIG, an insurance company known to be a big player in structured-finance markets. Washington Mutual, America's largest savings and loans institution, was downgraded to junk status by the ratings agencies Standard & Poor's and Moody's.

There was a flight to safety as investors switched their money into government bonds, and the yield on US Treasury bonds reached its lowest level since 1941. Even money market funds – mutual funds that invest in short-term debt instruments, previously considered the next best thing to government bonds when it came to low-risk investments – came under pressure as investors realised that the bonds in which they had invested were not totally secure. Net outflows from US money market funds totalled $197 billion in a single week after one of the oldest, Reserve Primary, said on 16 September that it would return only 97 cents in the dollar. It was the first money market fund in fourteen years to see its net asset value fall below a dollar, an occurrence known as 'breaking the buck'.[8]

The event that caused Reserve Primary such problems was the bankruptcy of Lehman Brothers, the bulge bracket investment bank in which Reserve Primary had a $785 million bond holding; Lehman's fall caused that holding to be revalued to zero. Lehman was one of the oldest names on Wall Street; had nearly gone under in 1994 in the bond market crash of that year but had made a strong recovery under the leadership of Richard Fuld. Fuld made a lot of the Lehman culture, with an emphasis on teamwork and employee stock ownership, but its profits were driven increasingly by its fixed-income division, which was fully exposed to the Vicious Circle described earlier as a result of its high-leveraged heavy involvement in real estate. It had trouble refinancing its business as credit markets seized up and the fall in the mortgage-backed securities market left it with $35 billion of bad real estate assets. On 11 September the ratings agencies threatened to downgrade its credit status, an event that would have made it impossible for Lehman to raise enough money to carry on, unless it found a buyer. Despite last-minute discussions with Bank of America and Barclays, no one stepped forward. Other Wall Street banks lacked the will or the way to buy up the toxic assets and on 15 September Lehman went down.

The coordinated rescue of another bulge bracket member, Bear Stearns, just six months before had suggested that big investment banks were considered too big to fail, but the decision to let Lehman fail confused the market and panic set in. Henry Paulson, US Treasury secretary, said, 'I never once considered it appropriate to put taxpayer money on the line in rescuing Lehman.'⁹ He believed that the financial system would not be jeopardised by Lehman's failure but the market's immediate reaction will cause historians to question this judgement.

Lehman's collapse on 15 September caused one other event to pass off with only mild comment when in normal times it would have shaken the financial world rigid. Merrill Lynch, the bank that had at one time used the slogan 'Bullish on America', found that America did not repay the compliment and merged with Bank of America in a $50 billion deal. After Stanley O'Neal left in 2007, Merrill had recruited the boss of the New York Stock Exchange and former Goldman Sachs partner John Thain as chief executive, but it had shocked the market with a further round of write-downs and a capital raising at the end of July. The share price on exit was only a third of Merrill's fifty-two-week high, a muted and previously unimaginable demise for one of the iconic firms of modern-day America.

The following day, 16 September, as the world got used to the fall of two of Wall Street's leading investment banks and considered the implications of the US Treasury's refusal to save Lehman, AIG, once the world's biggest insurer, hit the rocks. AIG is a good example of a company that was wrecked as a result of chasing alpha. Hank Greenberg, a hard-bitten veteran of the Second World and Korean Wars became chief executive in 1968 and built a formidable business that at its peak had nearly $1,000 billion of assets, made profits of $14 billion and employed over 100,000 people in 130 countries.¹⁰ It had a reputation for being prepared to insure anything and everything, and when the CDS market took off in the late 1990s AIG decided that bond insurance was a logical add-on to its core business of general insurance. A small team in London, by this time the leading international centre for credit derivatives trading, was given responsibility for expanding into this area. By the middle of 2007 AIG had insured $465 billion of high-grade CDSs, and its annual premium income from this business was over $200 million.

AIG had seen the real estate downturn coming and stopped offering credit insurance on bonds with a sub-prime mortgage exposure at the end of 2005. It was confident that it had neatly sidestepped the real estate slump and as late as August 2007 Joseph Cassano, the Wall Street veteran who headed up the London CDS unit, told investors that the firm would not lose a single dollar on its CDS book. In December 2007, by which time the CDS market had turned more volatile, the situation was described as 'manageable', but as the market turned down, AIG's auditors and risk managers took another look at the CDS portfolio. They decided that the insurance AIG had provided was insufficiently covered; book values were recalculated; and by the middle of 2008 accumulated losses of $25 billion on credit default protection were identified. There was a shareholder revolt, Cassano left and the credit rating agencies threatened to downgrade AIG's debt status, a change that would have triggered a claim for an additional $14.5 billion of collateral from its creditors. AIG's share price fell from over $12 to below $4 in a single day, and the company was about to collapse when the Federal Reserve stepped in. Unlike Lehman, AIG was considered too big to fail, and the Fed provided a two-year injection of $85 billion in return for an 80 per cent stake.

The decision to let Lehman fail terrified the markets. Inter-bank lending dried up completely and the cost of insuring corporate bonds on the CDS market rose to extreme levels. The rescue of AIG did little to calm nerves – the volte-face came so soon after the Lehman decision that investors assumed that the authorities knew more than they were owning up to – and as the week went on the pressure mounted on other financial institutions deemed to be at risk. Morgan Stanley's share price fell by a third in a single day. Goldman Sachs reported respectable third-quarter results but its share price was hammered nearly as hard. In order to restore market confidence, both companies became bank holding companies, giving them permanent access to Federal Reserve funds in return for tighter regulation, including restrictions on the amount of leverage they could deploy in their businesses. After fruitless discussions with various sovereign wealth funds and merger talks with the US regional bank

Wachovia, Morgan Stanley agreed to sell up to 20 per cent of itself for $9 billion to the Japanese institution Mitsubishi UFJ Financial Group.

The US authorities were shaken by the reaction to their decision to abandon Lehman – as shown by their different response to AIG's difficulties. On Thursday 18 September the Federal Reserve led an injection of $180 billion into global money markets, working with the Bank of England, the European Central Bank and other central banks. The following day the US government guaranteed money-market mutual funds with a $50 billion backing and Treasury secretary Paulson announced plans for a $700 billion fund to buy toxic assets off financial institutions operating in the US. Bear raiders were being blamed for exacerbating the crisis, and a temporary ban was imposed on short-selling financial stocks.

Confidence remained low throughout September as doubts grew about the $700 billion bail-out. The popular mood in America turned vitriolic towards bankers. Politicians on both sides of the House of Representatives were reluctant to be seen supporting any measure that appeared to let them off the hook and rejected Paulson's plan on 25 September. The pressure on financial institutions intensified as the House deliberated. Washington Mutual, a thrift or retail bank and one of America's largest institutions, was closed by the Office of Thrift Supervision and sold to J. P. Morgan Chase for $1.9 billion after savers withdrew 10 per cent of its deposits in eight days. Its stock market value had topped $30 billion just a year before.[11]

The pressure extended even to Paulson's former firm Goldman Sachs, the investment bank that had done most to avoid mortgage-related problems. It needed to raise cash, and the same day Congress turned down Paulson, Goldman unveiled Warren Buffett, America's most prestigious investor, as its new backer. Buffett bought $5 billion worth of preference shares yielding 10 per cent, and secured the right to buy 10 per cent of Goldman's equity for $5 billion. The confidence that Buffett's backing gave enabled Goldman to raise a further $5 billion from ordinary shareholders.

In the first week of October Congress passed a watered-down version of the $700 billion plan to buy up troubled mortgage-based assets and the Fed said it would buy short-term debt from banks for the first time.[12] As I explain more fully later, on 8 October the UK government made £400 billion available to British banks that strengthened their balance sheets to prescribed levels. This stablised the situation in Britain, but despite a coordinated cut in interest rates by six European and North American central banks world stock markets remained in a panic, recording falls of 24 per cent in Tokyo, 22 in Frankfurt, 21 in London and 23 in New York in the week ending 10 October. The US Treasury now realised that it had to move into overkill if it was to turn things round. A week after the British plan was announced it produced its own $250 billion plan to recapitalise the US banks and shortly afterwards offered to lend up to $540 billion to shore up the money-market mutual funds. Half of the $250 billion was to be injected into nine leading banks in return for non-voting preference shares and warrants on a smaller equity stake. Dividend policy for participating banks would in future need to be agreed with the US Treasury, and mild compensation restraints were imposed on the chief executives, chief financial officers and next three most highly paid employees of the banks. Other banks could apply to join the scheme on similar terms.

For a country founded on entrepreneurial spirit and an economy built on free-market principles, government intervention on this scale was a faith-shaking event. Treasury secretary Paulson said, 'Government owning a stake in any private US company is objectionable to most Americans, me included. Yet the alternative of leaving businesses and consumers without access to financing is totally unacceptable.'[13]

Unpalatable though they were, these measures restored some order to the world's financial markets and that phase of the panic subsided, but before the year was out there was a further blow to the battered pride of America's financial institutions. Citigroup, whose predecessor and constituent companies had invented mortgage-backed securities and pioneered securitisation, and whose expansion by acquisition under Sandy Weill had epitomised post-modern capitalism, had to be rescued by the US government. Its share price had been in freefall, sinking from $22.50 to $3.50 in the space of twelve months under the pressure of write-downs and funding difficulties, and it had to accept a US Treasury investment of $20 billion in high-yielding preferred stock and a government guarantee on $306 billion of its domestic assets in order to survive. The US banking sector, it seemed, was in intensive care.

BRITAIN

The credit crunch confirmed that the world now had a truly global financial system. The connection between mortgage arrears in New Jersey and bank deposits in Newcastle had previously seemed tenuous but it was now obvious and direct. Falling asset prices and liquidity problems in the US had triggered the Northern Rock crisis and continued to cause difficulties for Britain's banks in the final quarter of 2007 and throughout 2008. But first Northern Rock needed to be given a decent burial.

It had been originally intended that the UK government's liquidity support for Northern Rock announced on 14 September 2007 would be a backstop facility, but with a big securitisation looming, credit markets remaining tight and the loss of retail deposits, the company needed money immediately. The interim dividend for 2008 was cancelled to conserve £59 million of cash;[14] talk of Citigroup and several other banks forming a consortium to provide finance came to nothing; and by early December Northern Rock had drawn down £25 billion of the Treasury facility.[15]

Meanwhile the reconstruction of the company was under way, including the ousting of Northern Rock's discredited management. First to go was chairman Dr Matt Ridley, who resigned on 19 October having been accused by the Treasury Select Committee of 'clinging on to office'.[16] He was replaced by Bryan Sanderson, regarded as a safe pair of banking hands from his time as chairman of Standard Chartered Bank and with impeccable north-eastern roots. In December Adam Applegarth left with compensation for the year of £760,000 plus a further £25,000 of noncash benefits. The company provided £340,000 to top up his pension fund to £2.6 million, a package that provoked public anger. Andy Kuipers, a Northern Rock insider who had run the bank's marketing operations, replaced him as chief executive.[17]

European Union rules restricted state aid to private enterprise to a six-month period so there needed to be a conclusion to the Treasury's involvement by the end of February. Either Northern Rock would be acquired by a private-sector buyer or it would be taken into public ownership. The Treasury's second permanent secretary, a highly rated thirty-eight-year old career civil servant named John Kingman, was given the job of moving things along in conjunction with Goldman Sachs and the company's own advisers. These were led by some of the City's top mergers and acquisitions specialists including David Wormsely of Citigroup, Matthew Greenberg of Merrill Lynch and John Studzinski, by this time ensconced at Blackstone after his stay at HSBC. To begin with there was a flurry of interest, including several potential private-equity and trade buyers, and the advisers got to work meeting prospective bidders and drafting marketing documents. But by November Northern Rock was down to its last £11 billion; the share price was in freefall and on 11 December fell so far that it dropped out of the FTSE 100 index of leading companies.

The problem facing potential buyers was that under prevailing conditions in the credit markets they faced a difficult job securing the money to pay off the Bank of England. At the beginning of February 2008 there were just three parties still interested in Northern Rock. These were a consortium named Olivant, led by Luqman Arnold, former chief executive of UBS and Abbey National, which had the support of SRM and RAB, two hedge funds that owned 18 per cent of the bank's shares; Richard Branson's Virgin Group; and a management consortium led by Paul Thompson, a former investment banker and chief executive of the insurance company Resolution Life, who had joined the Northern Rock board as part of the reconstruction team. Olivant dropped out on 3 February because of the Treasury's refusal to extend its financing package beyond three years,[18] leaving two hats in the ring. Despite the backing of Five Mile, a US private equity group, the management consortium struggled to come up with the necessary funding for an equity injection into Northern Rock but sent in its final bid on Friday 15 February and was still in discussions with the Treasury and its advisers over the weekend.

Virgin had also submitted its final bid on the Friday and met the Treasury team over the weekend. Virgin's proposal would have injected £1.25 billion of equity, consisting of its Virgin Money business valued at £250 million, £500 million from partners and a planned rights issue worth £500 million in return for a 55 per cent stake. Virgin would repay £11 billion of the loans from the Bank of England immediately and the remainder over three years. Sir Brian Pitman, the highly regarded former chairman of Lloyds TSB, was leading the bid, and there were ambitious plans to revive Northern Rock under the Virgin Money brand name.

Goldman Sachs assessed the proposals from Virgin and the Northern Rock management and advised the Treasury that the proposed payback period was too long and the deal would give away too much of the upside. Frantic discussions took place as the bidders tried to work out if they could meet the Treasury's objections and at the same time squeeze out further concessions. Late on the Saturday evening Treasury official Kingman concluded that the gap between the two sides was too great. Early on the afternoon of Sunday 17 February Gordon Brown and Alistair Darling took the decision to nationalise Northern Rock.

An announcement was made that afternoon, and Ron Sandler, Zimbabwean-born former chief executive of Lloyd's of London and one of the City's non-domiciled taxpayers[19] took over as Northern Rock's new £90,000-per-month executive chairman. He assured customers that it would be business as usual. The branches would be open on time; customers would be able to deposit and withdraw money; and the government guarantees would remain in place. The following day legislation was brought before the House of Commons to take the company into public ownership and to appoint independent arbitrators to determine what the shares were worth. Dealing in the shares was suspended at the previous Friday's closing price of 90 pence, less than 10 per cent of their price at peak.

When the Northern Rock crisis first broke, its management was excoriated for pursuing a reckless business strategy. How could any responsible banker, critics said, allow such a large gap to open up between retail deposits and loans? But within weeks of Northern Rock's demise investors came to understand that Britain's other banks were also reliant on wholesale funding and securitisation to sustain their business. Between the end of 1998, when the top eight UK banks held more in deposits than they had lent out to borrowers, and the end of 2007, when loans exceeded deposits by over £500 billion, there had been a transformation in their business model.[20] The causes of this, including new banking regulations, the growth of securitisation and shareholder pressure, will be discussed in the final chapter, but the effect was to make the UK banks, like the US investment banks, highly leveraged organisations dependent on the money markets to bridge their funding gap.

What UK banks did was copy the techniques of the US investment banks in what they called their markets, treasury or investment banking divisions. It was a two-card trick. The first card involved packaging their own loans into CDOs and selling them to investors through SIVs and other conduits. The second card was to enhance profits and reduce funding costs by punting the American mortgage-backed securities market. Using a mixture of their own and borrowed capital, they invested in American mortgage-backed securities, holding some of them on their own books and repackaging others into CDOs, placing them in SIVs and selling them on to outside investors. In effect they were cutting their funding costs by borrowing capital at one price and lending it to home buyers and other borrowers at a higher price, while also taking a punt on the US housing market.

Between 2001 and 2006 it was a very easy trade, but it was riskier than it looked. If for any reason the underlying flow of interest payments to the SIV slowed down or if liquidity in the money markets dried up, underwriting agreements required banks to stand behind the SIVs. As we have seen in the preceding section, these conditions occurred in 2007–8, when the US real estate market cracked and the asset-backed commercial paper market on which the banks depended to fund their SIVs seized up.

UK analysts and investors were first alerted to the problems in the US property market in February 2007, when a trading statement from HSBC disclosed substantial sub-prime-related credit losses. HSBC was known to have a big consumer credit business in America, having made a number of acquisitions there, and the market was not unduly alarmed by its announcement. There was a second warning signal in August 2007, when HBOS decided to absorb Grampian, its off-balance-sheet funding vehicle. Grampian had assets of $37 billion including a significant amount of US mortgage-backed securities, but when the commercial paper market spiked HBOS decided that it was more cost effective to fund Grampian itself. Investors were surprised by this news – they knew very little about Grampian because under accounting rules HBOS did not have to disclose it in its annual report – but the bank described the matter as a business decision that would have 'no material adverse impact'. However, shareholders were more alarmed in February 2008, when in reporting profits for 2007 HBOS wrote down the value of mortgage-backed securities by £736 million and in

April, when it set aside a further £2.8 billion. It revealed that at the end of March 2008 it held mortgage-backed securities worth £20.7 billion, of which half related to US mortgages.[21]

The Northern Rock, HSBC and HBOS cases alerted investors to British banks' exposure to the troubling issues of securitisation, wholesale funding and mortgage-backed securities. During the first half of 2008 falling house prices and weakness in all forms of mortgage-backed securities led to fears that write-downs would leave the banks without enough capital to meet the levels required by banking regulators. In March 2008 these concerns caused banks' share prices to come under pressure, with HBOS and mortgage lenders Alliance & Leicester and Bradford & Bingley hit particularly hard, and in April there were stories of imminent rights issues and profit warnings from the UK banks.

The collapse of Bear Stearns across the Atlantic had been a chilling warning that liquidity problems could bring down big financial institutions, and in the light of the funding gap at the British banks the Bank of England decided to address the issue. On 21 April it announced its Special Liquidity Scheme, which would enable Britain's banks and building societies to exchange mortgage-backed securities for UK Treasury bills. There was no limit to the funds on offer, but the Bank indicated that it expected £50 billion to be exchanged over the next two months despite the stiff conditions and the high costs it imposed on participating banks.

It was a neat scheme since taxpayer money was at risk only if a bank went bust, and even then the public purse was protected by a safety margin built into the ratio between the Treasury bills issued and mortgage-backed securities received.[22] In August 2007 the Bank of England had seemed slow-footed in responding to the crisis. Sir John Gieve, the deputy governor of the Bank of England responsible for financial stability, had remained on holiday while the Northern Rock storm raged and the Bank's governor Mervyn King had indicated that banks should be able to work out their own problems. But having lagged behind other central banks, notably the Federal Reserve and the European Central Bank, in responding to the crisis in 2007, the Bank of England now appeared to have moved out ahead and to have done so without breaking its taboo on moral hazard, the risk that the promise of central bank support would encourage reckless behaviour. Mervyn King, who had worked out the Special Liquidity Scheme over the Easter weekend, felt confident that the initiative would solve their funding problem. 'Now is the time,' he said, 'to take the liquidity issue off the table in a decisive way.'[23]

Unfortunately, market conditions ensured that such issues stayed firmly on the table. The day after King's plan was revealed, RBS announced Europe's largest ever rights issue of £12 billion and said it planned asset sales of £8 billion to shore up its balance sheet. A week later HBOS announced a £4 billion rights issue and revealed the increase in its write-downs referred to above. Shareholders asked what a predominantly British-based mortgage lender had been doing speculating in such markets; the share price fell below the rights price and less than one in ten took up their rights.

Soon after the HBOS rights issue was launched, another mortgage bank, Bradford & Bingley, made the headlines. It had already surprised the market in February 2008, when it took £160 million of write-downs on trading assets such as CDOs held by its treasury department, and on 13 May it announced a deeply discounted £300 million rights issue. The funding was accompanied by a statement that Bradford & Bingley was trading in line with the guidance given at its recent AGM, but on 2 June it provided a real stunner by releasing a profit warning, revising the terms of the rights issue and bringing in the private-equity firm TPG as an investor. The bank was the UK's largest lender for buy-to-let mortgages and had been caught out by an unexpected increase in mortgage arrears. Angry shareholders wanted to know why the information was so slow in coming – an embarrassed management blamed its less-than-state-of-the-art technology – and why the investment banks Citigroup and UBS, which had been paid £37 million to underwrite the rights issue, had been let off the hook. A month later there was more drama when the ratings agency Moody's downgraded Bradford & Bingley's credit status, citing the weak housing market and the bank's high proportion of self-certified and buy-to-let loans. TPG walked away from its plans to invest, and the FSA organised a rescue plan with four of Bradford & Bingley's largest shareholders, Legal & General, M&G, Standard Life and Insight.

The banks' interim-results season in July and August was particularly horrific as write-downs scarred their profit and loss accounts and balance sheets. RBS revealed a loss of £691 million, having reported profits of over £5 billion in the corresponding period in 2007. Interim profits at Lloyds TSB and HBOS were each down over 70 per cent. Barclays – which had raised £4.5 billion from investors in June in a capital raising that was largely shunned by existing shareholders – and HSBC dropped in the region of 30 per cent, and only Standard Chartered, with its predominantly Asian and Middle Eastern customer base, managed to increase profits.

September 2008 was not a good month for the mortgage banks. Alliance & Leicester, previously one of Northern Rock's closest competitors, was taken over by Banco Santander for £1.3 billion, half its stock market value at the beginning of the year. Then Bradford & Bingley was nationalised after retail investors took out £200 million on a single day, 27 September, as rumours circulated that rising arrears threatened the business.[24] Banco Santander was involved again, buying the bank's £21 billion retail deposit book and branch network for £600 million, leaving the government to manage Bradford & Bingley's £42 billion mortgage book.

At the very end of the month HBOS, Britain's biggest mortgage lender, was forced to agree to be taken over by Lloyds TSB. It was another example of what can happen if institutions chase alpha too hard. Halifax was the UK's largest pure building society when it merged with the Leeds Permanent in 1995 and listed on the stock market in 1997. It merged with Bank of Scotland in 2001, but property lending remained a significant and distinct business for the enlarged bank. James Crosby, a clever actuary who had been a fund manager with Scottish Amicable before becoming a founder director of the wealth management company J Rothschild Assurance that later became St James's Place and then joining Halifax, where he rose to become chief executive in 1999, led HBOS.

That same year Halifax had recruited Andy Hornby, previously retail managing director at Asda, to head its retail business, a position he held for the new group after the merger. He was promoted to HBOS chief operating officer in 2005 and rose again in 2006, when he became chief executive after Crosby left to follow a portfolio of interests. Crosby, who had been knighted for his services to the financial services industry, had doubled HBOS's profits between 2001 and 2005, and he left it as the UK's biggest mortgage lender and savings bank. On leaving he said, 'Now I know what I know, I wish I'd been bolder.'[25]

In fact, Crosby's leadership of HBOS had been quite bold enough, and subsequent events would cause some to believe too bold. Rigorous cost cutting following the merger had been accompanied by an expansion of its consumer business through slick marketing and a focus on customer service. At its peak it had ten million customers, a current account market share of 13 per cent, 74,000 staff, 1,100 branches and as of 30 June 2008 retail deposits of £258 billion, over 15 per cent of the UK's total consumer savings. But consumer lending had been pushed more aggressively than savings, and by promoting buy-to-let and self-certified loans in which employment and other checks on borrowers were waived, HBOS often had a mortgage market share of 20 per cent. It had outgrown the matched-loan-and-deposit business model, and its retail and corporate deposits now covered little more than half its balance sheet, the rest coming from wholesale markets and securitisation. Managing this was the responsibility of HBOS's treasury department, a vast army of debt, derivatives and currency traders working in the bank's Old Broad Street dealing room. They had two functions. The first was to organise HBOS's funding and liquidity; the second was to work the markets in a unit described as Trading and Sales. This was a professional and well-regarded team, and management's confidence in it was such that HBOS ran a funding gap that by September 2008 was about £200 billion with an annual refinancing requirement of about £20 billion.

In the second half of 2008 this funding requirement was causing serious problems. Conditions were difficult enough anyway, but the Grampian saga, the write-downs, the failed rights issue and the ongoing problems in the global property and credit markets put HBOS on the market's watch list. Counterparties became reluctant to deal with HBOS; there was a bear raid on the shares during September in which speculators were suspected of targeted selling; and after the collapse of Lehman the price of credit default swaps on HBOS bonds soared. The share price sunk from 283 pence on Friday 12 September to 88 pence on Wednesday 17 September; it had been over 450 pence less than six months before.

By late September 2008 HBOS was no longer viable as an independent entity. A bank of its size and national importance could not be allowed to fail; it would either have to be nationalised or taken over. HBOS's preferred partner was Lloyds TSB, a conservatively run retail banking and insurance group with a low-risk business model and a strong balance sheet. Under the leadership of Sir Brian Pitman and from 2003 Eric Daniels, a former Citigroup banker known as the 'Quiet American', it had concentrated on its core businesses and unlike its UK clearing counterparts avoided building an investment bank or allowing its treasury to engage in excessive investment banking practices. As at 30 June 2008 Lloyds TSB was able to report no direct exposure to US sub-prime asset-backed securities, limited indirect exposure through asset-backed security CDOs and a modest exposure to SIVs and asset-backed commercial paper and SIVs of £120 million.[26] Its funding gap was estimated at £67 billion, about one third the level of HBOS, and its annual funding needs were in the region of £10 billion.

HBOS and Lloyds TSB had been in intermittent discussions for several years but had always concluded that a combined UK market shares of 28 per cent in mortagages, 35 per cent in current accounts and 22 per cent in savings would raise competition issues. But HBOS's situation was so dire that after the personal intervention of the prime minister and the Chancellor of the Exchequer, and with the encouragement of the FSA, the government agreed to waive any competition concerns. On 27 September the companies said that there would be an all-share takeover by Lloyds TSB on terms that were later revised after a further fall in the HBOS share price. HBOS chairman Lord Stevenson and chief executive Andy Hornby would leave after the merger was completed.

Events in Britain were matched elsewhere, for September 2008 was the month when the noose tightened around the world's financial system. Securitisations were impossible to achieve; inter-bank borrowing rates were several percentage points above central bank rates when they were normally only a few basis points higher, and the cost of insuring against credit defaults reached astronomical levels. In practice this meant that even if banks could get liquidity, the price they had to pay was such that they would lose money on loans they had already written, and this combined with the need to write down portfolios of loans and mortgage-backed securities left them haemorrhaging money.

By early October the problem had spread to Europe's financial institutions. On 28 September the governments of Belgium and the Netherlands rescued Fortis, the bank that had led the break-up of ABN

AMRO almost exactly a year before. The following day Iceland's government took control of Glitnir, the country's third largest bank; the German government organised a rescue of Hypo Real Estate and the Irish government guaranteed the deposits in that country's six largest banks. On 30 September Dexia, bankers to the local governments of France, had to be rescued, and on 2 October Greece guaranteed all its bank deposits. It was a crisis of such proportions that on 1 October Christine Lagarde, the French finance minister, put forward the idea of a European rescue fund.

The Bank of England had originally planned that its Special Liquidity Scheme would run for six months (although the draw-downs could run for up to three years) but when September 2008 turned into a rout in financial markets it was extended for a further three months. The suddenness of the deterioration can be illustrated by the fact that this announcement was made the week after Mervyn King told a parliamentary committee that the banks had been given ample access to the scheme since it had opened and there was no question of giving them more time. In additional moves, the Bank of England offered to lend £40 billion to banks until January 2009 and to accept AAA-rated mortgage-backed securities as collateral.[27]

But in the event not even this combination was sufficient to solve the liquidity issue, and a decisive move was made in October with the government-backed recapitalisation of the UK's banks. This was announced on the morning of Wednesday 8 October 2008 and had been under discussion for a week in urgent meetings between the government and the banks. On the evening of Monday 6 October the pace of these discussions picked up and became even more intense the following day when RBS, Lloyds TSB and Barclays indicated that action would be needed sooner rather than later.

The plan announced the following day aimed to tackle the two issues that threatened the banks' ability to survive: the adequacy of the capital cushion they had to protect themselves from asset write-downs and the funding gap between their deposits and loans. Under the plan the government would provide up to £50 billion of capital to raise banks' tier-one capital – equity capital and reserves, defined and measured by regulators – to help absorb any future losses. Half of this would be available to Britain's eight largest banks and a further £25 billion would be obtainable by other eligible financial institutions.

Government stakes in participating banks would be in the form of preference shares, and the banks that accepted government funding would have to accept restrictions on dividend payments and influence on senior executive compensation.

Once the banks had satisfied the government that they had fixed the capital reserves problem with either public or private funds, it would guarantee up to £250 billion of new bank debt in return for a fee. This would enable the banks to replace maturing debt on a solid long-term basis and thus get them out of the fix of having to depend on expensive and unreliable overnight funding. In addition, the size of the Special Liquidity Scheme would be doubled from £100 billion to £200 billion, and interest rates were cut by 50 basis points as part of the coordinated global action referred to in the section on America.

Britain's recapitalisation plan left a few questions unanswered – 'What do WE get for our blank cheque?' demanded the *Daily Mail* – but it did ease fears that a British bank would go bust, and the price of buying protection as measured in the CDS market fell. But it did not unblock inter-bank borrowing markets or calm investors. The FTSE 100 fell 8.9 per cent on the Friday, at the time the biggest single-day fall since Black Monday 1987; Asian and European markets saw heavy selling; and Wall Street turned in its biggest weekly fall since the Great Depression.

World leaders now rallied round in concerted action. A G7 meeting in Washington on Wednesday 9 October had resulted in the co-ordinated interest rate cuts referred to earlier and a commitment that no more banks would be allowed to fail. 'Trust me,' said US Treasury secretary Paulson. 'We're not wasting time; we're working round the clock.' European leaders got together the following Sunday, 12 October, when prime minister Gordon Brown joined the fifteen heads of the Eurozone countries in Paris in their first formal meeting since monet-ary union was launched in 1999. Brown's reputation as an experienced finance minister, the boldness of Britain's recapitalisation plan and the sheer depth of the crisis persuaded the European leaders to accept guidance from the UK, not one of the Eurozone countries. They agreed a €1,873 billion package of support across the Eurozone including €500 billion in credit guarantees and capital injections in Germany and €360 billion in credit guarantees and loan capital in France. The following week the US government came out with its own recapitalisation plan, and these measures drew a line under that phase of the banking crisis.

The following chapter will discuss how the British banks responded to this rescue, and where the year's events left them and the rest of the financial services industry. However, even the most conservative observer would have to concede that 8 October 2008 amounted to a catastrophic failure of private-sector banking in the UK and a chastening end to the City's golden decade.

11

WHERE THE CREDIT CRUNCH LEFT THE CITY

On a bright sunny Saturday morning in September 2008 I was driving from Cambridge to Leeds with the radio as company. The credit crunch was all over the papers, the banks were in crisis and savers wondered whether their deposits were safe. I flicked between the stations: a news quiz, a question-and-answer session with a live audience and a satirical take on the week's events. Every speaker on all three shows condemned the City, the financial services industry and the 'greedy bankers' who ran them. The more biting the criticism, the louder the applause. It was a striking illustration of how City bankers had moved from being the pin-ups of the knowledge economy to Britain's most wanted men and in one or two cases women.

POLITICIANS

The September crisis came at a delicate time for the UK's political parties. It was the middle of the party conference season and possibly less than twelve months away from the next general election. Labour was twenty points behind the Conservatives in the opinion polls and there was talk of a challenge to Gordon Brown's position as Labour leader. Brown was reckoned to have been one of Britiain's most successful Chancellors but the financial crisis threatened to undo that reputation and damage his credentials.

Fortunately for the prime minister, public attention focused more on the most egregious causes and effects of the problem than on party politics. The media slammed into City executives who drove their companies onto the rocks yet walked away with millions. Archbishop of Canterbury Rowan Williams criticised the contemporary dealing culture, attacked 'unbridled capitalism' and wrote, 'it is no use pretending that the financial world can maintain indefinitely the degree of exemption from scrutiny and regulation that it has got used to'.[1] Dr John Sentamu, archbishop of York, was even more extreme, likening short sellers to 'bank robbers and asset strippers'.[2]

The left of the Labour party got very excited about the problems in the financial sector and seized the opportunity to attack the City's bonus culture, tax rates and the role of the financial markets in modern society. Jon Cruddas, a leading left-wing MP, criticised 'casino capitalism', called for higher taxes on top earners and claimed, 'the era of neo-liberal economics is coming to an end'. Brendan Barber, general secretary of Britain's Trade Union Congress, urged the government to resist the 'intimidation of the siren voices in the City of London' that claimed higher taxes would drive financial services business away from London. Derek Simpson, joint general secretary of the two-million-member union Unite spoke directly to the Chancellor at the party conference: 'Alistair, these people want ordinary people to share their pain but they won't share their gain. If you can't regulate the bonus culture, then tax it out of existence.'[3]

New Labour needed to be careful how it responded. On the one hand it needed to connect with seething public opinion. After years of being told that the market needed to be left on its own to get on with things, now taxpayers were told that they would have to accept their money being spent on a grand scale to rescue the banks. On the other hand the government needed to be mindful of the pro-City stance it had taken and the importance of the City's role in the national economy. There was also the fact that with a general election due no later than May 2010, Labour would need donations from wealthy supporters in the City to help fund its campaign.

To begin with leading Labour politicians joined the criticism. Immediately after the rescue of HBOS prime minister Brown told the BBC, 'I think we've got to look at where there has been irresponsible behaviour, and I've said for some time that we need reforms in the system. I believe there's now an audience that agrees with me that we should do more. We've got to clean up the financial system, we don't want these problems recurring in the future.'[4] Labour's deputy leader Harriet Harman said, 'I think there is a level of outrage. Complaints have been building up because the huge bonuses in the City have meant mad house prices in the centre of London, which has had a ripple effect outside. It's . . . quite wrong that salaries are structured so that traders are incentivised to take unwarranted risks. This is about the incentivisation of risk but also about a fair and equal society.'[5] Speaking at a fringe meeting at the Labour Party conference, former Treasury minister Ed Balls said, 'Those who think the global market economy can be run without regulation or with self-regulation or light-touch regulation have been entirely routed.'[6]

The Conservatives could see an opportunity. Brown and his team had designed the tripartite arrangements between the Bank of England, the Treasury and the FSA back in 1997. After ten years in which British financial regulation had been widely praised as a model for the rest of the world, the banking crisis cast it in a different light. The system's architects were accused of failing to have defined precise responsibilities, and those charged with running it were alleged to have been asleep at the wheel. The shadow Chancellor George Osborne and the Conservative leader David Cameron landed a few heavy blows on the issue. Osborne accused Brown of 'trying to disown' the regulatory system he had created: 'He seems to forget that he is the man who in ten years as Chancellor created the current system of regulation.' He added, 'For ten years he boasted about his achievements. Today he is trying to disown them.'[7]

The Conservatives reminded journalists of a speech made by Ed Balls in 2006, when the then Treasury minister had told the British Bankers' Association, 'The government's interest in this area is specific and clear – to safeguard the light-touch and proportionate regulatory regime that has made London a magnet for international business.' They also dusted off Balls's earlier rejection of mandatory disclosure of hedge fund positions and contrasted it with a recently imposed requirement for investors to disclose short positions during rights issues and a ban on short selling financial stocks.[8] Osborne accused the government of trying to airbrush themselves out of blame for the financial crisis and said, 'With this government it is too much to expect ministers to agree with each other but at least they might agree with themselves.'[9]

There was an absence of clear thinking among Labour and Conservative politicians about what the financial sector was for, about the ways in which it had functioned well and the ways in which it had been dysfunctional. The confusion was summed up by comments made by the City minister Kitty Ussher at a Labour conference fringe meeting. She said, 'greed is bad, I think, maybe in some ways – though the profit motive can create wealth and jobs'.[10]

The Conservatives appeared equally muddled on what to do and say about the City. David Cameron stated that growth in the UK had become too dependent on finance (amongst other things)[11] but the Conservative mayor of London Boris Johnson said, 'I'm very much concerned when I read attacks on greed and spivs, attacks by neo-socialists on the culture of bonuses. Of course there have been excesses and of course there has been greed . . . but this is a great British industry and the last thing we want to do now is to throw the baby out with the bathwater with some form of [excessive] regulation.'[12] Gordon Brown accused the Conservatives of a laissez-faire stance on regulation, saying it would have left short selling (described by shadow Chancellor Osborne as a function of capitalism) unchecked and would have legitimised 'making money out of the misery of others'.[13]

The most consistent comments came from the Liberal Democrats, whose deputy leader and Treasury spokesman Vince Cable had been calling for banking reform and tougher controls on lending for years. As the crisis bit he called for an end to 'lavish' City bonuses and 'free-wheeling' financial markets.[14] He accused Gordon Brown of 'creating chaos out of order'. Having advocated the nationalisation of Northern Rock and state aid for the banks in advance of government policy, Cable said, 'My team and I have been right on top of how the government should approach the problem of the banking system – first with Northern Rock and latterly with recapitalisation.'[15] It was a good shout from Cable and the Liberal Democrats had come closest to getting it right, but there was no fully developed, enlightened and market-oriented critique on offer from any of the parties.

The government's response to criticism was to emphasise that the crisis was global and not of Britain's making. Speaking on the *Andrew Marr Show* on BBC television, Brown repeatedly referred to the world-wide nature of the problem and the need for a globally agreed solution. He said the world had changed as national financial markets had become global, and there would have to be international as well as national regulators to control it. He explained that that was what he had meant by his previous remarks about needing to clean up the City. On other occasions he referred back to a speech he had made in May 2008 in which he had urged the US to join him in seeking reform of major international institutions. He said he had been pressing this for many years and now other countries were coming into line.

The government stuck to its pro-business, pro-markets claims but laid into the bonus culture. Brown told Andrew Marr, 'There's an element of the bonus system that is unacceptable. Everyone knows there is going to have to be changes in that. I've been saying that when you get your bonuses and your salaries based on short-term deals that have no relationship to long-term performance, then you've got to look again at what the system is doing, because if it's encouraging the short-term fix and the deal rather than making the economy better in the long run [sic].'[16] Chancellor Alistair Darling told the Labour conference, 'It's essential that bonuses don't result in people being encouraged to take more and more risk without understanding the damage that might be done, not just to their bank but to the rest of us in the wider economy.'[17] The incoming chairman of the FSA Lord Turner said, 'There are some very important issues to be questioned about the time periods over which bonuses are paid out, the information on which they are measured'[18] and the regulator began a consultation with senior banking executives about what could be done.

The tripartite system of regulation, or at least the way it was operated in recent years, was thoroughly discredited. In June 2008 the government said it planned to introduce legislation to overhaul the way the tripartite authorities regulate the financial system. The Bank of England's role in ensuring financial stability would be precisely defined, including a new Financial Stability Committee chaired by the governor and attended by members of the Court, the FSA and the Treasury. The process by which the tripartite authorities intervened in the management of a struggling bank would also be tightened, and the Bank would be able to request information from the FSA if it was worried about the welfare of a specific bank and if necessary propose changes to the FSA's regulation framework.[19] The Chancellor also asked the FSA to conduct an 'urgent review' of banking regulation. The review was to include all aspects of banking regulation, including the role of the FSA itself, liquidity capital requirements and the remuneration system. Darling said, 'It's not a question of light-touch regulation against heavy-handed regulation. It's about effective regulation.'[20]

The government stepped up its direct involvement in the financial services industry, waiving competition issues that in normal times would have derailed the merger of HBOS and Lloyds TSB. Jeremy Heywood, the former investment banker who became the prime minister's right-hand man at 10 Downing Street, monitored the deal. The prime minister himself was seen talking to Lloyds TSB chairman Sir Victor Blank just before the deal was announced and is believed to have given support and assurances. Brown let it be known that he was taking a close personal interest in the financial crisis and that he had discussed the situation with President Bush in the US. Chancellor Alistair Darling was in regular contact with officials at the US Treasury and the Federal Reserve.

Irritatingly for Vince Cable, the government's version of the recapitalisation scheme that he had called for got the prime minister out of the mire. In contrast to the US, where the Treasury had seen the banks' bad debts as the first issue to be dealt with and even then had been unable to get Congress to support its original plan, the UK government identified the banks' capital position and the lack of liquidity in the wholesale banking markets as the priorities. The recapitalisation plan and the guarantees of British banks' debts tackled both problems and reintroduced some confidence into banking markets. The prime minister's role in helping Eurozone leaders address the crisis has already been noted and other European countries adopted many aspects of the British solution. Most gratifyingly of all for Gordon Brown, the US followed up its plan to buy up the banks' bad debts with a recapitalisation scheme of its own.

The opposition looked on aghast as Labour's role in hosting the party that had got out of hand was briefly forgotten in its initial success in cleaning up after it. George Osborne wrote, 'This is no triumph. It is a necessary but desperate last-ditch attempt to prevent catastrophe . . . the final sorry chapter of the Age of Irresponsibility.'[21] Vince Cable criticised the roll-out of the recapitalisation scheme, which turned out to be less onerous for the banks than had been first believed: 'it is becoming increasingly clear that the assurances that were given by the banks are completely and utterly worthless'.[22]

The Chancellor's pre-Budget statement in November 2008 revealed the appalling state of Britain's public finances as a result of the credit crunch and hinted at the painful measures that would be required in future to sort out the mess. It was a reminder of the issues still to be faced and punctured the prime minister's aura as the only man in the world who knew what to do. Nevertheless Gordon Brown ended 2008 with a certain amount of kudos as the world leader who had appeared to be most on top of the banking crisis during that chilly autumn.

THE REGULATORS

For most of the crisis Britain's financial services supervisors appeared to have lost control of the industry they were meant to be regulating. The initial Northern Rock crisis left all three members of the tripartite system looking foolish. The FSA missed several warning signals about Northern Rock, including the imbalance in its funding model, its rapid growth as a company and the falls in its share price from February 2007 onwards. The Treasury Select Committee, which had several field days interrogating hapless senior officials from the FSA, the Treasury and the Bank of England, regarded this 'as a substantial failure of regulation'.[23] The Bank of England did nothing to help Northern Rock or the banking system in August and the first half of September, in contrast to the Federal Reserve, which injected liquidity into the banking market, and the European Central Bank, which brought forward its supply of credit to Eurozone banks to bolster confidence. The Treasury Select Committee believed that the Bank of England had clung to its concerns about moral hazard for far too long and that 'the lack of confidence in the money markets was a practical problem and the Bank of England should have adopted a more proactive response.'[24] The Treasury was meant to pull all three regulators together, but there was clearly a lack of coordination and the Treasury Committee called the Northern Rock affair 'a significant failure of the tripartite system'.[25]

The regulators tried to regroup. It was fortunate for the FSA's attempts to repair its reputation that John Tiner and Sir Callum

McCarthy, chief executive and chairman respectively during the credit bubble, were due to leave in 2007 and 2008. This enabled a new management team to come in and reposition the regulator as 'proportionate' rather than light touch. Hector Sants, who had taken over as chief executive of the FSA the month before the Northern Rock problems surfaced, moved out those responsible for supervising it, and in April 2008 Clive Briault, who had been in charge of retail bank supervision, left by mutual consent. The FSA beefed up its supervision of high-impact financial institutions, promised to pay more attention to liquidity issues and supported global initiatives to strengthen the independence of the credit rating agencies and improve transparency in off-balance-sheet accounting.

The FSA upped its game. After years in which the official line had been 'let the market decide' it was now considered too dangerous to leave market forces to their own devices. In contrast to its behaviour at the time of the Northern Rock crisis, when it had done next to nothing to avert the impending problem, the FSA took the initiative in sounding out financial institutions that might be able to save another threatened mortgage bank, Bradford & Bingley, and finally instructed it to seek state help.[26]

After the run on the shares of Lehman, Goldman Sachs and Morgan Stanley in the US and HBOS in the UK, the FSA and its US counterpart the SEC introduced a temporary ban on short selling financial stocks. Hector Sants wrote a five-page letter to the chief executives of twenty-eight banks and building societies, urging them to take 'immediate action' to ensure that compensation was appropriately structured given the risks being run. The FSA said that it would increase regulatory capital requirements for banks that failed to do this, warning, 'if the policies are not aligned with sound risk management, that is unacceptable'.[27]

Following its appointment as the UK's independent monetary authority, the Bank of England had appeared wrapped up in interest-rate setting and taken its eye off the stability ball. For the first half of the crisis the Bank's governor had seemed too academic and overly preoccupied with moral hazard. The Special Liquidity Scheme of April 2008 marked a step change in the Bank's attitude, and thereafter it became more proactive and was more in tune with the gravity of the situation, for example slashing interest rates in October and November

2008. Sir John Gieve, deputy governor of the Bank with responsibility for financial stability, decided to step down from his post two years early but would not go until 2009.[28]

The Treasury's performance, which had also been strangely anaemic during the first part of the crisis, also improved. It finally moved ahead of the curve when it brokered the recapitalisation plan, an achievement that was recognised with a knighthood for the Treasury's Permanent Secretary Nicholas MacPherson for 'extraordinary work in response to the crisis in the financial services industry.' The recapitalisation plan helped the Treasury partly regain its status as the most blue-chip of government departments, the department that when Gordon Brown was Chancellor other civil servants said ran the country.

The regulators had made a spirited attempt at recovery. Responsibilities were more clearly defined; light touch was replaced by 'effective' as the new culture; and proaction not reaction was now the regulators' guiding light. The regulatory system appeared in better shape to anticipate and react to the next crisis, whatever that may be and whenever it may occur. But in the final analysis, the spectacle of London as a wonderful example of how the financial services industry could safely be left to look after itself, a spectacle that had been grabbing global attention in the opening years of the 21st century, was shown in 2007–8 to have been a mirage, an alluring figment of the imagination that had shimmered during the bull market years but then evaporated.

THE BANKS

'Exceptional circumstances can throw up exceptional requirements. Even a few months ago it would have seemed outlandish that the British Government would create a company to manage economic interests in banks with assets totaling £3,000 billion.'[29] But that was the situation on 14 November 2008 when UK Financial Investments (UKFI), the company set up to manage the government's banking investments, came into being. It was to be run by the authors of the opening quotation, Sir Philip Hampton, chairman of J Sainsbury and a former finance director at four FTSE 100 companies, and John Kingman, the Treasury official heavily involved in the mortgage and clearing bank rescues of 2007–8.

The government's recapitalisation plan of October 2008 had required the UK's largest banks to strengthen their capital position by a total of £25 billion if they were to take advantage of its £250 billion debt guarantee. The government would provide this capital if necessary but there would be strings attached. Bonuses and compensation for board members for 2008 would be limited and no payments would be made to departing executives deemed to have failed. Banks would have to maintain lending to home buyers and small and medium-sized enterprises at 2007 levels. The government would have an input on board appointments. The banks would not be allowed to pay dividends to ordinary shareholders until preference shares issued to the government had been paid off.

When officials sat down with the banks to discuss the details of the plan in the middle of October 2008, they heard two different stories. Barclays, HSBC, Standard Chartered and Abbey, the mortgage bank taken over by Banco Santander in 2004, said they would be able to raise the money from private capital, whereas Royal Bank of Scotland (RBS), HBOS and Lloyds TSB indicated that they would need government help to strengthen their balance sheets to the required levels.

Lloyds TSB, which took £5.5 billion of state aid to strengthen its capital reserves, was the surprise name in the latter group, given its reputation for prudence. Its focused approach had served it well, but it had long been using the wholesale banking markets to leverage its balance sheet. In 2008 it had an estimated funding gap of £67 billion and it had of course agreed a merger with HBOS. Lloyds TSB portrayed its participation in the scheme as taking an opportunity rather than needing a rescue. It pointed out that its own bailout was the smallest of those that were given and carried the fewest conditions. Its intended partner HBOS needed £11.5 billion of recapitalisation money, and its results for the third quarter, which showed that write-downs had doubled to £5 billion in the three months, illustrated the extent of its problems. HBOS's senior management, chairman Lord Stevenson and chief executive Andy Hornby would depart after the merger without leaving packages, a blow softened in the latter's case by a £60,000-per-month consultancy agreement.

RBS's third-quarter results also revealed exactly why it needed state help. There were further write-downs in its structured credit portfolio, taking the year's total to over £6 billion, and signals that there would be more to come in the fourth quarter. It raised £15 billion in equity and a further £5 billion in preference shares under the recapitalisation scheme in a deal that left the state owning nearly 60 per cent of the bank. Chairman Sir Tom McKillop and chief executive Sir Fred Goodwin apologised to shareholders for what had happened and stood down, the latter immediately and the former with effect from April 2009. They received no leaving packages.

It was a sorry end to a fast ride. Under Goodwin's leadership, RBS had conducted an aggressive acquisition strategy, including the hostile takeover of NatWest in 1999 and participation in the consortium break-up of ABN AMRO in 2007. This was achieved on the back of thin capital ratios and a leveraged balance sheet. The strategy had worked well in benign markets but the sea change in 2007 exposed the risks that had been run in the markets division and the high-rolling nature of an acquisition-led strategy. ABN AMRO was the deal that broke the camel's back. RBS paid a top-of-the-market price for a second-grade investment bank. The acquisition transformed RBS's global markets division from an aggressive and focused debt trading business into a diversified global investment bank. ABN AMRO's investment bank was not a member of the bulge bracket in terms of client reputation or profitability yet its headcount was equal to that of the industry leaders. The timing of the deal could not have been worse, coinciding with falling markets, mortgage-related write-downs and difficult funding conditions, all of which have been described previously. By December 2008 the market capitalisation of the entire British banking sector was little more than the price RBS and its consortium partners had paid for ABN AMRO in 2007. After £6 billion of write-downs, a £12 billion rights issue and a gap of £165 million between its retail deposits and loans, the falling share price showed that shareholders had lost confidence in RBS management long before the government was called in.[30]

Incoming chief executive Stephen Hester, a well-regarded banker from his time at Abbey National prior to its sale to Santander, said, 'the bank had overextended itself and got caught up in a bull market culture'.[31] Hester planned to review the bank from first principles and presumably to rationalise it to a more focused, less capital-intensive core. RBS indicated it was planning to cut 3,000 jobs in investment banking and other areas and it would shrink its markets division to a less risky, less capital-intensive business.[32] It seemed a far cry from the spring of 2007, when RBS was winning plaudits for the success of its markets division, and investment banking chief Johnny Cameron was boasting of its profitability and competitive position.

For HSBC and Barclays, the biggest of the banks that did not take part in the recapitalisation scheme, the events of the autumn of 2008 presented a threat and an opportunity. The dislocation in credit markets caused them to make write-downs and dodge the bullets, but the restructuring of the institutional landscape presented potential openings for strategic moves. In particular the collapse of two large investment banks, Lehman and Bear Stearns, and the availability of another, Merrill Lynch, for a cut-price merger, provided them with an opportunity to make the breakthrough into the bulge bracket that had been on and off their agendas at different times over the previous twenty years.

For HSBC the timing was bad. John Studzinski had not long gone, and it had only just wound down its latest attempt at organic growth in investment banking. It had spent some time explaining its slimmed-down strategy and an investment banking deal in the US would be an extremely tough sell to shareholders. HSBC's senior management must have debated the problem for some time. They knew that it was difficult if not impossible to achieve the required scale in investment banking through organic growth, and they knew that if an investment bank was to be purchased it was better to do so at the bottom of the market than the top. Now appeared close to the bottom of the market, but would the bank look ridiculous if it reversed its strategy less than two years after cutting back in investment banking? In the end it played safe and did nothing in 2008. Despite writing down almost $40 billion on sub-prime and other loans and facing a potential $1 billion hit from its exposure to Bernard Madoff's failed US investment fund, it ended the year with one of the strongest capital ratios in the sector and its chief executive Michael Geoghegan was able to afford the luxury of pontificating on the plight of his competitors and the risks of moral hazard: 'There is no question that guarantees have been given to failed managements. I hope these guarantees don't last too long because they may create the wrong type of behaviour by managements in those banks.'[33]

Barclays was in a much better position to take the investment banking opportunity. It was fortuitous that it had missed out on ABN AMRO – not for the want of trying – and had already identified investment banking as one of the global businesses it wanted to target. In Robert Diamond it had a manager with good credentials in investment banking, and in BarCap it had a business with a foot in the door. Diamond knew that BarCap was weak in the US, had no presence in equities and as such did not yet meet Barclays' global criterion. He had been looking closely at the US during 2007, and in February 2008 he moved one of his closest lieutenants, forty-six-year-old Canadian Jerry del Missier, to New York. Plan A was to grow organically. Several teams and many individuals were hired, but the bank was also watching out for an acquisition. It looked hard at Bear Stearns when that firm was in trouble in March 2008 but decided that it would not be ready in time and watched it go to J. P. Morgan. It then identified Lehman as a possible candidate, Barclays' chief executive John Varley telling analysts in September 2008, 'We thought some months ago that it was possible this opportunity might arise but we were clear we would only be interested in pursuing it at the right price.'[34]

Lehman's problems came to a head in the second week of September 2008. US Treasury secretary Hank Paulson was determined that the taxpayers would not bail out Lehman but tried to find a private buyer. On Thursday 11 September the US Treasury contacted Barclays to sound out its interest in Lehman, and the following day a team from Barclays went through Lehman's books. It rejected Lehman's $40 billion of commercial real estate assets but said it would be prepared to buy its asset management, investment banking, fixed-income and equities business. There was just one problem. It would take Barclays three months to get approval from its regulators and shareholders, and in the meantime would Lehman's counterparties continue to trade with it? The US Treasury refused to guarantee Lehman's obligations; Barclays walked away; and Lehman filed for Chapter 11.[35]

Lehman's executives continued to work hard to keep together as much of the business as possible. On the evening of Sunday 14 September, Bob Diamond, who had stayed in New York after the takeover talks failed, took a call from Bart McDade, Lehman's chief operating officer. McDade wanted to know whether Barclays would consider buying all or part of Lehman out of bankruptcy. Having already done extensive due diligence in respect of a takeover, Barclays knew its way round Lehman. Monday was spent updating calculations, rerunning models and horse-trading. By Tuesday 16 September Barclays had agreed to buy trading assets of $72 billion and liabilities of $68 billion for $250 million in cash, and for a further $1.5 billion three Lehman properties including its prestigious headquarters building near Times Square in New York. Bob Diamond was able to walk onto the trading floor at Lehman and announce to the bank's 10,000 US employees, 'You have a new partner.'[36]

It looked like a good deal for Barclays. It had paid $1.75 billion for the core business of a group that had been worth $45 billion on the stock market in early 2007.[37] It had avoided the most toxic part of Lehman's balance sheet, and the assets it took on had been written down by Lehman and pored over by Barclays' own people during due diligence. Barclays chief executive John Varley said, 'The acquisition of these businesses and assets significantly enhances BarCap's position in the US by a transaction that is derisked by excluding the over-whelming majority of Lehman's risk assets.'[38] The 10,000 people it took on indicated the scale of the top Wall Street firms and the diffi-culty of reaching critical mass through Barclays' previous strategy of organic growth. Barclays maintained the bonus pool that had been accrued for these staff and cut special deals for the top 200 to prevent them from being poached by competitors.[39]

Diamond claimed that there was little overlap between the two businesses: 'Lehman Brothers brings excellence, top tier excellence in M&A; equity sales and trading and equity capital markets; and in credit trading. Two of those three areas we are not in, one we are quite weak in. If you look at BarCap's strengths, it is commodities – top three in the world; FX – top three in the world; interest rate trading – top three in the world; in investment grade debt – top three in the world. Areas that Lehman Brothers has traditionally been in, but weaker. The two firms combined become top three in both prime services and leverage finance, areas neither were top three in.'[40] There would be integration issues and some redundancies to eliminate overlaps, but Barclays had pulled off a coup in achieving a presence on Wall Street in one fell swoop at what looked to be the bottom of the market.

There are some unanswered questions. Between its formation in

1997 and 16 September 2008 BarCap had made a virtue of avoiding cash equities. Its predecessor BZW had not made much of an impact on Wall Street when it tried a similar strategy in 1989, picking up a sizeable chunk of the US equities business of another failed US investment bank, Drexel Burnham Lambert. Barclays' retreat from equities in 1997 revealed a corporate distaste for the business and some bitterness towards it. Many Barclays top people regarded equities as a low-margin business that was more trouble than it was worth. Suddenly, according to Diamond, cash equities was a business to be admired: 'It is an absolute machine, it is extremely profitable. Jerry Danini and the team that run it have been there for a long time. Year after year it has got a completely integrated research, sales and investment banking business. It is fantastic.'[41]

Diamond may be disappointed. In reality, cash equities in the US securities industry is a commodity business that relies on high volumes, proprietary trading and derivatives to protect falling margins. The equities business at Lehman worked because it was stitched into a complete Wall Street bank; Barclays will have to work hard to replicate that structure. With only the US piece of the business – Diamond had hoped to buy the UK and European equities and corporate finance businesses too, but lost out to Nomura – Barclays does not have a complete presence in what is a global business. After it lost out to Nomura it made a play for some of the ex-Lehman people in Europe and Japan, and it seems likely that it will have to spend more money to round out the rest of its equities, equity capital markets and mergers and acquisition businesses to give the US the global support that it needs.

While they were concluding the Lehman deal, Barclays' senior management was also monitoring the bank's funding position. Barclays had been one of the banks that had urged the government to get a move on with the recapitalisation scheme in the middle of October 2008, and it was a surprise when it decided to strengthen its balance sheet without state aid. It scrapped its final dividend, saving about £2 billion, and raised privately the further £7 billion it needed to access the government's guaranteed debt package. The majority came from a placing with Middle Eastern investors, and ordinary shareholders were annoyed that they had not been given their pre-emption right to participate in the heavily discounted share issue. The Association of British Insurers, one of the UK's most influential shareholder organisations, described this as a serious breach of corporate governance. The executive directors waived their bonuses for 2008 and the entire board put itself up for re-election in April 2009. It had been a controversial exercise but the Barclays board probably wanted to avoid government influence on sensitive matters such as compensation and risk profile at a time when it was building a global investment bank.

Commentators were divided in their views on Barclays' position at the end of 2008. Barclays wrote down about $5 billion during the year as a result of impaired assets and was criticised by analysts for not marking down to market value its loans to private equity companies.[42] Rumours had circulated regularly that it was having difficulties funding its business and its share price had been hammered in the crisis along with the rest of them. Yet it avoided the indignity of state aid, and the acquisition of Lehman's American equities business gave it a chance to join the investment banking big league, the first British bank in over ten years to have that opportunity. Supporters agreed with Diamond's logic in progressing the deal. He said, 'We're in a consolidating world where there will be three or four or five bulge bracket firms. If we were sitting here watching Bank of America and Merrill Lynch and others merge, you'd have to question whether it was OK to sit on your hands.'[43]

Others were not so sure, including one investment banker I interviewed. He paid tribute to the development of BarCap and described Barclays as 'the biggest beneficiaries of securitisation because it enabled them to build a large debt-based investment bank'. But he saw dangers: 'BarCap is so profitable that it must be difficult for the board to challenge it. Raising all this capital privately means that there has not been a full public prospectus or underwriters' due diligence. It is difficult for outsiders to gain an informed view.'[44]

Sir Philip Hampton and John Kingman, chairman and chief executive respectively of UKFI, certainly got one thing right on their first day. As they said in the article with which we opened this section, these were exceptional circumstances for British banks. A large group of them including some of the biggest names in the High Street were in disarray. The business model they had been operating for nearly ten years had failed; several of their top executives had been ushered from office without thanks or favour; and their successors had a new and influential shareholder to consider in the form of Her Majesty's Government. They were no longer in full control of compensation, board appointments, dividends, risk profile and domestic lending. They will be pursuing less ambitious strategies for some years to come and according to Charlie Bean, deputy governor of the Bank of England, 'it may well turn out that further capital injections are required' in the UK banking sector.

Barclays, HSBC and the emerging markets specialist Standard Chartered were in a different position. They had a nasty fright – in November 2008 Standard Chartered announced a large and deeply discounted rights issue – and their share prices and balance sheets had taken a beating, but they were still intact. They next faced the very considerable challenge of staying that way.

HEDGE FUNDS

It was Meltdown Monday, 15 September 2008, thirty years to the day since I first started work in the City and the morning after two of Wall Street's biggest investment banks had collapsed – Lehman's into bankruptcy and Merrill Lynch into the arms of the Bank of America. I felt disoriented in a way that I had experienced only a few times in those thirty years: the fall of Barings in 1995, the stock market crash of 1987, the Big Bang agreement of 1983. I knew that the world was going to be different but I was not quite sure how.

I had a long-standing meeting arranged with David Yarrow, one of London's hedge fund pioneers and a man I knew well but had not seen since the credit crunch began. I walked up Victoria Street, cut through the maze of narrow streets around Westminster Cathedral and entered the offices of Yarrow's firm Clareville Capital through the back door that I had used many times before. I had no idea what to expect. Would the fund managers be scrambling to get out of their positions? Would Yarrow have taken a counter-view and be buying the market? Would the office be under siege from investors trying to withdraw their money?

In fact, as I looked across the room all was calm. A dozen people were hard at work, studying their screens, occasionally consulting colleagues. There was only one problem: none of them worked for

Clareville Capital. And when I looked closely, the room I was standing in was a fraction the size of Clareville's old dealing room. My disorientation was complete. Wall Street was falling apart and some of my best friends in the City appeared to have been blown away. A young man approached and asked if he could help. He worked for the architects that had taken over Clareville's old space and obligingly told me that the hedge fund had moved next door.

And there they were. The same screens, some familiar faces but now working in a room half the size. Yarrow himself was realistic. Despite Clareville's successful ten years, investors had pulled their money out as the credit crunch hit, two of his fund managers had spun off and a fledgling office in India had been shut down after a disastrous few months trading. Funds under management had slipped from around $1 billion to not much over $100 million and Yarrow had downsized the firm and sublet the office.

Clareville Capital had done nothing wrong but what happened to it happened to scores of other hedge funds in London during the crisis. Private investors and the family offices that looked after the affairs of the super-rich stampeded to get out of markets, and the hedge funds were hit by wave after wave of redemptions. Yarrow was one of the fortunate ones: his business survived. His funds' performance had been good; he had a long track record and he was quick to read the signs and downsize his business. Others rapidly fell below critical mass, closed their doors and joined the queues of people trying to get back into long-only asset management or the investment banks.

One of the most dramatic collapses was that of Peloton Partners, a fund started in 2005 by two former Goldman Sachs traders, Ron Beller and Geoff Grant. In 2007 the fund decided that US sub-prime mortgages would take a tumble and bet heavily against them, a decision that produced a return for the year of 87 per cent for its ABS fund, a performance that won it a credit fund of the year award early in 2008. On 4 February 2008 co-founder Ron Beller was profiled in the *Financial Times*. Photographed in the company's trendy Soho offices he was quoted as saying, 'These are terrific trading markets. There's a lot of volatility and uncertainty and these are the conditions where we find good trading opportunities.'[45]

Three weeks later he was in the *Financial Times* again. Peloton's flagship fund had leveraged its assets and bet billions of dollars that prime US mortgage-backed securities would recover. In fact, the credit squeeze forced prices down and Peloton's nervy banks asked for more collateral. Peloton had to sell its positions to raise cash for the banks; news of its problems spread; the banks seized some of Peloton's assets; others had to be sold at a loss and the fund was worthless. Investors, including the firm's own partners and staff, who had $127 million invested, lost all their money, and within a fortnight property agents were appointed to try to get Peloton out of the lease on its London offices.[46]

The episode contained many elements that were symptomatic of the grip that new finance and its people had on the world. Ron Beller and his wife Jennifer Moses moved seamlessly between the worlds of finance, philanthropy and public service. After leaving Goldman Sachs in 2001 Beller spent a year redesigning the New York school system for the city's mayor Michael Bloomberg, and Moses was later appointed to be an unpaid special advisor to prime minister Gordon Brown. Beller is co-chair of the ARK education charity in London and with his wife sponsored a new primary school in London. Beller and Moses first came to the public's attention in 2004 in a court case concerning Beller's secretary's theft of £1 million from them. Commentators made much of the fact that the theft of such a large amount had gone unnoticed for quite some time. The hedge fund Beller ran had many of the trappings of the industry: the London offices were open plan with wooden floors and Turkish-style meeting rooms decorated in gaudy colours with low sofas, and there was a satellite office in Santa Barbara, California. The people the fund employed were well qualified, smart and hard-working. The fund even had a zappy name, a peloton being the pack tucked in around the leader in cycle races. But in the end, leverage, flawed judgement and a touch of hubris brought everything down, leaving the feeling that, like the industry that spawned it, the firm just got a bit too clever for its own good.

Peloton was one of the earliest and most public of the hedge fund failures in the City during the credit crunch, but other credit funds were also hit hard. Cambridge Place, the structured-credit hedge fund founded by former Goldman Sachs bankers Martin Finegold and Boston-based Bob Kramer, was one of the first to show the pain. In November 2007 it wound down Caliber Global, its $900 million London-listed fund, suspended redemptions in some of its other funds in return for lowering fees and laid off a fifth of its staff. At about the same time, several SIVs set up by London hedge funds went into receivership when the credit crunch destroyed the value of their assets, the first being Cheyne Finance, a $6 billion SIV set up by Cheyne Capital. Cheyne also had to write down the value of its Queen's Walk vehicle, listed on the stock market at €10 in December 2005 and falling below €1 in December 2008.

High-profile equity funds also hit hard times. GLG, the UK hedge fund that listed in New York in November 2007, reported losses of $308 million for the first half of 2008 after a sharp drop in perform-ance fees and an outflow of funds in the second quarter, when Greg Coffey the firm's star emerging markets fund manager handed in his resignation. In August 2008 founder Noam Gottesman said that GLG's funds would have to gain more than $700 million before they resumed generating performance fees.[47] RAB Capital and SRM Global, the two hedge funds that became Northern Rock's biggest shareholders, also hit the rocks. RAB's share price fell by two thirds in the first nine months of 2008, and the value of its Special Situations fund halved. Co-founder Philip Richards stood down as chief executive to concen-trate on running the fund and investors were warned that the fund would have to be closed with further losses unless they stuck with it. SRM's 'high conviction' fund, in which fund manager Jon Wood and his team took a small number of big positions, halved between its launch in 2006 and the beginning of 2008. It was reported that The Children's Investment Fund lost more than $1 billion in June 2008, at the time its worst month ever.

The credit crunch certainly rubbed the sheen off hedge funds' reputation. Typical funds were down 15–20 per cent in 2008 in what was only the industry's second down year since 1990. Many funds proved unable to do what it said on the tin: they could not hedge effectively against volatile markets. Deprived of the prop of being able to borrow short and invest long by the freeze in credit markets and high short-term interest rates, yesterday's heroes looked distinctly ordinary. The private-equity boom disappeared; mergers outside the financials sector became rare; and opportunities for event-driven strategies that relied on a busy takeover market dried up. Aggressive short selling was curtailed by restrictions in the US and the UK. Investors were annoyed when funds froze their right to redeem or threatened them with massive value destruction if they tried to withdraw money. The stock market rating of listed hedge funds collapsed to below net asset value, and the buyers that had once been prepared to pay several times annual profits for hedge funds regretted their actions and marked down their holdings.

In the first phase of the credit cycle there was a flight to scale. During 2007, the first year of the crisis, the world's top hundred hedge funds increased their market share from 47 to 66 per cent.[48] The drivers were the funds of funds, organisations that placed money for retail investors, and pension funds. They and other institutions consolidated their investments around a few large hedge funds with a performance track record and a solid corporate infrastructure. In the teeth of the gale, Brevan Howard, a firm that had made its name as a macro-global investor betting on interest-rate and currency movements, raised close to $1 billion by listing a new fund on the stock market. Investors were attracted by Brevan Howard's track record – its first listed fund returned 41 per cent in its first year – and the reassuring figure in the chair of Lord Turnbull, formerly Britain's most senior civil servant.[49] Man Group, the world's biggest listed hedge fund manager, achieved record sales of $5 billion in the second quarter of 2008, easily outweighing redemptions from nervous investors and enabling it to achieve assets under management of nearly $80 billion at the end of June 2008.[50]

However, in the dark closing months of 2008 the bigger funds were smashed too. GLG recorded a third-quarter loss of $163 million to add to the first-half loss mentioned above, and shares in Man Group fell 31 per cent on 6 November 2008, the day it reported declines of 44 per cent in performance fees and 24 per cent in pre-tax profits in the first half of its year. In December, Centaurus Capital, the credit and equity fund launched by the two former BNP Paribas traders Bernard Oppetit and Randy Freeman, said it would run down its main fund after investors refused to agree to a prolonged lock-up in return for lower fees.

The credit crunch played havoc with the hedge fund industry. It revealed that leverage and the bull market, not fund management genius, was behind many hedge funds' success. Investors questioned the two-and-twenty fee structure and the sector's rationale, perceiving it as being unable to deliver the absolute return it had promised or hedge out market risk. Investors were also startled to find themselves locked into positions by 'gates' (hastily erected restrictions that limited withdrawals to a certain proportion of the funds invested) and 'side pockets', which limited withdrawals to liquid shares. They were shocked when funds suspended redemptions or told them that if they exercised their right to redeem their money, they would crater the fund by forcing it to accept knock-down prices in illiquid markets. Finally, toxic hard-to-sell assets were moved into special vehicles and investors were told that they could not withdraw their money.

Estimates of the number of hedge funds that will close vary between 25 and 50 per cent, and those that remain will be smaller and less leveraged. The most likely outcome will be clusters around the very large quasi-institutional funds at one end of the scale and smaller closed funds run by top fund managers charging premium fees. The middle ground will find it difficult to achieve the scale or command the fees to flourish. The investment banks and other professional services companies succoured by the hedge funds are restructuring the specialist teams and prime broking departments that service them in the expectation that lower business flows will persist for some time. The service providers have stopped fawning over the hedge funds, and prime brokers have used the funds' fall in value to renegotiate the terms on which they do business. David Yarrow, the hedge fund manager I visited at the start of this section, describes the changed circumstances: 'These are not normal times. Only the weekends are normal – albeit we behave in a more chastened and frugal manner than we once did.'[51]

It was, of course, the banks not the hedge funds that blew up the system. At the time of writing no hedge funds had needed government help in order to stave off systemic risk. Some hedge funds performed well in the crisis, and a few fund managers were able to add to their good track records. But much of the industry turned out to be an ordinary investment business that for a while fooled the punters into paying very high fees for very average performance. That is not entirely the fault of the hedge funds.

PRIVATE EQUITY

Sir Michael Rake's day job is chairman of BT Group, Britain's largest telecommunications company, but in November 2007 he took on a new part-time role as the first ever chairman of the committee policing the private equity industry's voluntary code on transparency. The code was the result of the deliberations of Sir David Walker's working party and applied to FSA-registered private equity firms that owned a large UK company and large companies bought by the private equity industry. For participating firms, private-equity-owned companies had to produce an annual report and private equity funds had to make public information about their structure, key people and portfolio holdings. The code was heavily criticised. Brendan Barber, general secretary of the Trades Union Congress, feared that it would prove 'toothless', and John McFall, chairman of the Treasury Select Committee, described it as 'inadequate'.[52] The final code had been watered down in the face of industry pressure, but thirty-two of the industry's biggest buyout firms signed up for it and over fifty of their portfolio companies produced annual reports.

But by the time the code came out in November 2007 no one really cared. The credit crunch had changed the terms of trade for private equity companies, and buyouts of the kind that had caused such a fuss between 2005 and 2007 were no more. In the first half of 2008 the value of UK buyouts was less than half the level seen in the same period in 2007. Multi-billion-dollar deals such as the Alliance Boots buyout and the attempted bid for J Sainsbury became history. The top four deals done in the UK in the first half of 2008 were Emap at £2 billion; Biffa, a waste management company at £1.2 billion; Abbot, an oilfield services business at £0.9 billion; and Northgate Information Solutions at £0.5 billion. It is noticeable that most of these and other large deals were in sectors believed to be defensive in a recession. Similar trends were seen in Europe, historically an important area for British private equity firms, where the buyout market was running at only a third the level of corresponding periods in 2006 and 2007 in the first half of 2008.[53]

The banks were no longer prepared to lend to buyout firms on such generous terms – if they were prepared to lend at all – and private equity deals, such as a plan to merge Emap with another company in private equity group Apax's portfolio, were cancelled.[54] As the economy got worse and financial markets tightened, private equity firms such as TPG, the US buyout firm that had pulled out of investing in Bradford & Bingley at the last minute, became more careful about where they put their money. Deals that had already been done came under pressure as stock market valuations fell. One high-profile example was the music group EMI, bought by Terra Firma for £4 billion with the aid of £2.6 billion of Citigroup debt in the middle of 2007 just before the credit crunch bit and the stock market fell. It proved a difficult turnround. The market value of EMI fell to below the level of the loan from Citigroup, according to *Financial Times* research, and Terra Firma had to inject capital into EMI's balance sheet to avoid breaching its banking covenants. Several of the team that Terra Firma put into EMI left after little more than a year.[55]

Listed private equity firms had to mark their holdings to market value. In the summer of 2008 SVG Capital, the biggest investor in Permira, reported the first fall in its private equity portfolio since the dot.com bubble burst seven years before. 'Quick flips', in which private equity firms relisted buyouts on the stock market a year or two after purchase, and recapitalisations, in which they paid themselves a fat dividend out of bank loans, became a distant memory.

Senior industry figures warned that private equity's traditional two-and-twenty fee structure would not be sustainable. Others spoke of a new and more difficult operating environment, including Guy Hands, head of Terra Firma, who told conference delegates in November 2008, 'I am afraid returns in private equity for the vast majority of firms are coming down not only for the deals done at high prices in 2006 and 2007 but also for future deals.'[56] In contrast to the fears raised in 2007, the barbarians had disappeared from the gate of the FTSE 100.

ASSET MANAGEMENT

Inevitably, asset management took a beating during the credit crunch. Retail investors retreated and the fund management industry's net retail sales, the difference between inflows and outflows, turned negative in the fourth quarter of 2007, compounding the fall in the value of assets under management due to falling markets. The impact on the industry's profits was severe. Analysts reckon that a 1 per cent fall in assets under management results in a 1 per cent fall in fund managers' profits, and senior management tried to restructure their businesses to cope. There was talk of moving from a high fixed-cost base to a more variable model, but like most other financial services businesses this was a people business and cost cutting meant redundancies. The cuts were not as deep as those being implemented in investment banking but nearly all firms were involved. For example, Fidelity planned to cut several hundred UK jobs as part of its global cost-cutting programme, and other big firms including BlackRock and Gartmore laid people off.

The results of listed companies showed the pressures that fund management houses were under. Schroders reported a fall in profits from £98 million to £78 million, and a decline in assets under management from £139 billion to £115 billion for the nine months to the end of September 2008, at which point its share price had more than halved over the previous year.

New Star, John Duffield's high-flying firm listed in 2005, endured a particularly torrid time in the closing months of 2007 and in 2008. Its appeal to investors was its stable of star fund managers and the freedom they were allowed in their investment decisions, but when some of the top names hit a bad run, there seemed to be no portfolio structure to protect performance. One of its most famous managers, Stephen Whittaker, was asked to leave in November 2008 after his fund performed much worse than its peer group, and other top names at New Star also had problems. New Star's assets under management fell by 38 per cent in the first eleven months of 2008 and the company planned to cut sixty jobs.

Unfortunately for investors, poor investment performance was not New Star's only problem. In April 2007 it borrowed £260 million from five banks in order to return cash to shareholders, notably the company's management. The lending banks became progressively concerned about their money as New Star's results deteriorated and conditions in the credit markets tightened. New Star had to renegotiate the terms of the loan, and after an embarrassing debacle in which the FSA refused the company's request for a share suspension, the five banks took 75 per cent of New Star's equity and cancelled all but £20 million of its debt. The share price, which had been as high as 248 pence towards the end of 2007, sank to just half a penny in early December 2008.

Other independent funds managed to avoid New Star's fate.

Aberdeen Asset Management continued its recovery from its involvement in the split capital trusts affair and reported increased profits for 2007–8. The management of Artemis exercised its right to compel Fortis, the bank that had bought out its majority shareholder ABN AMRO, to buy a third of the group at what appeared to be a rich price in 2008's market.

The fund management industry was a second-order player in the liquidity squeeze and credit crunch of 2007 and 2008. Falling markets led to redemptions by investors, declining assets under management and lower profits but at the time of writing the industry in the UK appears to have avoided meltdown and to have retained its reputation as one of the better-managed parts of the 21st-century financial services industry. Whether that situation persists depends on its success in restructuring without damaging its ability to deliver investment performance.

OVERVIEW

It had been a nightmare for the City. Its public reputation was in tatters. Some of its most important financial institutions were no longer free to take their own decisions. Shareholders and investors had lost a fortune and would be hard to please. Employees faced an uncertain future. The consensus was that the restructured financial services industry would be low risk, low reward and much reduced in influence.

These views are perfectly understandable. At the time of writing the City is like a deflating balloon – limp and dull when it was once all pumped up and shiny. When the figures for 2008 come out, the City's role in the economy will be seen to have reduced. Its contribution to GDP and invisible earnings will be lower in absolute and relative terms and it will be a smaller employer. The City's HR departments are going through their downsizing rituals as investment banking chiefs call for 10 per cent off headcounts and then another 5 per cent. Many hedge funds are quietly packing up their tents, and the survivors will be more compact versions of those of the glory days. Credible estimates put the likely fall in City jobs at 20 per cent taking the total from 370,000 to about 300,000, a level last seen in the 1990s.

The consequences for the wider economy are becoming apparent.

The City and Canary Wharf still throb on a Thursday night, but the pubs and restaurants in the financial districts report that business is slow and it is suddenly easier to get a table at the smart West End restaurants beloved by the hedge fund and investment banking crowds. Upmarket estate agents report an easing in demand for prime London houses and apartments. The effects of disappointing bonuses and disappearing jobs are spreading out to the Home Counties, knocking house prices, consumer spending and the building trades in the hourglass of City feeder districts in Essex and Hertfordshire to the north and Surrey and Kent to the south. And although the cranes in central London are still busy finishing the tower blocks commissioned at the peak of the boom, tenants will be slow to come forward and commercial rents are already falling.

The City's status has been knocked almost as much as its economic clout. Whereas as recently as 2007 it was regarded as an industry that Britain could be proud of, one that led the world and served as an example of the new knowledge industries, now it is a byword for greed and complacency. University careers advisers report a resurgence of interest in jobs in technology and the public sector from 2009 graduates, not surprising given the layoffs in the City and the cutbacks in hiring plans. Charities have had to reduce their expectations from financial services benefactors, and university alumni relations people already look back on the generosity seen in the opening years of the 21st century as a wonderful aberration.

The City's relations with the government and politicians have taken on a frostier note. After years of restraint towards personal taxation, a policy that had defined New Labour's attitude to the City, the government announced its intention to raise the top rate of tax from 40% to 45%, to increase national insurance contributions, and to impose a £30,000 charge on non-domiciles after they have been resident for seven years. The Treasury is in control of dividend policy at several banks; the government influences their boards and bonuses; the FSA is watching their risk profile and warning of a 'more intrusive approach to regulation';[57] and the Bank of England is back in the picture with a stronger remit for financial stability. The new City minister in the House of Lords, Paul Myners, is a fund manager not an investment banker and has a track record of taking on the big guns in banking and broking.

The role of finance in the post-modern world is being widely debated. Free-market values, deregulation and non-intervention, the principles and philosophies on which finance feeds, are under the microscope. Alan Greenspan has conceded that he may have gone too far in trusting market forces, and journals of economic liberalism such as *The Economist*, the *Financial Times* and the *Wall Street Journal* have ever so gently tempered their ideologies. Intelligent intervention not rampant deregulation is the new order of the day.

There are many issues for the financial services industry to deal with. The credit crunch is still playing out and it is as yet unclear whether the world is in for a short sharp recession or a longer 1930s style depression. 2009 seems likely to be another difficult year for the financial sector. It will take some time for banks to re-establish themselves as healthy, free-standing institutions and when they do they may well occupy a different place in the reconstituted global economy.

The outlook for investment banking, which commentators have written off as a high-profit, high-compensation industry appears particularly bleak. The US investment banks are now under the supervision of the Federal Reserve as a result of changes in ownership, or in the cases of Goldman Sachs and Morgan Stanley by converting to commercial banks, and as described above British banks are on a tighter leash. Reduced risk appetite from management and shareholders, restrictions on leverage and tougher rules on capital adequacy are expected to curtail activities. Under pressure from government, top management at many banks have waived their bonuses for 2008, the staff bonus pools are down and a greater proportion of compensation will be deferred, with the threat of claw back if trades booked today go wrong later on.

It is therefore tempting to dismiss the financial services industry in general and investment banking in particular but such conclusions might be premature. Despite the disappearance of investment banks, investment banking as a business still exists and its recovery powers may surprise. Competition has diminished. The collapse of Bear Stearns and Lehman creates opportunities for those still standing. Demand for investment banking products and services will eventually recover as depressed asset prices force some businesses to restructure and create opportunities for others. The banks have retained the integrated investment banking business model and, despite the likelihood of more regulation and more cautious attitudes, will be well placed to ride the next wave.

The broader financial services industry can take comfort from the probability that the free-market philosophies on which it depends will be modified rather than dumped. President Sarkozy's claim in September 2008, 'The all-powerful market which is always right is finished,' seems over the top.[58] The lead will come from America. It remains to be seen whether the view of outgoing US President George W. Bush that 'History has shown that the greater threat to economic prosperity is not too little government involvement in the market but too much' will be echoed by his successor but it will be harder for the Obama administration to match its tough rhetoric with effective radical action.[59] In Britain, Gordon Brown, who liked to be seen as the man who showed the world the way, assured bankers, 'We will not make the mistake of taking reflex and ill-considered actions when facing crises.'[60] The *Financial Times*, in a large-font, double-spaced leader article, conceded, 'This is a difficult time to defend free markets,' but added, 'Nevertheless they must be defended, not only on their matchless record when it comes to raising living standards but on the maxim that it is wise to let adults exercise their own judgment.'[61]

The UK needs a strong City, and politicians of all parties know this. Speaking in October 2008, Gordon Brown reaffirmed, 'This government will always work hard to advance London's central role in the world financial system.'[62] The Conservatives were also thinking about turning the crisis to London's advantage, Philip Hammond, shadow chief secretary to the Treasury, saying, 'if we are able to take a more objective view than our competitors and pitch this just right . . . we have the potential to come out of this stronger'.[63] The Conservative leader David Cameron's tub-thumping call for erring bankers to be brought to account was accompanied by the statement that 'I want to do all I can to make sure the City of London recovers from the crisis and leads the world again.'[64] Unpalatable though it may be to those who call for blood, Britain's service economy needs a strong financial sector, and governments of every political persuasion seem likely to continue to do their best to ensure that the City remains globally competitive.

It is also worth remembering that the financial services industry's practitioners are the mothers of reinvention. The next iteration of the industry will be different from the super-charged version of the early 21st century. It will be more regulated, less leveraged, will involve less lending, will be more liquid and less complex. Management, regulators and customers will insist on understanding in full and in detail the products being traded. Overblown originate and distribute banking is dead and old style lending with rigorous credit scoring and balance sheet retention will play a greater role in the banking industry of the future. But imaginative financiers will strive to come up with new products, forge new relationships and find themselves a perch on the government's right hand. If regulation gets too heavy-handed, they will point to America's Sarbanes-Oxley overreaction to the dot.com scandals of 2001–3. That crisis is a good example of how unexpectedly the financial services industry can bounce back. Wall Street had become synonymous with greed and sleaze; the investment banks were laying off people and reporting huge losses; and there was a widespread conviction that the system had to change. Yet through a skilful rearguard action the financial services industry deflected the criticism and protected its business model. After a couple of years of contrition it was reporting record profits and was back at the top table in Washington. As a worked example of the financial services industry's cunning and resilience, it is hard to beat. This time round the industry is starting from further back, the political environment is different and the industry will certainly have to adapt to new rules. But unless politicians' actions for once match their rhetoric I, for one, am not going to write it off.

12

OUR OWN POSITION IN TIME

WHAT CAUSED BRITAIN'S BANKING CRISIS?

It was modern market capitalism that did for us all. The origins of the crisis date back to 1971 and the dismantling of Bretton Woods, the post-war system of monetary policy to which the world's leading economic powers had signed up. After Bretton Woods the US dollar became the world's reserve currency and governments were freed from following exchange-rate-led monetary policies. Volatility returned to financial markets, and dynamic and innovative finance worked its way out of its Keynesian stranglehold.

Ideological leadership came from the Chicago school of economists led by Milton Friedman, which became influential in Washington, particularly during the presidency of Ronald Reagan, 1981–89. These economic liberals believed that when governments attempted to intervene in markets they got things wrong. They picked up the free-market ideas of the 18th-century Scottish philosopher Adam Smith and believed that the invisible hand of markets would cull the weak and nurture the strong, leaving the system itself stronger and fitter. It followed from this that non-intervention and deregulation were the best courses for governments to follow.

At the same time shareholder value became generally accepted as the primary objective for companies, following research by another American academic, Professor Alfred Rappaport of the Northwestern University Business School. Management consultancies such as the firm of Stern Stewart, with its concept of economic value added, developed these ideas into a new and complete creed for management. Once the notion of performance-based compensation was added, a development that came with the introduction of share options in the 1980s, the stage was set for three decades in which deregulation, shareholder value and incentives formed the template for business in the US and its economic disciples.

These ideas were adopted in Britain by the Conservative government that was elected in 1979, marking the start of the UK free-market era. All four prime ministers – Thatcher, Major, Blair and Brown – who have occupied 10 Downing Street since have practised macro-economic policies of non-intervention in business and markets. Industries such as telecommunications, utilities and energy were deregulated and mergers and acquisitions waved through.

The industry that was deregulated the most in the UK was financial services, and again the lead came from the US, where fixed commissions on Wall Street were abolished in 1975. American banks had been tightly regulated since the Glass Steagall Act of 1933 when in response to the Great Crash of 1929 deposit-taking banks and investment banks were kept apart. But in the last quarter of the 20th century this restriction was eroded by the development of new financial products that made old definitions outdated, and eventually in 1999 by legislation. American investment banks had always been given a lot of leeway to mix client and proprietary business and to advise on all sides of a deal; now they had the added firepower of big bank balance sheets behind them.

Financial services deregulation hit the UK in 1986. That was the year Big Bang ushered in the Americanisation of the City and the first Buildings Society Act opened the door to friendly-society demutualisations, the two events that came together in the banking collapses of 2007–8. Deregulation of the industry was essential for Britain. If Thatcherite reforms such as the abolition of exchange controls and the end of the stock exchange closed shop had not occurred, the UK would have been bypassed as the world's financial services industry modernised in the last quarter of the 20th century. There were plenty of European capitals ready to take London's place if the City had not been reformed. And the country needed it. Having missed the opportunity to modernise British industry during the Bretton Woods period of relative stability in global markets after the Second World War, successive governments depended on financial services. Employment in manufacturing was running down as new technology, automated production and emerging markets in the east undercut British producers. New industries such as life sciences and information technology were centred in the US not the UK, and developing the financial services industry was one of the few and possibly the only option for creating knowledge-economy jobs in the UK.

But necessary though these reforms were, the way they played out had unforeseen consequences. The combination of deregulation, nonintervention and shareholder value led to a revolution in corporate behaviour in the UK. Institutional shareholders' relationship with the corporate sector changed from passive long-term support for management, in which disapproval was expressed in discreet meetings or in extremis by selling the shares, to a more proactive engagement. During the 1980s the first corporate raiders and aggressive conglomerates such as Hanson and BTR picked off underperforming companies or those where the share price sat at a discount to asset value. In the 1990s hedge funds transformed shareholder activism from a minority pursuit practised by maverick raiders into a mainstream activity. Fund managers, under pressure from trustees and consultants to deliver results every quarter, eagerly accepted takeover bids, cashing in today and letting tomorrow look after itself. Investors become more outspoken in their criticism of management and less tolerant of underperformance, and companies followed the shareholders' lead in doing everything they could to deliver short-term results.

Unlike France and Germany, where governments used national interest considerations to protect strategic industries from takeover by foreign companies, foreign buyers were welcomed in Britain. The energy sector became dominated by the French firm EDF; Britain's airports were taken over by the Spanish group Ferrovial; and another Spanish company, Banco Santander, became a big player in the UK's housing market as the owner of the mortgage bank Abbey National even before it bought the distressed Alliance & Leicester and Bradford & Bingley.

One victim of the open-door policy was a small industry with strategic importance, which was sold lock, stock and nearly barrel to foreign buyers in the 1990s: investment banking. The firms that changed hands were not large businesses but their absence removed a potential safeguard against do-or-die capitalism. The American model of invest-ment banking, in which relationships with clients lasted only as long as the deal being worked on, replaced the City's traditional culture of independent advice and long-term relationships. The client–banker dialogue ceased to be about trust and the client's long-term interests and became more about today's profit. This meant that when a corpo-rate client asked an investment bank for advice, the reply was nearly always, 'Transact, and do it now.' The new relationship was summed up by the investment banks' terminology for analysing their clients. They categorised them by 'size of wallet', a crude but telling descrip-tion of what really mattered to them.

The investment banks became so profitable and powerful that they were able to buy in the very best talent to dream up and sell innovative new products. They used this talent to thrust these products down the throats of chief executives. Chief executives are not babes in the wood, but it was an unequal contest between fast-talking investment bankers with almost limitless resources and chief executives under pressure from shareholders to match the fastest growth rates in the market. In the UK there used to exist a breed of corporate financier that would advise a client not to transact if the deal looked wrong. Most of those advisers disappeared from the market once the Americans came to town, or had no option but to change tack and adopt hard-selling investment banking practices if they were to remain employed.

Belatedly, in the opening years of the 21st century senior bankers who had got fed up with the big bank mentality opened up advisory boutiques, but by then it was too late. The integrated investment banks had wrapped their tentacles all round the corporate sector. During two decades of anything-goes management they egged on chief executives to explore every conceivable avenue to grow earnings per share. Corporate executives listened intently. They were incen-tivised by share options schemes and could achieve life-changing rewards if they were able to get the share price above the price of their options. They redoubled their efforts to please the market using devices such as share buy-backs, buyouts, mergers, leverage and financial engineering.

Incentive-based compensation was an even bigger factor at the investment banks than it was in the rest of the corporate sector. Firms in the investment banking industry in the UK and US had started out as partnerships, and a culture existed of paying staff modest salaries and then a share of the year's profits as a bonus. This practice was continued when the banks and brokers incorporated in the 1970s in the US and the 1980s in the UK. As the industry became more profitable the bonuses became larger. Million-dollar and higher bonuses were already common in the US in the 1980s and million-pound plus bonuses were paid in London from the 1990s onwards.

Bonuses became a business risk in the financial services industry in the second half of the 1990s, when trading became more important and the complexity of deals grew. These developments changed the dynamic in two important ways. First, the number of people whose pay was tied to a trading book increased rapidly, encouraging reckless risk-taking on the part of traders who needed a strong end to the year to boost their bonus. Second, derivatives-based structured products had a long shelf life, but bonuses were paid out instantly. Fees booked upfront could be eroded if the bank was left holding positions in a falling market, but by then the originators of the deal might well have banked their bonuses and moved on. This gave traders every incentive to write business that generated fees upfront and to disregard the long-term risk.

This coincided with the era of light-touch regulation, particularly in the UK. There was no overt slackening of the rules, but British regulators believed that too much intervention stifled creativity. In addition to its supervisory function, the FSA had a mandate to promote financial innovation and London's competitiveness as a financial services centre. The financial services industry heaped praise upon the FSA for its enlightened approach and this confirmed the regulators' light-touch tendencies.

All of this left the UK corporate sector in a very dangerous place at the beginning of the 21st century. The investment banks were rampant; the corporate world was an activist jungle; the incentive structure encouraged executives to chase alpha; and the regulator seemed more concerned about protecting the City's global status than carrying out prudential supervision. It was an accident waiting to happen, and then global forces came along to make sure that it did.

Low interest rates encouraged a consumer credit boom, and the developing Asian economies and the wealthy oil-producing states provided the money to lend. Derivatives enabled financiers to connect the supply and demand of credit, and the shadow banking system enabled banks to reduce the amount of capital they had to hold on their balance sheets.

In the UK the full weight of free-market economics, deregulation, shareholder value, incentives and modern finance bore down on the banking sector. It was an intensely watched industry, and management was under pressure to keep up with the pack when it came to earnings growth. New regulations gave banks the incentive to move assets off the balance sheet. Investment bankers sold the securitisation model hard. The mortgage banks were particularly vulnerable. Abbey National had been the first building society to demutualise after the Building Societies Act of 1986. A second Buildings Society Act in 1997 triggered a wave of demutualisations that year including Alliance & Leicester, Halifax and Northern Rock, and Bradford & Bingley three years later. The timing was unfortunate. The individuals running these banks ran slap bang into financialisation in its pomp. Originate-and-distribute banking was all the rage. The investment bankers claimed to have 'transformed risk' through their new credit derivatives, off-balance-sheet vehicles and securitisations. Governments and regulators were easing off the brakes in respect of capital adequacy, disclosure and intervention. Benign economic conditions and low interest rates encouraged leverage and risk-taking.

All of this happened while the chief executives of Britain's mortgage banks were finding their feet as listed businesses. They saw other financial institutions including the clearing banks and the US investment banks growing earnings through aggressive financing schemes, and their shareholders pressed them to do the same. Banking regulations encouraged flexibility, and national regulators seemed unconcerned. Objective, independent advisers had been replaced by deal hungry whizz-kids, and shareholders wanted results and they wanted them now.

Britain's mortgage banks changed their business model and became heavily reliant on wholesale banking and securitisation. The economist John Kay, who was on the board of Halifax until 2000, regards 'the day it was decided that treasury should be a profit centre in its own right rather than an ancillary activity' as the defining moment in that organisation's history, and this is a fitting comment on the entire sector.[1] The new model was a mile away from the original friendly-society model, which lent out only what its members had deposited. The clearing banks were more savvy and less extreme in their business models but eventually they were also playing the high-risk high-reward game. Everyone was doing it. In the year 2000 there was no funding gap at British banks: they only lent out what they took in deposits. By 2007 the gap was an astronomical £500 billion.

There were situations in which people might have done better to prevent the crisis, but as Howard Davies, who became director of the London School of Economics after he left the FSA, has remarked, 'Harry Hindsight' is a wonderful thing.[2] It now seems obvious that over-reliance on wholesale markets and securitisation was running a massive liquidity risk. But the environment of the time was unashamedly bullish, and Britain's banks were bit players in a new system designed and run by Americans. It would have been practically impossible for a public company in the UK to have resisted the trend. When Morgan Stanley's chief executive Philip Purcell tried to follow a low-risk strategy he was hounded out of office by shareholders who wanted a more aggressive approach. It is very doubtful whether the shareholders of British banks would have tolerated a low-growth strategy in the 21st-century bull market.

A case in point is Andy Hornby, the much-criticised chief executive of HBOS from 2006 to 2008 and a man I have never met, spoken to or dealt with in any way. Hornby is the son of a Bristol headmaster, had a distinguished academic career at Oxford and the Harvard Business School, and was considered a rising star by Asda and then his bosses at HBOS after he moved there in 1999. As retail director he played his part in growing HBOS's consumer lending business and was appointed chief executive during a raging bull market for housing in which HBOS was the market leader. Now he might have said to shareholders, 'Wait a minute. This money market funding thing could disappear and the housing market could slump. I am going to shrink market share, build up deposits, and earnings per share will halve. Is that OK?' But if he had, he would probably have got a pretty rude answer. This young man in his first chief executive's job would have needed to turn the world on its head and tell the market, 'You are all wrong.' Adam Applegarth at Northern Rock had longer at the top of his organisation but he faced similar pressures. This was not the failure of a handful of individual executives; it was a system-wide failure.

Hubris of course played a part. The banks had been so successful for so long they believed they were infallible. Boards of directors including the non-executives who were meant to offer objective counsel got sucked in. The last time the capital markets had faced meltdown was during the oil crisis of 1973–4, before the careers of most 21st-century bankers, fund managers and chief executives had begun. The senior British journalist Christopher Fildes defines the moment of maximum economic danger as the point at which the last person to have lived through the last recession retires, a telling description of the situation in the opening years of the 21st century.[3] Financial services practitioners, non-executive directors who sat on their boards and regulators all forgot that liquidity is what keeps markets going. They were blinded by their own genius. It is significant that two of the banks that survived the 2008 crisis best were J. P. Morgan and Goldman Sachs, both hit heavily in the bond market crash of 1994 and who learned the lessons by introducing strong risk management systems and analytics.

For thirty years British governments of the left and right listened far too much to investment bankers and not enough to people in other industries, including other parts of the financial services industry such as accounting, fund management and management consultancy. They also listened too much to extreme economic liberals and not enough to writers such as Will Hutton, John Kay and John Plender, all of whom warned well in advance of the crisis of the risks of relying too heavily on markets.[4] Equally the regulators might have done better. The tripartite system was loosely defined; the governor of the Bank of England might have intervened in markets earlier; the FSA official in charge of supervising Northern Rock might have paid more attention to the warning signs. But ultimately it was the system that did it; unjustified faith in the power of markets and a mistaken belief that it was wrong for governments to intervene.

At the time of writing state intervention has stopped the tailspin. Government stakes in financial institutions of the size and importance of Citigroup in the US and RBS in the UK have created an extraordinary opportunity to redesign the global financial services industry. However, the precedents are not encouraging. A similar and only slightly less inviting opportunity to tighten up the system was missed by US regulators in 2003. The crisis in corporate governance at the time of the crash of Enron and the dot.com implosion had some of the same elements as the credit crunch, notably off-balance-sheet financing, hubris, and a belief that the good times would carry on to the end of time. When it all blew up, the regulators' response was to toughen up the rules at the micro-level but to leave the system intact. When the system blew up again five years later, the precise cause was different to what had happened in 2003, but the role of over-mighty banks and over-incentivised bankers was common to both crises.

Tinkering with the rules did not work in 2003 and it is doubtful whether it will make a lasting difference in 2009. Unfortunately, more tinkering is exactly what is being discussed at the time of writing. Market forces and perhaps some new regulations will constrain leverage, discourage risk-taking and ration capital for a certain period, but at the time of writing nothing has been done to curtail the range of activities permitted to the financial institutions. Unless such action is taken, this means that at some point they will become over-mighty once more, and the whole cycle will begin again. The author has suggested before the revival and modernisation of the Glass-Steagall Act that separated deposit-taking from securities trading and the case seems even more compelling now than it was then.[5]

Under this model financial institutions would have to choose whether to be investment banks that underwrote and traded securities or whether to be banks that took deposits from savers and lent to borrowers. Banks making loans would keep the risk on their balance sheets and would need to deal with investment banks on an arm's length basis if they wished to hedge risk or offer clients other services as agents. Concentrating risk on to banks' balance sheets in this way would have the positive effect of focusing their attention on it.

Investment banks would become providers of liquidity as pure trading houses. They would be able to trade for themselves as well as for clients but they would not be allowed to give advice to clients. That role would be reserved for advisory firms working for a fee and covering all asset classes and corporate advisory services.

Such a system would be transparent and free of conflict of interest. The risk of one component contaminating another would be minimal. Under this model, financial markets might be less liquid than institutions have come to expect and the cost of capital might rise but neither outcome is certain and in any case we have seen in recent years what excess liquidity and cheap capital can do to the world.

The larger British financial institutions such as Barclays and HSBC would have the opportunity to float off their markets businesses. Their remaining banking businesses would be conservative and solidly based. The return of objective advice for investors and corporate chief executives would improve the quality of decision-making and reduce their pressure to transact. The financial services industry would probably turn out to be a smaller part of the UK economy and the markets culture that has permeated British society for the last quarter of a century would be dissipated. Who is to say, given the events of 2008, that this would be a bad thing?

NOTES

PREFACE

1 I am grateful to Paul Mason for this analogy

1 THE BIG END OF TOWN: SUMMER 2007

1   Hm-treasury.gov.uk 14 June 2006
2   *Sunday Times* Rich List 2008, Giving List page 9
3   *Financial Times* 27 March 2006
4   *Sustaining New York's and the US's Global Financial Services Leadership*, 2007, 80. Subsequently referred to as McKinsey
5   *Financial Times* 14 March 2007
6   Ibid.
7   cityoflondon.gov.uk
8   *Sizing up the City*, Centre for the Study of Financial Innovation (CSFI), June 2003, 4
9   International Financial Services London (IFSL), *Economic Contribution of UK Financial Services 2007* September 2007
10 McKinsey, 63
11 IFSL, *International Financial Markets in the UK* May 2007
12 McKinsey, 72
13 Ibid. 44
14 Ibid. 19, 33, 34
15 *The Economist*, 22 September 2007
16 Philip Augar, *The Greed Merchants*, Penguin 2006, 84
17 *Financial Times* 30 June 2004

18   Ibid. 26 March 2006
19   *Observer* 29 October 2006

2 GROUND ZERO: 1987–97

1   Figures from *City Research Project* report quoted in David Kynaston, *The City of London*, volume 4, Chatto & Windus 2001, 769
2   *The City's Importance to the European Union Economy*, June 1998, Centre for Economics and Business Research and the Corporation of London
3   Will Hutton, *The State We're In*, Vintage 1996, 1, 5
4   *Institutional Investment in the UK; a Review*, HM Treasury 2001, 75 Subsequent references to this report noted as Myners
5   *Financial Times* 4 January 2002
6   Myners, 75
7   *Daily Telegraph* 31 October 2001; *BBC News Online* 5 November 2001; *Financial Times* 28 January 2002; *Financial Times* 25 February 2002
8   *Daily Telegraph* 31 October 2001
9   *Guardian* 25 January 2002
10   This account is based on an interview with Nicola Horlick in 2007
11   Author interview 2007
12   *Report of the Board of Banking Supervision into the Circumstances of the Collapse of Barings* 1995, 244–5
13   Ibid. 248
14   Ranald Michie, *The London Stock Exchange: A History*, Oxford University Press 1999, 608
15   Ibid. 616
16   Kynaston, 743, 776
17   Writing in *New Yorker* 1993, quoted ibid. 743

3 THE PERFECT CALM

1   *Financial Times* 26 September 2008
2   Ibid. 22 November 2004
3   *Prospect* November 2008
4   *Financial Times* 15 November 2008
5   *Securities Industry and Financial Markets Association Fact Book* 2008
6   McKinsey, 34
7   IFSL *International markets in the UK* May 2007, 4
8   McKinsey, 83

9   Ibid. 87

10 Ibid. 83

11 CSFI, *Sizing up the City* 2003, 9.

12 *Financial Times* 3 October 2007, 'Paris launches drive to challenge London as global financial hub,' *London and Paris as International Financial Centres in the Twentieth Century*, Cassis and Bussiere, chapter on Paris 1980–2000 by Andre Straus, Oxford University Press, 2005

13 CSFI, 1

14 Ibid. 14. 'Quants' are financial experts that base their investment decisions on mathematical models.

15 Ibid. 27

16 *Financial Times* 13 June 1997

17 Ibid.

18 Kynaston, 732

19 Quoted in John Newsinger, *International Socialism* 115, summer 2007, 'Gordon Brown: From Reformism to Neoliberalism'

20 Alan Greenspan, *The Age of Turbulence*, Allen Lane 2007, 284

21 Ibid. 283

22 Ibid.

23 John Plender, *A Stake in the Future*, Nicholas Brealey 1997, 12

24 Alastair Campbell, *The Blair Years*, Hutchinson 2007, 99–100

25 Paul Vallely, 'Enemies of the People', *The Independent*, 4 July 2000, quoted in Robin Ramsay, *The Rise of New Labour*, Pocket Essentials 2002, 89–90

26 Shann Turnbull, http://cog.kent.edu/archives/ownership/msg00778.html

27 Author interview 2007

28 George G. Blakey, *The Post-War History of the London Stock Market*, Management Books 1997, 424

29 Ibid. 426

30 Author interview 2007

31 Gordon Brown budget speech 1998

32 Author interview 2007

33 Ibid.

34 Ibid.

35 *Guardian Unlimited*, 11 April 2002, 'The golden rule that saves the super-rich millions'

36 HMT 2 July 1997, archive.treasury.gov.uk

37 Sir Howard Davies interview 2007. The Securities and Futures Authority (SFA) was the lead regulator for the securities industry under the old regime

38 Sir Steve Robson interview 2008

39   Ibid.

40   Geoffrey Robinson, *The Unconventional Minister*, Michael Joseph 2000, 37

41   Sir Steve Robson interview 2008

42   William Keegan, *The Prudence of Mr Gordon Brown*, John Wiley 2003, 184

43   Ibid. 183 *Financial Times* 22 May 1997

44   Sir Steve Robson interview 2008

45   *Financial Times* 21 May 1997

46   Robinson, 42

47   McKinsey, 90

48   McKinsey, 84

49   Ibid. 80

50   FSA, *Annual Report* 2005–6, Chief Executive's Report

51   FSA, *Annual Report* 2006–7, 15

52   Ibid. 16

53   Letters from Hector Sants, 17 September 2004 and 10 November 2005, FSA.gov.uk

54   Author interview 2007

55   fsa.gov.uk, AIFA Conference, 21 November 2007

56   McKinsey, 84

57   Author interview 2007

58   Author interview 2008

59   McKinsey, 46–52

60   2005 MOU, http://www.hm-treasury.gov.uk/6210.htm

4 HEDGE FUNDS

1   Kynaston

2   Philip Augar, *The Death of Gentlemanly Capitalism*, Penguin 2000

3   Myners, 157–8

4   IFSL, *Hedge Funds* April 2007, 2 and author estimate

5   IFSL, *Hedge Funds* June 2004, 2 and author estimate

6   Author estimate

7   Author interview 2008. 'Put and call' is a technical term from the options market and means 'Heads we win, tails you lose.'

8   Author interview 2007

9   Employment and revenue figures based on author estimates

10   Author interview 2007

11   *Financial Times* 25 July 2002

12   IFSL, *Hedge Funds* April 2007

13 Author interview 2007
14 Kynaston, 750–1
15 British Bankers' Association, *Credit Derivatives Report* 2006
16 *Financial Times* 23 May 2008
17 Ibid. 5 October 2007
18 Ibid. 22 May 2007
19 Ibid. 25 September 2007
20 *Evening Standard* 17 May 2006, 'The City set who control £2 trillion'
21 *Sunday Times* Rich List 2008, 70
22 *The Economist* 4 October 2005
23 *Independent* 23 July 2002
24 *The Economist* 27 February 2007
25 FSA.gov.uk 25 July 2002
26 Ibid. 12 September 2002
27 Research carried out by the London Business School, *Financial Times* 22 June 2008
28 IFSL, *Hedge Funds* April 2007, 4
29 FSA Financial Risk Outlook, 2006
30 *Financial Times* 24 November 2008
31 Ibid. 10 August 2004
32 Ibid. 7 January 2008
33 Ibid. 7 May 2007
34 Ibid. 8 September 2007
35 Ibid. 11 June 2007
36 Ibid. and 19 December 2007
37 Ibid. 1 August 2005
38 Ibid. 24 April 2007
39 Ibid. 10 June 2007
40 Ibid. 6 October, 11 May 2006
41 Ibid. 27 March 2006
42 *Update of FSF Report on Highly Leveraged institutions* 9 May 2007, 2
43 Ibid. 3
44 Author interview, 2008
45 *Financial Times* 25 September 2007
46 Ibid. 28 May 2007
47 Ibid. 11 October 2007

5 ASSET MANAGEMENT

1 Institutional investment management consisted of three sectors: insurance funds, with half of the total assets under management,

pension funds with a third of the assets and collective retail investments such as unit trusts, open-ended investment companies and
investment trusts with the remainder.

2   Myners, 28
3   Association of British Insurers Research Paper 3, *Understanding
    Companies' Pension Benefits* 3
4   Myners, 32
5   Ibid.
6   Ibid. 28 Between 1963 and 1998 pension funds achieved average
    annual returns of 12.1 per cent, nearly five percentage points more
    than inflation over the same period
7   Ibid. 54
8   Investment Management Association, *Annual Survey* 2007, 27. This
    is subsequently referred to as IMA
9   *Financial Times* 18 June 2007
10 Ibid. 28 March 2004
11 IMA, 24 – excluding in-house corporate pension fund assets
12 *Financial Times* 4 January 2002. The pooled funds managed by the
    big four did manage to produce absolute returns in 1997, only to
    be expected given that the Financial Times All Share index rose
    23.6 per cent in that year, but none achieved returns above 14 per
    cent
13 Rory Cellan-Jones, *dot.bomb: The rise and fall of dot.com Britain*,
    Aurum, 2001, page 5
14 Alan Greenspan, *The Age of Turbulence*, Allen Lane 2007, 176–7
15 BBC News Inline, 'Dot.com doomster sees more share falls',
    12 March 2002
16 Barry Riley, *Financial Times* 14 March 2008
17 Peter Stormonth Darling, *City Cinderella*, Weidenfeld & Nicolson
    1999, 256
18 Ibid. 110 and jacket
19 *Financial Times* 14 February 2006
20 *The Times* 22 April 2006
21 *Financial Times* hedge funds survey, 27 April 2007
22 Ibid. 4 September 2007
23 Ibid.
24 Ibid. 24 January 2006
25 Ibid. 27 April 2007
26 Ibid. 27 May 2006
27 Ibid. 19 January 2002
28 Ibid. 8 November 2004
29 Ibid.

30 Ibid.

31 Ibid. 19 January 2002

32 Ibid. 8 November 2004

33 Ibid. 17 May 2005

34 Ibid. 3 March 2007

35 Ibid. 22 February 2006

36 In 2006 gross margins reached 59 basis points, compared with 54 basis points in 2005 and 41 basis points in 2001 while profits exceeded the record levels of 1999. Ibid. 3 March 2007

37 Myners, 75

38 Although general insurance companies held investment funds to smooth out the volatile underwriting cycle in their core business, the vast majority of its £1.2 trillion of funds under management were life insurance funds

39 Policies were either 'with profits', based on the investment returns of a pooled fund and a share of the life company's profits, or 'unit linked', based on the performance of a specified index such as the FTSE 100

40 IMA, Chart 5

41 *Financial Times* 20 October 2006 and 7 April 2008

42 Author interview 2008

43 Ibid.

44 There was £650 billion of retail money, a fifth of the total assets under management in the UK at the end of 2006

45 IMA page 35

46 *Financial Times* 15 May 2007

47 Ibid. 27 June 2004

48 Artemisonline.co.uk

49 *Daily Telegraph* 5 February 2007; *Guardian* 12 June 2005; *Financial Times* 1 February and 29 September 2007

50 *Financial Times* 15 May 2007; 21 March 2007 and 24 March 2007

6 PRIVATE EQUITY

1 Gmb.org.uk. In another high-profile stunt the union handed out sick bags to those attending the launch of the Private Equity Foundation, an industry-wide charity of which Buffini was a prominent supporter. In 2006 the GMB sent its members a Christmas card with a photo of Buffini and the words 'Merry Christmas from your multi-millionaire AA boss Damon Buffini as he heads for the exit with his millions'

2 Gmb.org.uk

3   ft.com and economist.com; *Sun* 4 July 2007

4   FSA Discussion Paper 6/06, *Private Equity*, 2006, 4

5   Ibid. 3–4

6   *Financial Times* 4 and 18 June 2007

7   House of Commons Treasury Committee, 'Private Equity', Tenth Report of Session 2006–7, 5–6

8   *Financial Times* 13 June 2007

9   Ibid. 21 June 2007

10   Ibid. 4 July 2007

11   'Myths and realities of private equity', Lerner and Gurung, World Economic Forum Website, 2008

12   Myners, 153

13   Bryan Burrough and John Helyar, *Barbarians at the Gate*, Jonathan Cape, 1990

14   Maggie Mahar, *Bull!*, HarperBusiness 2003, 53

15   Sudi Sudarsanam, *Creating Value from Mergers and Acquisitions*, Pearson Education 2003, 271–2

16   'World's top ten private equity deals', Times online, 2 April 2007; *Financial Times Private Equity Supplement*, 24 April 2007, 4. Figures derived from Thomson Financial

17   KKR website, 'Who we are'. Figures as of September 2007

18   Dan Briody, *The Iron Triangle*, John Wiley & Sons, 2003 xxvi

19   Carlyle Group website

20   Myners, 158–9, Centre for Management Buy-out Research, Management Buy-Outs 1986–2006, 6–7, Mike Wright et al

21   Centre for Management Buy-out Research, June 2006, 'Private Equity and Buy-outs: Jobs, Leverage, Longevity and Sell-offs'. Centre for Management Buy-out Research, Management Buy-Outs 1986–2006, Mike Wright et al., 17

22   *Financial Times Private Equity Supplement*, 24 April 2007

23   In 2007 private equity-backed companies employed 1.1 million people – 8 per cent of private sector employees and about 5 per cent of the total workforce

24   Private-equity-backed firms paid £35 billion in taxes: £4.6 billion in corporation tax, £13.8 billion in PAYE and National Insurance, £11.9 billion VAT and £4.6 billion in excise and other specific taxes

25   British Venture Capital Association (BVCA), *The Economic Impact of Private Equity in the UK*, 2008. London accounted for 57 per cent of total European private equity investment in 2006

26   Sir David Walker consultation document, walkerworkinggroup.com, 11. Subsequently referred to as Walker. Only a third of the money raised by Britain's private equity firms was actually invested in the UK

27 BVCA, *The Economic Impact of Private Equity in the UK*, 2008. In 2007 UK based banks accounted for 10 per cent of investment banks' global private equity fees

28 Ibid. Private-equity-sourced work accounted for 12 per cent of financial services industry turnover by 2007

29 Author interview 2008

30 Ibid.

31 *Financial Times* 28 March 2007

32 Author interview 2008

33 *Financial Times* 15 May 2007

34 'Myths and realities of private equity', Lerner and Gurung, World Economic Forum website, 2008. Studied all of the UK's 142 public-to-private buyouts between 1998 and 2005

35 FSA *Private Equity Discussion Paper*, 46

36 Walker, 12

37 Evidence to Treasury Select Committee, 'Private Equity', 24 July 2007

38 Walker, 11

39 BVCA report, 2006, 29–30; 37 per cent came from North American investors, 23 per cent from Europeans

40 Discussion Paper 6/06, FSA *Private Equity*, 2006, 4, 40

41 Author interview, 2008

42 *Financial Times* 18 June 2007; *The Economist* 23 June 2007; Treasury Select Committee, 'Private Equity', 24 July 2007, 36

43 Treasury Select Committee, 'Private Equity', 24 July 2007, 38. The GMB claimed that Alliance Boots would be able to offset interest payments of £500 million against expected profits of £480 million, saving itself £144 million in corporation tax along the way.

44 BVCA, *The Economic Influence of Private Equity in the UK*, 2008

45 Management Buy-outs, 1896–2006, Mike Wright et al., Centre for Management Buy-out Research, June 2006, 'Private Equity and Buy-outs: Jobs, Leverage, Longevity and Sell-offs'

46 Josh Lerner and Anuradha Gurung, 'Myths and realities of private equity', World Economic Forum, executive summary

47 Treasury Select Committee, 'Private Equity', 24 July 2007, 17

48 Centre for Management Buyouts Research, MBOs 1986–2006, Mike Wright et al., 14; Bank of England Financial Stability Report April 2007; Treasury Select Committee report on Private Equity, 24 July 2007, 19

49 FSA Discussion Paper 06/06, *Private equity*, 2006, 48

50 *Financial Times* 6 August 2007

51 Ibid. 19 June 2007

52 Ibid. 1 August 2007

53 bbc.co.uk 25 June 2007
54 *Financial Times* 14 June 2007
55 Ibid. 29 December 2007
56 Ibid. 20 August 2007
57 *Guardian* 28 September 2007

7 INVESTMENT BANKING

1 Author interview 2007
2 McKinsey 34; IFSL, Banking 2008
3 *Financial Times* 19 July 2007
4 Outlined in Chapter 2.
5 Author interview 2008
6 *Financial Times* 31 March 2003, 15 July 2007 and 7 August 2007
7 Gillian Tett, 'The dream machine', *Financial Times* 24 March 2006
8 Robin Blackburn, 'The Sub-Prime Crisis', *New Left Review* 50, March–April 2008, 63
9 Author interview 2008
10 Rory Cellan-Jones, *dot.bomb*, Aurum Press 2001, 8
11 Securities Industry Association, *Fact Book* 2006, 35
12 BBC website, 12 November 2002
13 *Sunday Times* 23 April 2006; *Financial Times* 28 March 2006 and 16 January 2007
14 *Financial World*, October 2006
15 *FSA Financial Risk Outlook*, January 2007 page 37
16 Martin Vander Weyer, *Falling Eagle*, Weidenfeld & Nicolson 2000, 215
17 Ibid. 224
18 Ibid. 227
19 Ibid. 11–12
20 Ibid. 17–18
21 *Guardian Weekend* 16 February 2008; *Financial Times* 14 March 2007
22 *Financial News* 15 June 2006, quoted on BarCap website
23 Ibid.
24 Johnny Cameron interview 1 March 2007 RBS website
25 *Financial Times* 12 August 2005
26 *The Banker* 2 June 2004
27 Johnny Cameron interview 1 March 2007, RBS website
28 *Financial Times* 17 May 2006 and 18 January 2008

29   Icap website; *Guardian* 14 December 2007; *Financial Times* 21 November 2007 and 25 January 2008
30   *Guardian* 15 February 2007
31   *Financial Times* 7 April 2007
32   Ibid. 17 January 2006
33   Ibid. 10 July 2007

8 THE MANSION HOUSE DINNER 2007

1   Unless otherwise stated all quotes in this chapter are from the speeches made by Gordon Brown and Mervyn King at the Mansion House Dinner 2007
2   Bank of England, *Financial Stability Review* July 2006, 7 and April 2007, 5

9 NORTHERN ROCK

1   House of Commons Treasury Select Committee, 'The run on the Rock', Volume 1, 24 January 2008, 11, subsequently referred to as TSC
2   Chairman's statement, 2005 annual report
3   *Independent* 6 September 1997
4   TSC, 12
5   Ibid. 13
6   Richard Tomlinson and Ben Livesey, *The Age* 20 March 2008. Northern Rock Annual Reports and Accounts
7   TSC, 15
8   'Financial Stability and Transparency', House of Commons Treasury Committee, 26 February 2008, 25, subsequently referred to as FST
9   FST, 28, speech in Chicago 17 May 2007
10   IMF, *Global Financial Stability Report* October 2007, 9, cited ibid. 31
11   Ibid. 32
12   *Financial Times* 26 April 2007
13   Ibid. 29 July 2007
14   *Daily Telegraph* 19 July 2007
15   FST, 34
16   FST, 35
17   FST, 36–7
18   *Financial Times* 22 January 2008

19   TSC, 15
20   Ibid. 41, Charts 2 and 3
21   Ibid. 51–2
22   Mervyn King letter to the TSC 12 September 2007, cited in TSC, 39
23   Bank of England news release, 'Liquidity support facility for Northern Rock plc' 14 September 2007
24   TSC, 67
25   HMT press release, 'Statement by the Chancellor of the Exchequer on financial markets' 17 September 2007
26   *The Age*, 20 March 2008
27   Alex Brummer, *The Crunch*, Random House Business Books, 2008, 93
28   Ibid. 91
29   onlinemortgages.co.uk
30   Brummer, 93
31   Northern Rock, Annual Report 1998
32   Brummer, 88

10 SEPTEMBER 2007–DECEMBER 2008

1   *Financial Times* 31 October 2007
2   Ibid. 5 November 2007
3   Ibid. 7 January 2008
4   Ibid. 3 April 2008
5   Robin Blackburn, 'The Sub-prime Crisis', *New Left Review* 5 April 2008, 63
6   *Financial Times* 28 August 2008
7   Ibid. 1 August 2008
8   Ibid. 23 September 2008
9   Ibid. 13 October 2008
10   AIG account based on 'Inadequate cover', Francesco Guerrera and Andrea Felsted, *Financial Times* 6 October 2008
11   Ibid. 26 September 2008
12   The troubled assets plan was quietly dropped the following month in favour of recapitalising the banks and supporting the commercial paper market
13   *Financial Times* 15 October 2008
14   Ibid. 26 September 2007
15   TSC, 135
16   *Financial Times* 20 October 2007
17   Ibid. 15 and 22 January 2008
18   Ibid. 4 February 2008

19   TSC, 141
20   *Financial Times* 3 October 2008
21   Ibid. 21 and 23 August 2007 and 30 August 2008
22   Bank of England, Market Notice 21 April 2008, 'Special Liquidity Scheme'
23   *Financial Times* 22 April 2008
24   Evidence to TSC, *Financial Times* 19 November 2008
25   *Financial Times* 28 July 2006
26   Lloyds TSB offer document for HBOS, 223
27   *Financial Times* 17 September 2008

11 WHERE THE CREDIT CRUNCH LEFT THE CITY

1   *Spectator* 26 September 2008
2   Speech to Worshipful Company of International Bankers, archbishopofyork.org/1981
3   *Financial Times* 23 September 2008
4   BBC website 18 September 2008
5   *Guardian* 19 September 2008
6   *Financial Times* 23 September 2008
7   Conservative Party website
8   FSA statement on disclosure regime for significant short positions during rights issues 13 June 2008 and FSA Statement on short positions in financial stocks 18 September 2008, fsa.gov.uk
9   *Financial Times* 23 September 2008
10   Ibid. 22 September 2008
11   Ibid. 18 September 2008
12   Ibid. 24 September 2008
13   Ibid.
14   BBC website 18 September 2008
15   *Guardian* 28 October 2008
16   *Financial Times* 22 September 2008
17   Ibid. 23 September 2008
18   Ibid. 22 September 2008
19   *Daily Telegraph* 20 June 2008
20   *Financial Times* 23 September 2008
21   *Evening Standard* 13 October 2008
22   *Financial Times* 14 November 2008
23   House of Commons Treasury Committee, 'The run on the Rock', government's response 2 July 2008, 2
24   Ibid. 4

25   Ibid. 18

26   Ibid. 23 September 2008

27   Dear CEO letter 13 October 2008, fsa.gov.uk

28   *Financial Times* 19 June 2008

29   *Financial Times* 14 November 2008

30   Ibid. 18 September 2008

31   Ibid. 5 November 2008

32   Ibid. 14 October, 15 November 2008

33   Ibid. 11 November 2008

34   Barclays website September 2008, transcript of analysts' conference call

35   *Financial Times* 15 September 2008

36   Ibid. 20 September 2008

37   *Wall Street Journal* 17 September 2008

38   Barclays website, analysts conference call

39   *Financial Times* 22 September 2008

40   Barclays website, analysts' conference call

41   Barclays website, analysts' conference call

42   *Financial Times* 15 September and 20 September 2008

43   Ibid. 20 September 2008

44   Author interview 2008

45   *Financial Times* 4 February 2008

46   Ibid. 28 February, 1, 5, 6 and 10 March 2008

47   Ibid. 8 August 2008

48   *The Economist* 26 July 2008

49   *Financial Times* 6 March and 23 May 2008

50   Ibid. 10 July 2008

51   Pegasus investors' report, *Surviving the chaos* 11 November 2008

52   *Financial Times* 20 November 2007

53   Centre for Management Buy Out Research quoted in *Financial Times* 25 June and 28 August 2008

54   *Financial Times* 22 August 2008

55   Ibid. 25 October and 4 December 2008

56   Ibid. 21 November 2008

57   Hector Sants speaking to the *Financial Times* 1 December 2008

58   *Financial Times* 25 September 2008

59   Ibid. 15 November 2008

60   Ibid. 14 October 2008

61   Ibid. 27 September 2008

62   Ibid. 14 October 2008

63   Ibid.

64   *Financial Times* 16 December 2008

12 OUR OWN POSITION IN TIME

1   *Financial Times*, 23 September 2008
2   Ibid. 30 September 2008
3   *Evening Standard* 1 October 2008
4   Will Hutton, *The State We're In*, Vintage 1996; John Plender, *Going Off the Rails*, John Wiley 2003; John Kay, *The Truth About Markets*, Allen Lane 2003; See also Larry Elliott and Dan Atkinson, *The Gods That Failed*, Bodley Head 2008
5   Philip Augar, *The Greed Merchants*, Allen Lane 2005, 213–214

INDEX